PASSIONATE
CONVICTION

PASSIONATE CONVICTION

Contemporary
Discourses on
Christian
Apologetics

editors:
PAUL COPAN and **WILLIAM LANE CRAIG**

Nashville, Tennessee

978-0-8054-4538-1

Published by B&H Publishing Group
Nashville, Tennessee

Dewey Decimal Classification: 239
Subject Heading: Apologetics/Theology

3 4 5 6 7 8 9 10 • 17 16 15 14 13
VP

CONTENTS

PREFACE

Over the last forty years there has been an ongoing revolution in Anglo-American philosophy. As the old, antimetaphysical prejudices have waned, there has been a renaissance of Christian philosophy. One of the fruits of this renaissance is the Evangelical Philosophical Society, the largest society of Christian philosophers in the world and publisher of *Philosophia Christi*, the only professional journal devoted to philosophical inquiry from an evangelical perspective.

The EPS has as its mission influencing both the academy and the church. In an effort to bring the fruits of evangelical scholarship out of the ivory tower to the layman in the pew, the EPS began four years ago to hold apologetics conferences in local churches in conjunction with the EPS annual convention each November. Each conference features a stellar array of more than twenty evangelical scholars from different disciplines who, as their gift to the church, provide pro bono training in the defense of the Christian faith. For those fortunate enough to live near the city where the annual convention is being held, such an opportunity is truly unprecedented and unlikely to come again for many years.

The first such conference, entitled "Set Forth Your Case," was held at Johnson Ferry Baptist Church in suburban Atlanta. The following year the conference was held at Parkhills Baptist Church in

San Antonio and called "To Everyone an Answer." The third conference, "Reason for the Hope within," was hosted by Branch Creek
Community Church in Valley Forge. The conference in 2006, held at
McLean Bible Church just outside Washington, D.C., "Loving God
with All Your Mind," drew the largest attendance yet with more than
fifteen hundred participants. The testimony of people at these remarkable conferences is that they have been truly life changing for many
participants, who for the first time in their lives have come to discover
a part of the body of Christ—namely Christian scholars—that they
did not even know existed. These gatherings uniquely feature scholars
from different fields—history, philosophy, biblical studies, science, religious studies, theology, archaeology, ethics—who capably defend the
Christian faith.

This volume is, we hope, the first of an ongoing series of cutting-
edge, accessible essays in Christian apologetics taken from these conferences. May God use this book to encourage your faith, strengthen
your mind, and embolden your witness!

Paul Copan
William Lane Craig

Part 1

WHY APOLOGETICS?

Chapter 1

IN INTELLECTUAL NEUTRAL

William Lane Craig

A number of years ago, two books appeared that sent shock waves through the American educational community. The first of these, *Cultural Literacy: What Every American Needs to Know*, by E. D. Hirsch, documented the fact that large numbers of American college students do not have the basic background knowledge to understand the front page of a newspaper or to act responsibly as citizens. For example, a quarter of the students in a recent survey thought Franklin D. Roosevelt was president during the Vietnam War. Two-thirds did not know when the Civil War occurred. One-third thought Columbus discovered the New World sometime after 1750. In a recent survey at California State University at Fullerton, over half the students could not identify Chaucer or Dante. Ninety percent did not know who Alexander Hamilton was, despite the fact that his picture is on every ten-dollar bill.

These statistics would be funny if they weren't so alarming. What has happened to our schools that they should be producing such dreadfully ignorant people? Alan Bloom, who was an eminent educator at the University of Chicago and the author of the second book I referred to above, argued in his *The Closing of the American Mind* that behind the current educational malaise lies the universal conviction of students that all truth is relative and, therefore, that truth is not worth pursuing. Bloom writes:

There is one thing a professor can be absolutely certain of: almost every student entering the university believes, or says he believes, that truth is relative. If this belief is put to the test, one can count on the students' reaction: they will be uncomprehending. That anyone should regard the proposition as not self-evident astonishes them, as though he were calling into question 2 + 2 = 4. These are things you don't think about. . . . That it is a moral issue for students is revealed by the character of their response when challenged—a combination of disbelief and indignation: "Are you an absolutist?," the only alternative they know, uttered in the same tone as . . . "Do you really believe in witches?" This latter leads into the indignation, for someone who believes in witches might well be a witch-hunter or a Salem judge. The danger they have been taught to fear from absolutism is not error but intolerance. Relativism is necessary to openness; and this is the virtue, the only virtue, which all primary education for more than fifty years has dedicated itself to inculcating. Openness—and the relativism that makes it the only plausible stance in the face of various claims to truth and various ways of life and kinds of human beings—is the great insight of our times. . . . The study of history and of culture teaches that all the world was mad in the past; men always thought they were right, and that led to wars, persecutions, slavery, xenophobia, racism, and chauvinism. The point is not to correct the mistakes and really be right; rather it is not to think you are right at all.[1]

Since there is no absolute truth, since everything is relative, the purpose of an education is not to learn truth or master facts; rather it is merely to acquire a skill so that one can go out and obtain wealth, power, and fame. Truth has become irrelevant.

Now, of course, this sort of relativistic attitude toward truth is antithetical to the Christian worldview. For as Christians we believe that

[1] Alan Bloom, *The Closing of the American Mind* (New York: Simon & Schuster, 1987), 25–26.

all truth is God's truth, that God has revealed to us the truth, both in His Word and in Him who said, "I am the Truth." The Christian, therefore, can never look on the truth with apathy or disdain. Rather, he cherishes and treasures the truth as a reflection of God Himself. Nor does his commitment to truth make the Christian intolerant, as Bloom's students erroneously inferred; on the contrary, the concept of tolerance entails that one does not agree with that which one tolerates. The Christian is committed to both truth and tolerance, for he believes in Him who said not only, "I am the truth," but also, "Love your enemies."

At the time that these books were released, I was teaching in the Religious Studies Department at a Christian liberal arts college. So I began to wonder: how much have Christian students been infected with the attitude that Bloom describes? How would my own students fare on one of E. D. Hirsch's tests? *Well, how would they?* I thought. *Why not give them such a quiz?* So I did.

I drew up a brief, general knowledge quiz about famous people, places, and things and administered it to two classes of about fifty sophomores. What I found was that although they did better than the general student population, still there were sizable portions of the group who could not identify—even with a phrase—some important names and events. For example, 49 percent could not identify Leo Tolstoy, the author of perhaps the world's greatest novel, *War and Peace*. To my surprise, 16 percent did not know who Winston Churchill was. One student thought he was one of the founding fathers of our nation! Another identified him as a great revival preacher of a few hundred years ago! Twenty-two percent did not know what Afghanistan is, and 22 percent could not identify Nicaragua. Twenty percent did not know where the Amazon River is. Imagine!

They fared even worse with things and events. I was amazed that a whopping 67 percent could not identify the Battle of the Bulge. Several identified it as a dieter's problem. Twenty-four percent did not know what the Special Theory of Relativity is (mind you, just to *identify* it—even as, say; "a theory of Einstein"—not to *explain* it).

Forty-five percent couldn't identify Custer's Last Stand; it was variously classed as a battle in the Revolutionary War or as a battle in the Civil War. And I wasn't really surprised that 73 percent did not know what the expression "Manifest Destiny" referred to.

So it became clear to me that Christian students have not been able to rise above the dark undertow in our educational system at the primary and secondary levels. This level of ignorance presents a real crisis for Christian colleges and seminaries.

But then an even more terrible fear began to dawn on me as I contemplated these statistics. *If Christian students are this ignorant of the general facts of history and geography,* I thought, *then the chances are that they, and Christians in general, are equally or even more ignorant of the facts of our own Christian heritage and doctrine.* Our culture in general has sunk to the level of biblical and theological illiteracy. A great many, if not most, people cannot even name the four Gospels. In a recent survey one person identified them as Matthew, Mark, and Luther! In another survey Joan of Arc was identified by some as Noah's wife! The suspicion arose in my mind that the evangelical church is probably also caught somewhere higher up in this same downward spiral.

If we do not preserve the truth of our own Christian heritage and doctrine, who will learn it for us? Non-Christians? That hardly seems likely. If the church does not treasure her own Christian truth, then it will be lost to her forever. So how, I wondered, would Christians fare on a quiz over general facts of Christian history and doctrine?

Well, how would they? I now invite you to get out a pen and paper and take the following quiz yourself. (Go on, it'll only take a minute!) The following are items I think any mature Christian in our society ought to be able to identify. Simply provide some identifying phrase that indicates that you know what the item is. For example, if I say, "John Wesley," you might write: "the founder of Methodism" or "an eighteenth-century English revivalist."

Quiz

1. Augustine
2. Council of Nicea
3. Trinity
4. Two natures united in one person
5. Pantheism
6. Thomas Aquinas
7. Reformation
8. Martin Luther
9. Substitutionary atonement
10. Enlightenment

How did you do? If you're typical of the audiences to whom I've given this quiz, probably not too well. If that is the case, you might be tempted to react to this quiz defensively: "Who needs to know all this stuff anyway? This junk isn't important. All that really counts is my walk with Christ and my sharing Him with others. Who cares about all this other trivia?"

I truly hope that will not be your reaction, for that will close you off to self-improvement. This little exercise will have been of no profit to you. You will have learned nothing from it.

But there's a second, more positive reaction. You may see, perhaps for the first time in your life, that here is a need in your life for you to become intellectually engaged as a Christian, and you may resolve to do something about it. This is a momentous decision. You will be taking a step which millions of American Christians need to take.

No one has issued a more forceful challenge to Christians to become intellectually engaged than did Charles Malik, former Lebanese ambassador to the United States, in his address at the dedication of the Billy Graham Center in Wheaton, Illinois. Malik emphasized that as Christians we face two tasks in our evangelism: saving the soul and saving the mind, that is to say, not only converting people spiritually but converting them intellectually as well. And the church is lagging dangerously behind with regard to this second task. Our churches are filled with people who are spiritually born again but who still think like non-Christians. Mark his words well:

> I must be frank with you: the greatest danger confronting American evangelical Christianity is the danger of anti-intellectualism. The mind in its greatest and deepest reaches is not cared for enough. But intellectual nurture cannot take place apart from profound immersion for a period of years in the history of thought and the spirit. People who are in a hurry to get out of the university and start earning money or serving the church or preaching the gospel have no idea of the infinite value of spending years of leisure conversing with the greatest minds and souls of the past, ripening and sharpening and enlarging their powers of thinking. The result is that the arena of creative thinking is vacated and abdicated to the enemy.[2]

Malik went on to say:

> It will take a different spirit altogether to overcome this great danger of anti-intellectualism. For example, I say this different spirit, so far as philosophy alone—the most important domain for thought and intellect—is concerned, must see the tremendous value of spending an entire year doing nothing but poring intensely over the *Republic* or the *Sophist* of Plato, or two years over the *Metaphysics* or the *Ethics* of Aristotle, or three years over the *City of God* of Augustine. But if a start is made now on a crash program in this and other domains, it will take at least a century to catch up with the Harvards and Tübingens and the Sorbonnes—and by then where will these universities be?[3]

What Malik clearly saw is the strategic position occupied by the university in shaping Western thought and culture. Indeed, the single most important institution shaping Western society is the university. At the university our future political leaders, our journalists, our lawyers, our teachers, our scientists, our business executives, our artists

---

[2] Charles Malik, "The Other Side of Evangelism," *Christianity Today*, 7 November 1980, 40.
[3] Ibid.

will be trained. At the university they will formulate or, more likely, simply absorb the worldview that will shape their lives. And since these are the opinion makers and leaders who shape our culture, the worldview they imbibe at the university will be the one that shapes our culture.

Why is this important? Simply because the gospel is never heard in isolation. It is always heard against the background of the cultural milieu in which one lives. A person raised in a cultural milieu in which Christianity is still seen as an intellectually viable option will display an openness to the gospel which a person who is secularized will not. You may as well tell the secular person to believe in fairies or leprechauns as in Jesus Christ! Or, to give a more realistic illustration, it is like a devotee of the Hare Krishna movement approaching you on the street and inviting you to believe in Krishna. Such an invitation strikes us as bizarre, freakish, even amusing. But to a person on the streets of Delhi, such an invitation would, I assume, appear reasonable and cause for reflection. I fear that evangelicals appear almost as weird to persons on the streets of Bonn, Stockholm, or Toronto as do the devotees of Krishna.

Part of the broader task of Christian scholarship is to help create and sustain a cultural milieu in which the gospel can be heard as an intellectually viable option for thinking men and women. Therefore, the church has a vital stake in raising up Christian scholars who will help to create a place at the university for Christian ideas. The average Christian does not realize that there is an intellectual war going on in the universities and in the professional journals and scholarly societies. Christianity is being attacked as irrational or obsolete; and millions of students, our future generation of leaders, have absorbed that viewpoint.

This is a war we cannot afford to lose. The great Princeton theologian J. Gresham Machen warned on the eve of the fundamentalist controversy that if the church loses the intellectual battle in one generation, then evangelism would become immeasurably more difficult in the next:

False ideas are the greatest obstacles to the reception of the gospel. We may preach with all the fervor of a reformer and yet succeed only in winning a straggler here and there, if we permit the whole collective thought of the nation or of the world to be controlled by ideas which, by the resistless force of logic, prevent Christianity from being regarded as anything more than a harmless delusion. Under such circumstances, what God desires us to do is to destroy the obstacle at its root.[4]

The root of the obstacle is to be found in the university, and it is there that it must be attacked. Unfortunately, Machen's warning went unheeded, and biblical Christianity retreated into the intellectual closets of Fundamentalism, from which it has only recently begun to re-emerge. The war is not yet lost, and it is one which we must not lose: souls of men and women hang in the balance.

So what are evangelicals doing to win this war? Until recently, very little indeed. Malik asked pointedly:

Who among evangelicals can stand up to the great secular or naturalistic or atheistic scholars on their own terms of scholarship? Who among evangelical scholars is quoted as a normative source by the greatest secular authorities on history or philosophy or psychology or sociology or politics? Does the evangelical mode of thinking have the slightest chance of becoming the dominant mode in the great universities of Europe and America that stamp our entire civilization with their spirit and ideas? . . .

For the sake of greater effectiveness in witnessing to Jesus Christ Himself, as well as for their own sakes, evangelicals cannot afford to keep on living on the periphery of responsible intellectual existence.[5]

These words hit like a hammer. Evangelicals really have been living on the periphery of responsible intellectual existence. Most prominent

---

[4] J. Gresham Machen, "Christianity and Culture," *Princeton Theological Review* 11 (1913): 7.
[5] Malik, "Other Side of Evangelism," 40.

evangelical scholars tend to be big fish in a small pond. Our influence extends little beyond the evangelical subculture. We tend to publish exclusively with evangelical presses, and therefore our books are likely to go unread by nonevangelical scholars; and instead of participating in the standard professional societies, we are active instead in the evangelical professional societies. As a result, we effectively put our light under a bushel and have little leavening effect for the gospel in our professional fields. In turn, the intellectual drift of the culture at large continues to slide unchecked, deeper into secularism.

We desperately need Christian scholars who can, as Malik said, compete with non-Christian thinkers in their fields of expertise on their own terms of scholarship. It can be done. There is, for example, a revolution going on right now in the field of philosophy, which, as Malik noted, is the most important domain for thought and intellect, since it is foundational to every other discipline at the university. Christian philosophers have been coming out of the closet and defending the truth of the Christian worldview with philosophically sophisticated arguments in the finest secular journals and professional societies. The face of American philosophy has been changed as a result.

Fifty years ago philosophers widely regarded talk about God as literally meaningless, as mere gibberish, but today no informed philosopher could take such a viewpoint. In fact, many of America's finest philosophers today are outspoken Christians. To give you some feel for the impact of this revolution, let me quote an article which appeared in the fall of 2001 in the journal *Philo* lamenting what the author called "the desecularization of academia that evolved in philosophy departments since the late 1960s." The author, himself a prominent atheist philosopher, writes:

> Naturalists passively watched as realist versions of theism
> . . . began to sweep through the philosophical community, un-
> til today perhaps one-quarter or one-third of philosophy pro-
> fessors are theists, with most being orthodox Christians. . . .

In philosophy, it became, almost overnight, "academically respectable" to argue for theism, making philosophy a favored field of entry for the most intelligent and talented theists entering academia today. . . .

God is not "dead" in academia; he returned to life in the late 1960s and is now alive and well in his last academic stronghold, philosophy departments.[6]

This is the testimony of a prominent atheist philosopher to the change that has taken place before his eyes in American philosophy. I think that he is probably exaggerating when he estimates that one-quarter to one-third of American philosophers are theists, but what his estimates do reveal is the *perceived impact* of Christian philosophers on this field. Like Gideon's army, a committed minority of activists can have an impact far out of proportion to their numbers. The principal error he makes is calling philosophy departments God's "last stronghold" at the university. On the contrary, philosophy departments are a beachhead from which operations can be launched to impact other disciplines at the university for Christ.

The point is that the task of desecularization is not hopeless or impossible, nor do significant changes need to take as long to achieve as one might think. This sort of Christian scholarship represents the best hope for the transformation of culture that Malik and Machen envisioned, and its true impact for the cause of Christ will only be felt in the next generation, as it filters down into popular culture.

It can be done if we are willing to put in the hard work. Machen observed that in his day "many would have the seminaries combat error by attacking it as it is taught by its popular exponents" instead of confusing students "with a lot of German names unknown outside the walls of the university." But to the contrary, Machen insisted, it is essential that Christian scholars be alert to the power of an idea before it has reached popular formulation. Scholarly procedure, he said,

is based simply upon a profound belief in the pervasiveness of ideas. What is today a matter of academic speculation begins

[6] Quentin Smith, "The Metaphilosophy of Naturalism," *Philo* 4/2 (2001).

tomorrow to move armies and pull down empires. In that second stage, it has gone too far to be combated; the time to stop it was when it was still a matter of impassionate debate. So as Christians we should try to mold the thought of the world in such a way as to make the acceptance of Christianity something more than a logical absurdity.[7]

Like Malik, Machen also believed that "the chief obstacle to the Christian religion today lies in the sphere of the intellect"[8] and that objections to Christianity must be attacked in that sphere. "The church is perishing to-day through the lack of thinking, not through an excess of it."[9]

What is ironic about the mentality which says that our seminaries should produce pastors, not scholars, is that it is precisely our future pastors, not just our future scholars, who need to be intellectually engaged and to receive this scholarly training. Machen's article was originally given as a speech entitled "The Scientific Preparation of the Minister." A model for us here ought to be a man like John Wesley, a Spirit-filled revivalist and at the same time an Oxford-educated scholar.[10] Wesley's vision of a pastor is remarkable: a gentleman, skilled in the Scriptures and conversant with history, philosophy, and the science of his day.

How do the pastors graduating from our seminaries compare to this model? Church historian and theologian David Wells has called our contemporary generation of pastors "the new disablers" because they have abandoned the traditional role of the pastor as a broker of truth to his congregation and replaced it with a new managerial model drawn from the professional world which emphasizes leadership abilities, marketing, and administration. As a result the church has produced a generation of Christians for whom theology is irrelevant and whose lives outside the church do not differ practically from those of atheists. These new managerial pastors, complains Wells, "are

[7] Machen, "Christianity and Culture," 6.
[8] Ibid., 10.
[9] Ibid., 13.
[10] John Wesley, *The Works of John Wesley* (1959; repr., Peabody, MA: Hendrickson, 1984), 6: 217–31.

failing the Church and even disabling it. They are leaving it vulnerable to all the seductions of modernity precisely because they have not provided the alternative, which is a view of life centered in God and his truth."[11] We need to recover the traditional model which men like Wesley exemplified.

But finally, not only Christian scholars and pastors need to be intellectually engaged if the church is to make an impact in our culture. Christian laymen, too, must become intellectually engaged. Our churches are filled with Christians who are idling in intellectual neutral. As Christians, their minds are going to waste. J. P. Moreland in his challenging book *Love Your God with All Your Mind* has called them "empty selves." An empty self is inordinately individualistic, infantile, and narcissistic. It is passive, sensate, busy, and hurried, incapable of developing an interior life. In what is perhaps the most devastating passage in his book, Moreland asks us to envision a church filled with such people. He asks:

> What would be the theological understanding, . . . the evangelistic courage, the . . . cultural penetration of such a church? . . . If the interior life does not really matter all that much, why spend the time . . . trying to develop an . . . intellectual, spiritually mature life? If someone is basically passive, he or she will just not make the effort to read, preferring instead to be entertained. If a person is sensate in orientation, music, magazines filled with pictures, and visual media in general will be more important than mere words on a page or abstract thoughts. If one is hurried and distracted, one will have little patience for theoretical knowledge and too short . . . an attention span to stay with an idea while it is being carefully developed. . . .
>
> And if someone is overly individualistic, infantile, and narcissistic, what *will* that person read, if he or she reads at all? . . . Christian self-help books that are filled with self-serving content, . . . slogans, simplistic moralizing, a lot of

---

[11] David F. Wells, *No Place for Truth* (Grand Rapids, Mich.: Wm. B. Eerdmans, 1993), 253.

stories and pictures, and inadequate diagnosis of issues that place no demand on the reader. Books about Christian celebrities. . . . What will not be read are books that equip people to . . . develop a well-reasoned, theological understanding of the Christian religion, and fill their role in the broader kingdom of God . . . [Such] a church . . . will become . . . impotent to stand against the powerful forces of secularism that threaten to bury Christian ideas under a veneer of soulless pluralism and misguided scientism. In such a context, the church will be tempted to measure her success largely in terms of numbers—numbers achieved by cultural accommodation to empty selves. In this way, . . . the church will become her own grave digger; her means of short-term "success" will turn out to be the very thing that marginalizes her in the long run.[12]

What makes this description so devastating is that we don't have to imagine such a church; rather this *is* an apt description of far too many American evangelical churches today.

Sometimes people try to justify their lack of intellectual engagement by asserting that they prefer having a "simple faith." But here I think we must distinguish between a childlike faith and a childish faith. A childlike faith is a whole-souled trust in God as one's loving heavenly Father, and Jesus commends such a faith to us. But a childish faith is an immature, unreflective faith, and such a faith is not commended to us. On the contrary, Paul says, "Do not be children in your thinking; be babes in evil, but in thinking be mature" (1 Cor 14:20 RSV). If a "simple" faith means an unreflective, ignorant faith, then we should want none of it. In my own life I can testify that, after many years of study, my worship of God is deeper precisely because of, and not in spite of, my philosophical and theological studies. In every area I have intensely researched—creation, the resurrection, divine omniscience, divine eternity, divine aseity—my appreciation of God's truth and my awe of His personhood have become more profound. I

[12] J. P. Moreland, *Love Your God with All Your Mind* (Colorado Springs: NavPress, 1997), 93–94.

am excited about future study because of the deeper appreciation I am sure it will bring me of God's personhood and work. Christian faith is not an apathetic faith, a brain-dead faith, but a living, inquiring faith. As Anselm put it, ours is a faith that seeks understanding.

Furthermore, the results of being in intellectual neutral extend far beyond one's own self. If Christian laymen do not become intellectually engaged, then we are in serious danger of losing our youth. In high school and college, Christian teenagers are intellectually assaulted by every manner of non-Christian philosophy conjoined with an overwhelming relativism. As I speak in churches around the country, I constantly meet parents whose children have lost their faith because there was no one in the church to answer their questions. In fact, George Barna estimates that 40 percent of the youth in our churches, once they leave for college, will never darken the door of a church again.

There can be no question that the church has dropped the ball in this area. But the structures are in place in the church for remedying this problem if only we will make use of them. I am speaking, of course, of adult Sunday school programs. Why not begin to use Sunday school classes to offer laymen serious instruction in such subjects as Christian doctrine, church history, New Testament Greek, apologetics, and so forth? Think of the potential for change! Why not?

I believe that our culture can be changed. I am excited about the renaissance in Christian philosophy in my generation, which bodes well for the next. Whether God is calling you to become a Christian scholar on the front lines of intellectual battle, a Christian pastor to serve as a broker of truth to your congregation, or a Christian parent or layman who is always ready to give a reason for the hope that is in you, we have the awesome opportunity of being agents of cultural change in Christ's name. For the church's sake, for your own sakes, for your children's sake, do not squander this opportunity! So if, up until now, you've just been coasting, idling in intellectual neutral, now is the time to get it in gear!

Answers to the Quiz

1. Church father (354–430) and the author of *The City of God* who emphasized God's unmerited grace.

2. The church council that in 325 officially ratified the doctrine of the equal deity of the Father and the Son as opposed to the view held by the Arian heretics.

3. The doctrine that in God there are three persons in one being.

4. The doctrine enunciated at the Council of Chalcedon (451) affirming the true deity and true humanity of Christ.

5. The view that the world and God are identical.

6. A medieval Catholic theologian (1225–1274) and the author of *Summa Theologica*, whose views have been determinative for traditional Roman Catholic theology.

7. The origin of Protestantism in the sixteenth century in the efforts of men such as Luther, Calvin, and Zwingli to reform the doctrine and practice of the Roman Catholic church; it emphasized justification by grace through faith alone and the exclusive authority of the Bible.

8. The Roman Catholic monk (1483–1546) who started the Protestant Reformation and was the founder of Lutheranism.

9. The doctrine that by His death on our behalf and in our place Christ reconciled us to God.

10. The intellectual revolt in Europe during the seventeenth and eighteenth centuries against the authority of church and monarchy in the name of human autonomy; also called the Age of Reason.

Chapter 2

LIVING SMART

J. P. Moreland

In recent years there has been a growing curiosity among Jesus' followers about "the integration of faith and learning." This way of putting it already demeans the cognitive status of Christianity's truth claims because what is being integrated is *learning* (extrabiblical claims assessable to rational assessment) and *faith* (privatized biblical ideas accepted without argument). But however the issue is labeled, the push toward integration is an important one. The word *integration* means "forming or blending into a whole, uniting." We humans naturally seek to find the unity that is behind diversity; and, in fact, coherence is an important mark of rationality. In conceptual integration one's theological beliefs, especially those derived from careful study of the Bible, are blended and unified with important, reasonable ideas from one's profession or extrabiblical subject matter into a coherent, intellectually satisfying worldview. As Augustine wisely advised, "We must show our Scriptures not to be in conflict with whatever [our critics] can demonstrate about the nature of things from reliable sources."[1] One of the goals of integration is to maintain or increase both the conceptual relevance of and rational justification for Christian theism.

[1] Augustine, *De genesi ad litteram* 1.21. Cited in Ernan McMullin, "How Should Cosmology Relate to Theology?" in *The Science and Theology in the Twentieth Century*, ed. Arthur R. Peacocke (Notre Dame: University of Notre Dame Press, 1981), 20.

But is there more to integration than this? *After all, you may think, it's hard enough to get through an average week with some energy left over for family, friends, and church. Now I'm being asked to do extra work— integration, whatever that is—just because I'm a Christian! And even if there are plenty of good reasons to care about integration, what does it look like in detail? How do I go about it in my area of teaching, employment, or interest?* In this essay I shall attempt to answer these questions, especially those regarding the importance of and priorities for integration, as well as the goals and methods of integration.

Five Reasons Integration Is Crucial to Christian Discipleship

1. *Vocation and the holistic character of discipleship.* As disciples grow, they learn to see, feel, think, desire, believe, and behave the way Jesus does in a manner fitting to the kingdom of God and their own station in life. With God's help I seek to live as Jesus would if He were I (e.g., if He were a philosophy professor at Biola University married to Hope and father of Ashley and Allison).

Two important implications flow from the nature of discipleship. For one thing, the lordship of Christ is holistic. The religious life is not a special compartment in an otherwise secular life. Rather, the religious life is an entire way of life. To live Christianly is to allow Jesus Christ to be the Lord of every aspect of my life. There is no room for a secular-sacred separation in the life of Jesus' followers. Jesus Christ should be every bit as much at home in my thinking and behavior when I am developing my views in my area of teaching or employment as He is when I am in a small-group fellowship.

Further, as a disciple of Jesus, I do not merely have a job; I also have a vocation. A job is a means for supporting myself and those for whom I am responsible. For the Christian a vocation (from the Latin *vocare*, which means "to call") is an overall calling from God. Harry Blamires correctly draws a distinction between a general and a special vocation:

> The general vocation of all Christians—indeed of all men
> and women—is the same. We are called to live as children of

God, obeying his will in all things. But obedience to God's will must inevitably take many different forms. The wife's mode of obedience is not the same as the nun's; the farmer's is not the same as the priest's. By "special vocation," therefore, we designate God's call to a man to serve him in a particular sphere of activity.[2]

As I seek to discover and become excellent in my special vocation, I must ask, How would Jesus approach the task of being a history teacher, a chemist, an athletic director, a mathematician, a homeschooling parent? It is not always easy to answer this question, but the vocational demands of discipleship require that we give it our best shot!

Whatever we do, however, it is important that we restore an image of Jesus Christ to our students as an intelligent, competent person who spoke authoritatively on whatever subject He addressed. The disciples of Jesus agreed with Paul when he said that all the wisdom of the Greeks and Jews was ultimately wrapped up in Jesus Himself (Col 2:2–3). For them Jesus was not merely a Savior from sin; He was the wisest, most intelligent, most attractive person they had ever seen. Interestingly, in the early centuries of Christianity, the church presented Jesus to unbelievers precisely because He was wiser, more virtuous, more intelligent, and more attractive in His character than Aristotle, Plato, Moses, or anyone else. It has been a part of the church's self-understanding to locate the spiritual life in a broader quest for the good life (i.e., a life of wisdom, knowledge, beauty, and goodness). So understood, the spiritual life and discipleship unto Jesus were seen as the best way to achieve a life of truth, beauty, and goodness than any other form of life. Moreover, the life of discipleship was depicted as the wisest, most reasonable form of life available so that a life of unbelief was taken to be foolish and absurd. Our discipleship needs to recapture

[2] Harry Blamires, *A God Who Acts* (Ann Arbor, Mich.: Servant Books, 1957), 67. Not everyone agrees that there is such a thing as a special vocation. While I am on the side of those who accept such a calling, my presentation to follow does not require acceptance of a special vocation. All my points require is that one agrees with the idea that a Christian should try to live and think Christianly in every aspect of life, including what he or she does forty or more hours a week.

and propagate this broader understanding of following Christ if it is to be thoroughly Christian in its approach to disciple-making.

2. *Biblical teaching about the role of the mind in the Christian life and the value of extra-biblical knowledge.* The Scriptures are clear that God wants us to be like Him in every facet of our lives. He desires commitment from our total being, and that includes the intellectual life. We are told that we change spiritually by having the categories of our minds renewed (Rom 12:1–2), that we are to include an intellectual love for God in our devotion (Matt 22:37–38), and that we are to be prepared to give others a reasonable answer to questions they ask us about why we believe what we believe (1 Pet 3:15). As the great eighteenth-century Christian thinker and spiritual master William Law put it, "Unreasonable and absurd ways of life . . . are truly an offense to God."[3]

Now learning and developing convictions about the teachings of Scripture are absolutely central to these mandates. However, many among Jesus' contemporary followers have failed to see that an aggressive pursuit of knowledge in areas outside the Bible is also relevant to these directives.

God has revealed Himself and various truths on a number of topics outside the Bible. As Christians have known throughout our history, common sense, logic, and mathematics, along with the arts, humanities, sciences, and other areas of study, contain important truths relevant to life in general and to the development of a careful, life-related Christian worldview.

In 1756, John Wesley delivered an address to a gathering of clergy on how to carry out the pastoral ministry with joy and skill. In it Wesley cataloged a number of things familiar to most contemporary believers—the cultivation of a disposition to glorify God and save souls, a knowledge of Scripture, and similar notions. However, at the first of his list, Wesley focused on something seldom expressly valued by most pastoral search committees: "Ought not a Minister to have,

---

[3] William Law, *A Serious Call to a Devout and Holy Life* (1728; repr., Grand Rapids: Eerdmans, 1966), 2.

First, a good understanding, a clear apprehension, a sound judgment, and a capacity of reasoning with some closeness?"[4]

Time and again throughout the address, Wesley unpacked this remark by admonishing ministers to know what would sound truly odd and almost pagan to the average congregant today: logic, metaphysics, natural theology, geometry, and the ideas of important figures in the history of philosophy. For Wesley, study in these areas (especially philosophy and geometry) helped train the mind to think precisely, a habit of incredible value, he asserted, when it comes to thinking as a Christian about theological themes or scriptural texts. According to Wesley, the study of extrabiblical information and of the writings of unbelievers is of critical value for growth and maturity. As he put it, "To imagine none can teach you but those who are themselves saved from sin, is a very great and dangerous mistake. Give not place to it for a moment."[5]

Wesley's remarks were not unusual in his time. A century earlier the great Reformed pastor Richard Baxter was faced with lukewarmness in the church and unbelief outside the church. In 1667 he wrote a book to meet this need; and in it he used philosophy, logic, and general items of knowledge outside Scripture to argue for the existence of the soul and the life to come. The fact that Baxter turned to philosophy and extrabiblical knowledge instead of small groups or praise hymns is worth pondering. In fact, it is safe to say that throughout much of church history, Scripture and right reason directed at extrabiblical truth were considered twin allies to be prized and used by disciples of Jesus.

In valuing extrabiblical knowledge, our brothers and sisters in church history were merely following common sense and Scripture itself. Repeatedly, Scripture acknowledges the wisdom of cultures outside Israel, e.g., Egypt (Isa 19:11–13), the Edomites (Jer 49:7), the Phoenicians (Zech 9:2), and many others. The remarkable achievements produced by human wisdom are acknowledged in Job 28:1–11.

[4] John Wesley, "An Address to the Clergy" in *The Works of John Wesley* (Grand Rapids: Baker, 1972), 481.
[5] John Wesley, *A Plain Account of Christian Perfection* (London: Epworth Press, 1952), 87.

The wisdom of Solomon is compared to the wisdom of the "sons of the east" and Egypt in order to show that Solomon's wisdom surpassed that of people with a long-standing, well-deserved reputation for wisdom (1 Kings 4:29–34). Paul approvingly quotes pagan philosophers (Acts 17:28), and Jude does the same thing with the noncanonical book *The Assumption of Moses* (Jude 9). The book of Proverbs is filled with examples in which knowledge, even moral and spiritual knowledge, can be gained from studying things (e.g., ants) in the natural world. Once Jesus taught that we should know we are to love our enemies, not on the basis of an Old Testament text but from reflection on God's general revelation: the rain and sunshine upon the just and the unjust reveal a merciful Creator (Matt 5:44–45).

In valuing extrabiblical knowledge, our brothers and sisters in church history were also living out scriptural teaching about the value of general revelation. As believers, we must never forget that God is the God of creation and general revelation just as He is the God of Scripture and special revelation.

The Christian teacher should do everything he can to gain and teach important and relevant knowledge in his area of teaching. At the level appropriate to one's station in life, the Christian teacher is called to be a Christian intellectual, at home in the world of ideas.

3. *The cost of a secular-sacred division resulting from a neglect of integration.* While few would actually put it in these terms, faith is now understood as a blind act of will, a sort of decision to believe something that is either independent of reason or that makes up for the paltry lack of evidence for what one is trying to believe. By contrast, biblical faith is a power or skill to act in accordance with the nature of the kingdom of God, a trust in and commitment to what we have reason to believe is true. Understood in this way, faith is built on reason. We should have good reasons for thinking that Christianity is true before we give complete dedication to it. We should have solid evidence that our understanding of a biblical passage is correct before we go on to apply it, and so on.

Unfortunately, our contemporary understanding of faith and reason treats them as polar opposites. A few years ago I went to New

York to conduct a series of evangelistic messages for a church. The series was in a high school gym, and several believers and unbelievers came each night. The first evening I gave arguments for the existence of God from science and philosophy. Before closing in prayer, I entertained several questions from the audience. One woman, a Christian, complained about my talk, charging that if I "proved" the existence of God, I would leave no room for faith. I responded by saying that if she were right, then we should pray that currently available evidence for God would evaporate and be refuted so there would be even more room for faith! Obviously, her view of faith utterly detached it from reason.

If faith and reason are deeply connected, then a teacher needs to explore her entire intellectual life in light of the Word of God. But if faith and reason are polar opposites, then the subject matter of one's teaching is irrelevant to one's growth in discipleship. Because of this view of faith and reason, a secular-sacred separation has emerged in our understanding of the Christian life with the result that Christian teaching and practice are privatized. The withdrawal of the corporate body of Christ from the public sphere of ideas is mirrored by our understanding of what is required to produce an individual disciple. Religion is personal, private, and a matter of how I feel about things. Clearly, there is no time like the present to recapture this integrative task. Given the abandonment of monotheism, the ground is weakened for believing in the unity of truth. This is one reason our *uni*-versities are turning into *multi*-versities. The fragmentation of secular education at all levels, along with its inability to define its purpose or gather together a coherent curriculum is symptomatic of what happens when monotheism is set aside. At this critical hour, the Christian has something increasingly rare and distinctive to offer our culture, and integration is at the heart of who we are as Christian thinkers/disciples.

4. *Integration and the nature of spiritual warfare.* Today spiritual warfare is widely misunderstood—briefly, that warfare is a conflict among persons (disembodied malevolent persons, namely, demons and the devil), human beings, and God Himself. Now persons control others by getting them to accept certain beliefs and emotions as

correct, good, and proper. This is precisely how the devil primarily works to destroy human beings and thwart God's work in history, namely, by influencing the idea structures in culture. That is why Paul makes the war of ideas central to spiritual conflict:

> For though we walk in the flesh, we do not war accord-
> ing to the flesh, for the weapons of our warfare are not of the
> flesh, but divinely powerful for the destruction of fortresses.
> We are destroying speculations and every lofty thing raised
> up against the knowledge of God, and we are taking every
> thought captive to the obedience of Christ (2 Cor 10:3–5).

Spiritual warfare is largely, though not entirely, a war of ideas; and we fight bad, false ideas with better ones. That means that truth, reason, argumentation, and so forth, using both Scripture and general revelation, are central weapons in the fight. Since the centers of education—schools, publishing houses, media, churches—are the centers for dealing with ideas, they become the main location for spiritual warfare. Solid, intelligent education, then, is part of our mandate to fight in spiritual conflict.

5. *Integration and spiritual formation.* Finally, it is crucial that we reflect a bit on the relationship between integration and the spiritual/devotional life. To begin with, there is a widespread hunger throughout our culture for genuine, life-transforming spirituality. This is as it should be. People are weary of those who claim to believe certain things when they do not see those beliefs having an impact on the lives of the heralds. Among other things integration is a spiritual activity—we may even call it a spiritual discipline—but not merely in the sense that often comes to mind in this context. Often Christians express the spiritual aspect of integration in terms of doxology: Christian integrators hold to and teach the same beliefs about their work or area of reflection that non-Christians accept but go on to add praise to God for the subject matter. Thus, the Christian biologist simply asserts the views widely accepted in the discipline but makes sure that class closes with a word of praise to God for the beauty and complexity of the living world.

Now the doxological approach is good as far as it goes; unfortunately, it doesn't go far enough in capturing the spiritual dimension of integration. We draw closer to the core of this dimension when we think about the role of beliefs in the process of spiritual transformation. Beliefs are the rails upon which our lives run. We almost always act according to what we really believe. It doesn't matter much what we say we believe or what we want others to think we believe. When the rubber meets the road, we act out our actual beliefs most of the time. That is why behavior is such a good indicator of a person's beliefs. The centrality of beliefs for spiritual progress is a clear implication of Old Testament teaching on wisdom and New Testament teaching about the role of a renewed mind in transformation. Thus, integration has as its spiritual aim the intellectual goal of structuring the mind so a person can see things as they really are and strengthening the belief structure that ought to inform the individual and corporate life of discipleship unto Jesus.

Integration can also help an unbeliever accept certain beliefs crucial to the Christian journey and aid a believer in maintaining and developing convictions about those beliefs. This aspect of integration becomes clear when we reflect on the notion of a plausibility structure. People will never be able to change their lives if they cannot even entertain the beliefs needed to bring about that change. By "entertain a belief" I mean to consider the *possibility* that the belief *might* be true. If people are hateful and mean to their fellow employee, these people will have to change what they believe about their coworkers before they will treat them differently. But if these hateful people cannot even entertain the thought that their coworkers are good and worthy of kindness, they will not change.

A person's plausibility structure is the set of ideas the person either is or is not willing to entertain as possibly true. For example, no one would come to a lecture defending a flat earth because this idea is just not part of our plausibility structure. We cannot even entertain the idea. Moreover, our plausibility structure is largely (though not exclusively) a function of the beliefs we already have. Applied to accepting or maintaining Christian belief, J. Gresham Machen got it right when he said:

God usually exerts that power in connection with certain prior conditions of the human mind, and it should be ours to create, so far as we can, with the help of God, those favorable conditions for the reception of the gospel. False ideas are the greatest obstacles to the reception of the gospel. We may preach with all the fervor of a reformer and yet succeed only in winning a straggler here and there, if we permit the whole collective thought of the nation or of the world to be controlled by ideas which, by the resistless force of logic, prevent Christianity from being regarded as anything more than a harmless delusion.[6]

If a culture reaches the point where Christian claims are not even part of its plausibility structure, fewer and fewer people will be able to entertain the possibility that they might be true. Whatever stragglers do come to faith in such a context would do so on the basis of felt needs alone, and the genuineness of such conversions would be questionable to say the least. And believers will not make much progress in the spiritual life because they will not have the depth of conviction or the integrated noetic structure necessary for such progress. This is why integration is so crucial to spirituality. It can create a plausibility structure in a person's mind, favorable conditions as Machen put it, so that Christian ideas can be entertained by that person. As Christian teachers, our goal is to make Christian ideas relevant to our subject matter appear to be true, beautiful, good, and reasonable to our students.

Current Integrative Priorities for the Christian Disciple

But how does a Christian decide on what to spend his energies in the integrative task? There are so many areas of study. What criteria are there to help one prioritize his efforts? Is there a taxonomy of issues that express some priorities that Christian scholars ought to adopt? I'm afraid I have a lot more thinking to do on this before I am prepared to

---

[6] J. Gresham Machen, "Christianity and Culture," *Princeton Theological Review* 11 (1913): 7. This article was originally an address delivered on September 20, 1912, at the opening of the 101st session of Princeton Theological Seminary.

offer anything approximating an adequate answer to these questions. Any taxonomy here would likely express the interests and biases of the taxonomist, and I am no exception to this rule. Obviously, one's own sense of personal calling and one's own curiosities will and should play an important role here.

But besides this, I think the following three criteria are not too wide of the mark. First, integration should be focused on those areas of study that seem to be intrinsically more central or foundational to the Christian theistic enterprise. The deeply imbedded metaphysical, epistemological, and axiological commitments that constitute mere Christianity should be preserved. Second, integration should be focused on areas that are currently under heavy attack. A third and, perhaps, less important criterion is this: integration should be focused on those areas of study in which such activity is underrepresented relatively speaking.

It is up to Christian teachers in each discipline to decide how these criteria inform their intellectual work. However, I think points one and two converge so as to yield an integrative mandate for contemporary Christians, especially those who work on the interface between science and Christianity. Christians must face an important cultural fact when they undertake the task of integration: There simply is no established, widely recognized body of ethical or religious knowledge now operative in the institutions of knowledge in our culture (e.g., the universities). Indeed, ethical and religious claims are frequently placed into what Francis Schaeffer used to call the upper story, and they are judged to have little or no rational authority, especially compared to the authority given to science to define the limits of knowledge and reality in those same institutions. This raises a pressing question: Is Christianity a knowledge tradition or merely a faith tradition, a perspective which, while true, cannot be known to be true and must be embraced on the basis of some intellectual state weaker than knowledge?

I agree with those who see a three-way worldview struggle in academic and popular culture among ethical monotheism (especially Christian theism), postmodernism, and scientific naturalism. As

Christians seek to promote Christianity as a knowledge tradition in their academic discipline, profession, or area of intellectual interest, they should keep in mind the impact of their work on this triumvirate. Both space considerations and my own view of priorities forbid me to say much about postmodernism here. I recognize it is a variegated tunic with many nuances. But to the degree that postmodernism denies the objectivity of reality, truth, value, reason (in its evidentiary if not psychological sense); to the degree that it rejects dichotomous thinking about real/unreal, true/false, rational/irrational, right/wrong; to the degree that it takes intentionality to create the objects of consciousness; to that degree it should be resisted by Christians.

Scientific naturalism also comes in many varieties; but, very roughly, a major form of it is the view that the spatiotemporal cosmos containing physical objects studied by the hard sciences is all there is and that the hard sciences are either the only source of knowledge or else vastly superior in proffering rationally justified beliefs compared to nonscientific fields. In connection with scientific naturalism, some have argued that the rise of modern science has contributed to the loss of intellectual authority in those fields like ethics and religion that, supposedly, are not subject to the types of testing and experimentation employed in science. Rightly or wrongly, science has in three ways been perceived as a threat to the intellectual credibility of Christianity:

1. Some scientific claims call into question certain interpretations of biblical texts (e.g., Gen 1–2) or certain theological beliefs (e.g., that humans have souls or are made in the image of God).

2. Some scientific claims, if correct, demote certain arguments for the existence of God (e.g., if natural, evolutionary processes can explain the origin or development of life, then we do not "need" to postulate a Creator/Designer to explain these things). There may be other reasons for believing in God, but the advances of science have robbed Christians of a number of arguments that used to be effective.

3. The progress of science vis-à-vis other disciplines like philosophy or theology justifies scientism, either the view that science and science alone offers true, justified beliefs (strong scientism) or that while other fields may offer true, justified beliefs in general, the degree of certainty

in science vastly outweighs what these other fields offer (weak scientism). As evolutionary naturalist George Gaylord Simpson put it:

> There is neither need nor excuse for postulation of non-material intervention in the origin of life, the rise of man, or any other part of the long history of the material cosmos. Yet the origin of that cosmos and the causal principles of its history remain unexplained and inaccessible to science. Here is hidden the First Cause sought by theology and philosophy. The First Cause is not known and I suspect it will never be known to living man. We may, if we are so inclined, worship it in our own ways, but we certainly do not comprehend it.[7]

Now Christians must respond to these three problem areas. One solution is the complementarity view according to which propositions, theories, or methodologies in theology and another discipline may involve two different, complementary, noninteracting approaches to the same reality. On this view theology and science interact much like the color and shape descriptions of an apple. Theology and science (or, for that matter, any discipline besides theology) interact in an additive way such that the whole truth is the sum of the contributions of both; but neither has direct, straightforward implications for the other. In my opinion the complementarian approach is inadequate as a total integrative model because, among other things, it contributes to the widespread philosophical naturalism that dominates much of the contemporary academy and broader culture. As Philip E. Johnson has pointed out:

> Politically astute scientific naturalists feel no hostility toward those religious leaders who implicitly accept the key naturalistic doctrine that supernatural powers do not actually affect the course of nature. . . . The most sophisticated naturalists realize that it is better just to say that statements about God are "religious" and hence incapable of being more than expressions of subjective feeling. It would be pretty

---

[7] George Gaylord Simpson, *The Meaning of Evolution* (New York: Bantam Books, 1971), 252.

ridiculous, after all, to make a big deal out of proving that Zeus and Apollo do not really exist.[8]

Elsewhere, Johnson observes:

> The conflict between the naturalistic worldview and the Christian supernaturalistic worldview goes all the way down. It cannot be papered over by superficial compromises. . . . It cannot be mitigated by reading the Bible figuratively rather than literally. . . . There is no satisfactory way to bring two such fundamentally different stories together, although various bogus intellectual systems offer a superficial compromise to those who are willing to overlook a logical contradiction or two. A clear thinker simply has to go one way or another.[9]

Johnson's remarks serve as a reminder that Christian complementarians run the risk of achieving integration between science and Christian theism at the price of placing the epistemological authority and certain important metaphysical claims of Christianity in some private, upper story. Whether intentional or not, when employed too broadly, the complementarity approach contributes to the scientism that controls contemporary culture. Thereby, it inadvertently fosters a separation of the secular and sacred because careful biblical exegesis does little intellectual work in the areas of study where complementarity is employed. The effect of this is to marginalize Christian doctrine in the marketplace of ideas.

In my view Christian complementarians give up too much intellectual ground too quickly in light of the pressures of philosophical naturalism. I am neither a sociologist nor the son of one, but I still opine that philosophical naturalism is sustained in the academy and broader culture by sociological and not distinctly rational factors. In my discipline, philosophy, signs indicate that important figures are finally acknowledging this. For example, naturalist Thomas Nagel has recently written:

[8] Phillip E. Johnson, *Defeating Darwinism* (Downers Grove, Ill.: InterVarsity, 1997), 100–1.
[9] Ibid., 111.

> In speaking of the fear of religion . . . I am talking about
> . . . the fear of religion itself. I speak from experience, being
> strongly subject to this fear myself: I want atheism to be true
> and am made uneasy by the fact that some of the most intelli-
> gent and well-informed people I know are religious believers.
> It isn't just that I don't believe in God and, naturally, hope
> that I'm right in my belief. It's that I hope there is no God! I
> don't want there to be a God; I don't want the universe to be
> like that. . . . My guess is that this cosmic authority problem
> is not a rare condition and that it is responsible for much of
> the scientism and reductionism of our time. One of the ten-
> dencies it supports is the ludicrous overuse of evolutionary
> biology to explain everything about life, including everything
> about the human mind.[10]

Along similar lines, in his 1996 presidential address for the Pacific
Division of the American Philosophical Association, Barry Stroud
noted that

> "Naturalism" seems to me in this and other respects rather
> like "World Peace." Almost everyone swears allegiance to it,
> and is willing to march under its banner. But disputes can
> still break out about what it is appropriate or acceptable to do
> in the name of that slogan. And like world peace, once you
> start specifying concretely exactly what it involves and how
> to achieve it, it becomes increasingly difficult to reach and to
> sustain a consistent and exclusive "naturalism."[11]

In light of these statements, it is time for Christians to be bold and
courageous in rejecting the authority of science to dictate in monologue fashion to theology what it can and cannot rationally affirm.
Christians must regain a respect for the cognitive authority of theology on the same par as our culture respects science.

[10] Thomas Nagel, *The Last Word* (New York: Oxford University Press, 1997), 130–31.
[11] Barry Stroud, "The Charm of Naturalism," *Proceedings and Addresses of the American Philosophical Association* 70 (1996): 43–44.

Intellectual Aims of Integration

As noted earlier, the word *integration* means forming or blending into a whole, uniting. One of the goals of integration is to maintain or increase both the conceptual relevance of and epistemological justification for Christian theism. To repeat Augustine's advice, "We must show our Scriptures not to be in conflict with whatever [our critics] can demonstrate about the nature of things from reliable sources."[12] We may distinguish three different aspects of the justificatory side of integration: direct defense, polemics, and Christian explanation.

1. *Direct Defense.* In direct defense one engages in integration with the primary intent of enhancing or maintaining directly the rational justification of Christian theism or some proposition taken to be explicit within or entailed by it, especially those aspects of a Christian worldview relevant to one's own discipline, work, or area of study. Specific attention should be given to topics that are intrinsically important to mere Christianity or currently under fire in one's field of teaching. Hereafter, I will simply refer to these issues as "Christian theism." I do so for brevity's sake. "Christian theism" should be taken to include specific views about a particular area of study that one takes to be relevant to the integrative task.

There are two basic forms of direct defense, one negative and one positive.[13] The less controversial of the two is a negative direct defense where one attempts to remove defeaters to Christian theism. If you have a justified belief regarding some proposition P, a defeater is something that weakens or removes that justification. Defeaters come in two types.[14] A rebutting defeater gives justification for believing ¬P ("not P")—in this case, that Christian theism is false. For example, attempts to show that the biblical concept of the family is dysfunctional and false or that homosexuality is causally necessitated by genes or brain states and that, therefore, it is not a proper object for moral appraisal are cases of rebutting defeaters. An undercutting defeater does

---

[12] Augustine, *De genesi ad litteram* 1.21.

[13] See Ronald Nash, *Faith and Reason* (Grand Rapids: Zondervan, 1988), 14–18.

[14] For a useful discussion of various types of defeaters, see John Pollock, *Contemporary Theories of Knowledge* (Totowa, N.J.: Rowman & Littlefield, 1986), 36–39; Ralph Baergen, *Contemporary Epistemology* (Fort Worth, Tex.: Harcourt Brace and Company, 1995), 119–24.

not give justification for believing ¬P but rather seeks to remove or weaken justification for believing P in the first place. Critiques of the arguments for God's existence are examples of undercutting defeaters. When defeaters are raised against Christian theism, a negative defense seeks either to rebut or to undercut those defeaters.

By contrast, a positive direct defense is an attempt to build a positive case for Christian theism. Arguments for the existence of God, objective morality, the existence of the soul, the value and nature of virtue ethics, and the possibility and knowability of miracles are examples. This task for integration is not accepted by all Christian intellectuals. For example, various species of what may be loosely called Reformed epistemology run the gamut from seeing a modest role for a positive direct defense to an outright rejection of this type of activity in certain areas (e.g., justifying belief in God and the authority of Holy Scripture).

2. *Philosophical Polemics.* In philosophical polemics, one seeks to criticize views that rival Christian theism in one way or another. Critiques of scientific naturalism, physicalism, pantheism, and normative ethical relativism are all cases of philosophical polemics.

3. *Theistic Explanation.* Suppose we have a set of items x_i through x_n that stand in need of explanation, and we offer some explanation E as an adequate or even best explanation of those items. In such a case, E explains x_i through x_n, and this fact provides some degree of confirmation for E. For example, if a certain intrinsic genre statement explains the various data of a biblical text, then this fact offers some confirmation for the belief that the statement is the correct interpretation of that text. Now Christian theists ought to be about the business of exploring the world in light of their worldview and, more specifically, of using their theistic beliefs as explanations of various desiderata in the intellectual life. Put differently, we should seek to solve intellectual problems and shed light on areas of puzzlement by using the explanatory power of our worldview. For example, for those who accept the existence of natural moral law, the irreducibly mental nature of consciousness, natural human rights, or the fact that human flourishing follows from certain biblically mandated ethical and religious

practices, the truth of Christian theism provides a good explanation of these phenomena. And this fact can provide some degree of confirmation for Christian theism.

Models Employed in Integration

When problem areas surface, there is a need for the Christian educator to think hard about the issue in light of the need for strengthening the rational authority of Christian theism and placing it squarely within the plausibility structure of contemporary culture. Let us use the term *theology* to stand for any Christian idea that seems to be a part of a Christian worldview derived primarily from special revelation. When one addresses problems like these, a number of different ways will emerge that theology can interact with an issue in a discipline outside theology. Here are some of the different ways that such interaction can take place.

1. *The Two Realms View.* Propositions, theories, or methodologies in theology and another discipline may involve two distinct, nonoverlapping areas of investigation. For example, debates about angels or the extent of the atonement have little to do with organic chemistry. Similarly, it is of little interest to theology whether a methane molecule has three or four hydrogen atoms in it.

2. *The Complementarity View.* Propositions, theories, or methodologies in theology and another discipline may involve two different, complementary, noninteracting approaches to the same reality. Sociological aspects of church growth, certain psychological aspects of conversion may be sociological or psychological descriptions of certain phenomena that are complementary to a theological description of church growth or conversion.

3. *The Direct Interaction View.* Propositions, theories, or methodologies in theology and another discipline may directly interact in such a way that either one area of study offers rational support for the other or one area of study raises rational difficulties for the other. For example, certain theological teachings about the existence of the soul raise rational problems for philosophical or scientific claims that deny

the existence of the soul. The general theory of evolution raises various difficulties for certain ways of understanding the book of Genesis. Some have argued that the big bang theory tends to support the theological proposition that the universe had a beginning.

4. *The Presuppositions View.* Theology tends to support the presuppositions of another discipline and vice versa. Some have argued that many of the presuppositions of science (e.g., the existence of truth; the rational, orderly nature of reality; the adequacy of our sensory and cognitive faculties as tools suited for knowing the external world) make sense and are easy to justify given Christian theism but are odd and without ultimate justification in a naturalistic worldview. Similarly, some have argued that philosophical critiques of epistemological skepticism and defenses of the existence of a real, theory-independent world and a correspondence theory of truth offer justification for some of the presuppositions of theology.

5. *The Practical Application View.* Theology fills out and adds details to general principles in another discipline and vice versa, and theology helps one practically apply principles in another discipline and vice versa. For example, theology teaches that fathers should not provoke their children to anger, and psychology can add important details about what this means by offering information about family systems, the nature and causes of anger, etc. Psychology can devise various tests for assessing whether one is or is not a mature person, and theology can offer a normative definition to psychology as to what a mature person is.

In sum, we have looked at the importance of and priorities for integration, as well as the goals and methods of integration. It becomes clear that Christian disciples need encouragement to sustain a self-understanding of their vocation as an intellectual calling, among other things. Moreover, it also becomes clear that Christians will need to think more creatively as to how to develop an integrated Christian worldview that can penetrate secular currents of thought shaping our culture. Will it be difficult? Indeed. It is hard to think of something more challenging. Is it worth the effort? The question answers itself.

Part 2

GOD

Chapter 3

WHY DOESN'T GOD MAKE HIS EXISTENCE MORE OBVIOUS TO US?

Michael J. Murray

The Problem of Hiddenness

Whether you are a Christian or not, one thing seems clear: if there is a God, He could make His existence much more clear to us than He does. For Christians, God's apparent distance or, some might feel, absence, leads to profound anxiety and disappointment with God. We can sense such despair, for example, in the words of Job:

> But if I go to the east, he is not there;
> if I go to the west, I do not find him.
> When he is at work in the north, I do not see him;
> when he turns to the south, I catch no glimpse of him.
> (Job 23:8–9 NIV)

Furthermore, the psalmist exclaims in apparent frustration, using words later uttered by Jesus on the cross: "My God, my God, why have you forsaken me? Why are you so far from saving me, so far from the words of my groaning? O my God, I cry out by day, but you do not answer" (Ps 22:1–2 NIV).

But not only theists have complained about the hiddenness of God. The late Norwood Hanson, philosopher of science at Yale University, once argued that his reason for disbelieving in God is that

God would make His existence known to us if He really exists; the fact that He doesn't do so is a good reason for disbelief. Hanson states his case vividly:

> "God exists" *could* in principle be established for all factually—it just happens not to be, certainly not for everyone! Suppose, however, that next Tuesday morning, just after breakfast, all of us in this one world are knocked to our knees by a percussive and ear-shattering thunderclap. Snow swirls; leaves drop from the trees; the earth heaves and buckles; buildings topple and towers tumble; the sky is ablaze with an eerie, silvery light. Just then, as all the people of this world look up, the heavens open—the clouds pull apart—revealing an unbelievably immense and radiant-like Zeus figure, towering above us like a hundred Everests. He frowns darkly as lightening plays across the features of his Michelangeloid face. He then points down—*at* me!—and explains, for every man and child to hear: "I have had quite enough of your too-clever logic-chopping and word-watching in matters of theology. Be assured, N. R. Hanson, that I most certainly do exist." . . .
>
> Please do not dismiss this as a playful, irreverent Disney-oid contrivance. The conceptual point here is that *if* such a remarkable event were to occur, *I* for one should certainly be convinced that God does exist. That matter of fact would have been settled once and for all time. . . . That God exists would, through this encounter, have been confirmed for me and for everyone else in a manner every bit as direct as that involved in any non-controversial factual claim.[1]

More recent atheists have explicitly invoked the hiddenness of God as sufficient reason for rejecting the existence of God, and this argument has some initial force. Because of this, I expect that this argument, one of two fairly new arguments for atheism, will, in the next

---

[1] Norwood Russell Hanson, *What I Do Not Believe and Other Essays* (New York: Humanities, 1971), 313–14.

generation, be taken by many to be the most compelling reason to accept atheism. In this essay we will critically examine this argument to see if it is as powerful as many atheists believe.

Arguing for Atheism

Before we take a look at that argument, it is worth pausing briefly to think about the project of arguing for atheism. It is good to start here because many people seem to think that it makes no sense to talk about arguing for the *nonexistence* of something. We understand what it would mean to argue *for* the existence of something. But can we also construct arguments for the *nonexistence* of something? We can, in two ways.

One way we can argue for the nonexistence of something is by showing that the thing described is *impossible*. If I tell you I have a round square in my pocket, you would know that I am wrong. You know there is no round square in my pocket (or anywhere else) because you know there *cannot be* round squares. Round things necessarily *lack* corners while squares necessarily *have* corners. One thing can't both have and lack corners. So there can be no such thing as a round square.

Of course it is rare to find people believing in things that are as obviously impossible as round squares. Yet there are other cases of believing in the existence of impossible things where the impossibility is not as obvious. For example, let's imagine that you are training to be a hairstylist. One of your classes in cosmetology school is entitled: Famous Hairstylists in History. In the class your professor tells you of a famous barber who lived in the European region of Saxony. This barber was enormously famous and incredibly busy. In fact, he was so popular that in Saxony he cut the hair of every single person (except those who cut their own hair). *That* is one famous and prosperous barber! The professor goes on to give an inspiring lecture, telling you that if you study and work hard, you too can become as famous and prosperous as the ancient barber of Saxony.

Now what is the point of this example? It is this: I know that there was no barber of Saxony. How? Because he is as impossible as the round square. To see why, remember that everyone in Saxony fits into one of two categories: cuts his own hair or has his hair cut by the barber. Now consider this question: which category is our barber in? Any answer to this question leads to a paradox. If he does *not* cut his own hair, then he *must cut his own hair* (since he cuts the hair of every person who does not cut his own hair). But if he *does cut his own hair*, then he doesn't cut his own hair since our barber doesn't cut the hair of people who cut their own. As a result, something impossible follows whether we suppose he cuts his own hair or not. And so our imagined barber is impossible; he can't exist.

Some people argue for the impossibility of God in similar fashion, claiming that no being, God included, can be, for example, both *all-powerful* and *unable* to do evil, or *free* in choosing among worlds to create and yet *compelled* to do the best he can. This is one way to argue for atheism though not the way we will pursue here.

A second way we can argue for the nonexistence of something is to show that certain *telltale signs* are absent which would be present if the thing in question actually did exist (or that certain telltale signs are present which would be absent if the thing in question actually did exist). If there had been a thunderstorm last night, your driveway would be wet this morning. If it is dry, you can safely conclude that there was no thunderstorm last night. The dry driveway is a telltale sign that leads you to infer the nonexistence of a thunderstorm.

Some atheists similarly argue for the nonexistence of God using these telltale signs arguments. The most widely known argument of this sort is the argument from evil: if there were a God, there would be no evil; but there is evil, so there must be no God. Evil is a telltale sign that there is no God. However, the argument we are going to focus on here is a different telltale sign argument—the argument from divine hiddenness: if there were a God, he would not be hidden; but he is hidden, so there must be no God. We turn to that argument presently.

The Argument from Hiddenness

The most notable contemporary defender of the argument from hiddenness is the philosopher John Schellenberg. In his book *Divine Hiddenness and Human Reason*, Schellenberg puts the argument as follows:

1. If there is a God, he is perfectly loving.
2. If a perfectly loving God exists, then no one could be a reasonable atheist.
3. But there are people who are reasonable atheists.
4. Thus, no perfectly loving God exists.
5. Thus, there is no God.[2]

The argument is clear and simple. And the conclusion follows from the premises. So now the question is, is there anything wrong with these premises?

We can take issue with only two premises, and they are premises 2 and 3. Initially, many theists are inclined to reject 3. For them, anyone who fails to believe that God exists must simply be failing to see the evidence that God has plainly set before us. Because of this failure, all atheists must count as unreasonable.

However, just because God makes evidence available to us that is sufficient for belief isn't enough for us to conclude that all atheists are unreasonable. Instead, to reject premise 3 we would need to be able to credibly claim that the evidence God has provided is so clear, telling, and unmistakable that someone would have to be unreasonable to fail to see it. That is a strong claim. Of course the mere fact that it is a strong claim doesn't make it wrong. In fact, a number of Christians have taken this strong claim to be directly supported in Scripture, which teaches that the creation makes the existence, invisible attributes, and nature of God known in such a way that those who fail to see these things are "without excuse" (Rom 1:18–20). Perhaps that is a good enough reason to reject premise 3 and thus the argument as a whole.

[2] John Schellenberg, *Divine Hiddenness and Human Reason* (Ithaca, N.Y.: Cornell University Press, 1993).

Schellenberg is convinced otherwise. He claims that while some atheists might reject the existence of God for no reason or perhaps even for bad reasons, many others reject the existence of God for good reasons. Some of these atheists have given long, hard attention to the arguments for and against the existence of God; and, after fair-mindedly weighing the evidence, they have come down against it. Since Schellenberg thinks that we cannot count such atheists as unreasonable, he also thinks premise 3 cannot be denied. As a result, he thinks the argument stands or falls with premise 2.

Assessing the Argument

In the rest of this essay, I intend to show two things. First, the argument from hiddenness depends on a certain flawed logic. Once we show this, we will see why the argument from hiddenness fails to demonstrate the truth of atheism. But showing that won't take away the lingering unease we feel about the fact that God is as hidden from us as He appears to be. As a result, after we see what is wrong with this argument, we will consider this phenomenon of hiddenness and see what explanations theists might be able to offer for it.

To begin, let's reconsider premise 2. Why does the atheist think, as the premise states, that if God exists there would be no reasonable atheists? The answer is that if a loving God exists, He would want His creatures to enter into a loving relationship with Him. And if you want people to be in loving relationship with you, they first need to know that you exist. Thus God would make His existence clear and obvious to us, as a necessary precondition for having this all-important relationship with us. Furthermore, because of the importance of having this relationship with God, then God would provide us with evidence so unmistakable that we could only fail to see it if we are being unreasonable.

Notice that the reasoning offered in favor of this premise invites us to think about what God would or should do in order to achieve certain aims that God has. Specifically, it invites us to think that God *should make His existence obvious to us* as a way of achieving His *goal of establishing human-divine relationships.* However, whenever you hear someone make an argument of any sort that starts from what we ought to expect God would or should do in order to achieve His aims, you have to ask yourself this question: "How could these critics be sure about what God would or should do in order to achieve some goal or other that He might have?" Many times simply asking yourself the question makes the answer plain: they can't. God's wisdom and insight so vastly exceed our own that it would be the height of folly to assume that we could discern the various possible ways God might be able to achieve His goal. As a result, it is also the height of folly for us to presume to know how God *should* go about trying to achieve His aims.

We can see the same phenomenon at work when we consider the argument for atheism that takes the existence of evil as its starting point. Those defending this argument claim that there are certain things we can expect of God as a result of our knowledge that God is a perfectly good being who aims to do His best—for example, we can expect that He would prevent all evil. But reasoning this way ignores the possibility that there might be some *good reason* for God to allow those evils that we think He wouldn't or shouldn't allow. Maybe a good God wants to do away with evil. But maybe He also wants a world with free creatures that can make morally significant choices. Allowing such free creatures just might *require* putting up with their choosing and causing evil, at least for a time. And thus, what we initially expect of God—that He would prevent all evil—turns out to be mistaken on further consideration. God had reasons for permitting it that we just weren't initially aware of.

The same thing that is true with respect to evil might be true with respect to hiddenness. In fairness we need to say not that God would not permit there to be any reasonable atheists but rather that God would not permit there to be any reasonable atheists unless *He has some good reason for doing so.* Once we see the need to add this extra condition, we can see that the argument from hiddenness needs to be modified as follows:

(1) If there is a God, he is perfectly loving

(2+) If a perfectly loving God exists, then there would not be reasonable atheists unless God has some good reason for allowing there to be reasonable atheists.

(3) There are people who are reasonable and who are atheists.

(3+) There is no good reason for God to allow there to be such atheists.

(4) Thus, no perfectly loving God exists.

(5) Thus, there is no God.

While the logic of the argument is impeccable, defending premise (3+) is no small task! How, we should wonder, do (or could) atheists—or anyone else for that matter—know that premise (3+) is true? Interestingly, when atheists are pressed on this question, they answer as follows: we have thought about this issue for a long time, and we don't see any possible good reason for God to allow there to be reasonable atheists. Philosophers call arguments of this sort "noseeum" arguments since they hold that since I don't see any good reason for God to allow this sort of thing, there isn't any good reason. Are noseeum arguments any good?

Sometimes they are. If your roommate asks you to get the milk from the refrigerator and you open the door, look carefully, and don't see any milk there, it is reasonable for you to conclude that there is no milk in the refrigerator *because you don't see it.* That is a good noseeum argument. But not all noseeum arguments are good. Imagine that you go to the doctor to get your immunizations. The doctor removes the protective sleeve from the needle and is about to inject you with it when he accidentally drops it on the floor. He picks it up and appears ready to continue when you object: "Doctor, I think that needle might be dirty; there might be germs on it!" The doctor holds the needle up to the light, closes one eye, and stares at it intently. After a few seconds he says, "I have looked closely, and I don't see any germs on it; there's nothing to worry about." This doctor has made a noseeum inference, and it is a *bad one.*

What separates good noseeum inferences from bad ones? For a noseeum inference to be good, two conditions must be met. First, it must be the case that you are *looking for the thing in question in the right place*. If your roommate asks you if there is any milk and you look in the oven, you are looking in the wrong place. Your failing to see it *there* would not be good evidence that you don't have any milk. Second, it must be the case that *you would see the thing in question if it really were there*. If your roommate asks if there are ants in the yard and you look at the window and say, "Nope. I don't see any," you have made a bad noseeum inference. You are looking in the right place, but ants are too small to be seen by you even if they are there.

Is the argument in favor of (3+) more like the argument of the roommate looking for milk or the doctor looking for germs? The answer is clear: more like the doctor. To see why, consider our two conditions of a good noseem argument. First, when atheists are looking for the reasons that God might allow Himself to remain somewhat hidden, are those atheists *looking in the right place*? Well, it is hard to know because it is hard to know what the right place would be. In any case, it seems highly unlikely that the right place to look is in the introspective consciousness of the atheist. Why would atheists take their powers of imagination to exhaust all the possible good reasons God might have for allowing hiddenness? Second, if an atheist were looking in the right place for such reasons, is it clear that the atheist would find them? There is certainly no reason to think so. Perhaps the reasons are so complex and difficult to unscramble that we wouldn't grasp them even if they were, so to speak, staring us in the face. As a result, the argument for (3+) is a failure, and so the argument from hiddenness is as well.

Still some people might think this doesn't settle the matter. Is it fair simply to throw up our hands and say, "How are we supposed to know why God would allow hiddenness to occur?" After all, ignorance of this sort doesn't *explain* hiddenness, and the atheist is simply demanding such an explanation.

True enough, our pleading ignorance doesn't explain hiddenness. But here we need to make two important points. First, the argument from hiddenness itself does not oblige the theist to explain hiddenness. Rather, it is the atheist who needs to be able to defend that claim that *God has no good reason for allowing hiddenness* to make the argument from hiddenness work. That, after all, is one of the premises of the argument. The atheist has not adequately defended that claim because there is no way we could know such a thing. Second, despite this, it is true that nothing we have said here explains why God is as hidden as he is. Because of this, some of the existential anxiety that we feel when confronted with hiddenness still remains. So can the Christian go further and try to propose some reason that would explain hiddenness? Yes! And in the final section, we will look at one such explanation.

An Explanation of Divine Hiddenness

It seems clear that one of the things God wants in His creation is creatures who can, at least for a time, freely choose to love Him or reject Him. What does the world have to be like to allow that? First, it needs to contain creatures with the ability to make free choices. Second, those creatures must exist in conditions where that freedom can be exercised. What sorts of conditions might those be?

It turns out that there are a number of them, but we need to focus on only one of them here: an absence of *pervasive coercion*. Everyone has had the experience of driving down the highway, perhaps going just a little bit faster than the posted speed limit allows, and spying a police car off in the bushes on the side of the road. What is our reaction? Immediately we hit the brakes and slow down to a speed below the limit. The presence of the police officer causes us to fear a penalty for violating the law that forces us to slow down. And that is, of course, exactly why the officer is there. But things aren't always like that. There are plenty of times when no one is watching over our shoulder, ensuring that we do what we should. Under those conditions, no external threat constrains us, allowing us freely to choose to obey the law or not.

Now imagine what things would be like if there were, so to speak, moral police officers on every corner, threatening to fine or imprison us for any violation of our moral duties. In such a world not only would people be coerced into obeying the speed limit; they would be coerced into behaving morally under every imaginable condition. A world like that would be a world filled with *pervasive coercion*, and in such a world no morally significant free choice would be possible.

How is this relevant to divine hiddenness? To see how, consider the sort of world that Schellenberg or Hanson seems to think God should create. They think that God ought to reveal Himself in a way that makes possible the loving relationship He wants with creatures. They think this would mean, (a) making it unmistakably clear that God exists. But surely an all-good God would want to make more than *that* clear to us. If God really loves us and wants us to experience true fulfillment, God would want to tell us in equally clear and unmistakable terms (b) how we can have good lives; and this would mean revealing to us His moral will, and how following His moral will alone brings us happiness, and how failing to follow it will lead us into misery and destruction.

But consider for a moment what would really happen if God brought about (b). Were God to make those things described in (b) unavoidably and unmistakably clear to us, what would be the result? Undoubtedly, God would become the equivalent of the moral police, patrolling every corner of your life. God would be directly present in our lives, making clear to us that loving obedience is the only way to experience happiness and that sin and evil will lead to swift and unavoidable punishment. Under conditions like that, we would be subject to *pervasive coercion* in our daily lives. And in those conditions, morally significant freedom becomes impossible. As a result, it seems that God cannot make Himself known to us in the ways specified in (a) and (b).

At this point one might think that something in my assessment of the argument from hiddenness has gone wrong here. After all, like Schellenberg and Hanson, Christians think that God must, and can, and does make His existence and will known to us. But they don't think that His doing so undermines our ability to act freely. How is that possible? That is, how can God make His existence and will known to us without introducing *pervasive coercion?* Here is where some hard thinking is needed. To answer this question, we need to give careful attention to coercion and to how it works.

Coercion occurs when threats are made which put what we might call "coercive pressure" on us. When we unpack the concept of coercive pressure with some care, we can see that it results from the interplay of at least five factors:

1. The strength of the threat: that is, how bad the threatened consequence appears to be.
2. The "imminence" of the threat. This factor has three elements:
   a Probabilistic: the likelihood that the threatened consequence will actually be carried out.
   b Temporal: how quickly the threatened consequence will be carried out.
   c Epistemic: the extent of the "felt awareness" of the threatened consequence (more will be said on this below).
3. Threat indifference: the extent to which the person threatened feels indifferent to threats.

In order for God to preserve the preconditions necessary for creaturely freedom, the coercive pressure that comes with the knowledge of His existence and moral will must be mitigated. Which of these factors can God "monkey with" to lower coercive pressure and thus safeguard creaturely freedom?

It does not appear that God can mitigate (1) since the strength of the "threat" for disbelieving or disobeying God seems fixed. If one fails to come to know God or obey His moral will (including the command to trust Christ for our salvation), that person is destined for eternal separation from God. It does not appear that mitigating this consequence is possible. The second factor, probabilistic imminence, is equally fixed. If God promises some result for failing to know or obey Him, the probability that the threatened consequence will be carried out is 100 percent. How could it be less? Only if God might be fooled or forget or change His mind. None of those are possible.

Temporal imminence can be mitigated in some sense since at least some of the consequences of failure to believe or obey are pushed into the afterlife. But notice two things about this. First, for any given person, even the afterlife might begin in the next instant. So does delaying the punishment "until the afterlife" really reduce the "temporal imminence of the threat"? It seems not. Second, even if these punishments were seen as temporally distant, it is hard to imagine that this would make any difference given the extreme nature of the threatened consequence—eternal separation from God.

Let's skip epistemic imminence for a moment. What about (3) threat indifference? Could God mitigate indifference as a way of mitigating coercive pressure? It seems not. After all, the extent to which we are indifferent to threats seems to be something that arises from our own free choosing. Some people develop resistance to threats by working hard at it (bullies). Others do not (those who routinely allow themselves to be bullied). In either case the indifference seems to result from our own free choice. God could only attune this factor by (objectionably) interfering with our own free choice.

As a result we are left only with epistemic imminence. But what exactly is epistemic imminence? It is the factor that explains why, for example, television spots that show horrible accident scenes caused by drunk drivers actually succeed in deterring people from drinking and driving. These spots don't provide the viewers with any new information. No one thinks, after watching such a spot, "Gee, I never knew drunk driving could cause accidents." Rather, what they do is take information that we already know and present it to us in a way that is emotionally gripping and compelling. What such television spots do is change the "epistemic imminence" of the "threatened consequence."

Since God cannot mitigate coercive pressure by mitigating the other four factors that contribute toward coercive pressure, God must do it by modifying the epistemic imminence of His existence and moral nature. When He does so, however, the result is the phenomenon we have been describing as divine hiddenness.

Notice that decreasing the epistemic imminence (and thus becoming more hidden) does not mean that there will be *no evidence* or only *weak evidence* available to us concerning the existence of God. We can see this again by considering the television spots that serve to reduce the incidence of drunk driving. People who are moved by these spots already know full well that drinking and driving is dangerous. That evidence was already fully available to them. But the information imparted by the evidence lacked the epistemic imminence to compel them to stop drinking and driving. It took the television spots to do that. Likewise, God could make all sorts of information available to us concerning His existence and moral will (such as a written revelation, an Incarnate Son, etc.). As long as the information is not imparted in such a way as to make this information epistemically imminent (and thus coercive) God will succeed in safeguarding our morally significant freedom.

Conclusion

The argument from hiddenness represents a challenge to the truth of theism that is being voiced with increased urgency by defenders of atheism. However, atheists using this argument have failed to see that making it work requires the assumption—a large assumption indeed—that God could have no good reason for allowing there to be reasonable atheists. We have seen that this claim is based on a noseeum inference that fails the two tests that good noseeum inferences must pass. In addition, these atheists fail to see that there are indeed some good reasons that God should allow His existence to be partially hidden or veiled to us. One reason we have examined here is that such hiddenness seems necessary to safeguard creaturely moral freedom. As a result, the argument from hiddenness clearly fails to provide a good reason for accepting atheism.

Chapter 4

TWO VERSIONS OF THE COSMOLOGICAL ARGUMENT

R. Douglas Geivett

I had that world-weary feeling you sometimes get when traveling. So, hunkered down in my window seat, it was mildly comforting to know that the next seat over was unoccupied. The young woman on the aisle appeared to favor a quiet, conversation-free flight—another positive. But in my gut I knew this arrangement wouldn't last. The plane was filling up, and the nice buffer I had hoped for would no doubt be taken by another passenger. Now I feared that it would be someone with a talkative streak. In fact, a shadow of conviction spread over me that whoever it was would *definitely* be an extrovert. The book I had with me would come in handy. I could look like I was reading and not to be interrupted, even if the words on the page were a blur to my tired eyes and mind. I could also break open my laptop in the event of an emergency.

I set my props in place for the forthcoming act and peered over the edge of the book. I wanted to monitor the entrance to the plane and see if I could identify my predestined seatmate without the benefit of indisputable evidence. I had this powerful intuition that I should expect some jaunty young fellow or perhaps a perky octogenarian. Some minutes later a guy bounced onboard, full of vigor and bonhomie. He was exuberance itself. That had to be the one. It was.

Without delay I buried myself in the lifesaving book. And for most of the journey, it worked. But the act required total concentration.

Exuberance guy was watchful, ready to pounce on the slightest opportunity to engage. The trick was to turn the unread pages at a natural rate and carefully avoid eye contact. And the plan would have worked until touchdown if it hadn't been for the kindness of a flight attendant, who, in complete innocence, offered me water. As I reached to accept this small gift—I assure you, the act was as brief as it could be—exuberance guy interposed himself between us and looked me in the eye, saying, "Hey, what's that you're reading there?"

I answered with less than admirable compactness: "It's a book."

Not to be put off, he pressed, "What's it about?"

"It's a book in philosophy." This did not have the customary effect.

"Are you a philosopher?"

"Yes."

"Really!" he said, with truly over-the-top enthusiasm. "I've always wanted to talk to a philosopher! I have so many questions."

Resigned to my fate, I asked the inevitable question: "What would you like to talk about?"

Turns out he had a friend at work that enjoyed debate, mostly about religion and politics. The two would disagree on most things. Exuberance guy told me that one topic came up most frequently. He said his friend believed in God; so he wanted to know if I could give him some ammunition that would blow up the case for God's existence. I said I might be able to help, but I needed to ask a couple of questions.

"Fire away," he said (or something to that effect).

"OK, you say your friend believes in God; so apparently you do not. What do you believe instead?"

"Oh, I believe in a higher power," he answered matter-of-factly and without hesitation—not an utterly clear and distinct concept.

So I asked, "What do you mean by a higher power?"

For a moment he looked genuinely perplexed, like, "What kind of a fool philosopher doesn't know what a higher power is?" My impassive expression must have told him that I really did expect an answer. Here's what he said; I remember his exact words. "A higher power is

. . . a power . . . that is . . . really high!" He spread his arms to gauge the magnitude of the power in question. I must confess, this struck me as a pretty superficial response, one for which I was, just possibly, overtrained.

I had one question left: "Why do you believe in a power that is really high?"

At that point things improved. He said, "Look around. All of this must have been caused by something."

I glanced through the window and looked down at the majestic landscape, stretched out some forty thousand feet below us. I couldn't disagree. I looked back at him and said, "If you believe that, then I'm not sure why you don't believe in God."

We were now fully engaged. The rest of our conversation was interesting, sometimes even a little animated. But the details are irrelevant for the purposes of this chapter. The important point is that this guy, who didn't believe in God, had just stated a low-tech version of the *cosmological argument* for the existence of God: the universe must have had a cause, and that cause must have been equipped with a load of power.

Kinds of Cosmological Arguments

All cosmological arguments reason from the *cosmos* to the existence of God, or cosmos-Maker. More precisely, cosmological arguments infer the existence of God from the need to *explain* the existence of the physical universe.

These arguments begin with observation of the obvious and at least a moderate degree of curiosity about the obvious. The observation: *There is a physical universe*. What could be more obvious? We don't expect much disagreement about that. For many, though, the existence of the physical universe is so obvious it never strikes them as odd that there should be such a thing. It's simply taken for granted. And why not, as long as they wake up in the same world each day and the familiar laws of nature (like gravity) continue working in the usual way.

I can relate. Even for me, a philosopher by trade, the practical problems of life can muscle aside my inclination toward philosophical rumination. Maybe if I woke up in one of Robert Heinlein's parallel universes and wanted to hitchhike my way back to this one, the space-time coordinates of this world would matter more to me.[1]

During a quiet moment you might ask yourself this question: *"Why is there something rather than nothing at all?"* You don't have to be a trained professional to go there. You can do it at home on your own.

You'll soon realize that this question is an extension by many degrees of a question most of us do contemplate at least occasionally: "Why do *I* exist? I might *not* have existed, but here I am." We know that we would not exist if the universe did not exist. So there's a connection of interest between my existence and the existence of the cosmos. We might well reflect, "Why does the cosmos exist? It might not have existed. But here it is." Part of solving the mystery of our own existence is solving, if we can, the mystery of the existence of the cosmos, the physical environment where we conduct our lives and which determines the potentialities of our existence.

So what is it about the physical universe that needs explaining? Its *existence*, of course. But why? For two reasons: because of *what sort of thing* the universe is and because of the *temporal longevity* of the universe. These two reasons give us two broad categories of cosmological arguments. Within each category there are various formulations. There are far too many versions of the cosmological argument to do justice to more than two of them here. In my opinion, they are "best of breed."

A Contingency Argument for the Existence of God

The first broad category of cosmological arguments zeroes in on a specific feature of the universe: its *contingency*. Contingency is a mode of existence: an entity is contingent if it is not a necessary being, if it does not exist *necessarily*. Every actually existing entity is either

[1] See, for example, Robert Heinlein, *Job: A Comedy of Justice* (New York: Del Ray, 1985) and his *The Number of the Beast* (New York: Ballantine, 1980) or Isaac Asimov, *The Gods Themselves* (West Sussex, England: Gollanz, 2000).

necessary or contingent. (All "entities" that could exist but do not would also be contingent if they existed since the fact that they are possible but not actual guarantees that they are not necessary.)

How are we to determine whether an entity is contingent or necessary? Our criterion is just this: if it is in the nature of a thing to exist, then its existence is necessary, and it is a necessary being; otherwise, it is a contingent entity, depending for its existence on something else. But how to tell whether it is in the nature of a thing to exist? Certainly, if a thing begins to exist or passes out of existence, it is a contingent thing. It is not in the nature of the thing for it to exist; it is not necessary. On the contrary, it depends on something else for its existence. If it were not for some appropriate cause, any entity that is contingent simply would not exist.

There are three major components in any contingency argument for the existence of God:

1. Establish the contingency of the physical universe.
2. Show how the contingency of the universe entails the existence of a necessary being.
3. Show that this necessary being is God.

The argument I've selected to represent this type of cosmological argument was developed in the eighteenth century.

Samuel Clarke's Cosmological Argument

Samuel Clarke (1675–1729), an English philosopher and Anglican minister, produced an influential version of the cosmological argument that has enjoyed the attention of philosophers for three centuries. Everyone agrees that it is an argument from the contingency of the universe. But in the formulation I present, following Clarke's own language closely, I use the terms *dependent* and *dependently*, rather than *contingent* and *contingently*.[2]

---

[2] Clarke's brief exposition of this argument appears in *A Discourse Concerning Natural Religion* (1705). It is conveniently excerpted under the title "Samuel Clarke: The Argument from Contingency," in Louis P. Pojman, ed., *Philosophy of Religion: An Anthology*, 4th ed. (Belmont, Calif.: Wadsworth, 2003).

1. Something must have existed from all eternity.

2. If something has existed from all eternity, then either there has always existed one unchangeable and independent Being, or there has been an infinite succession of changeable and dependent beings.

3. Either there has always existed one unchangeable and independent Being, or there has been an infinite succession of changeable and dependent beings.

4. An endless series of dependent beings either is caused by something external to itself, or it contains within itself the reason for its own existence (i.e., it is self-existent).

5. If an endless series of dependent beings is self-existent, then at least some one thing in the series must be self-existent.

6. Every being within an endless series of dependent beings depends for its existence on some other being in the series.

7. An endless series of dependent beings cannot be self-existent. [5, 6]

8. An endless series of dependent beings must be caused by something external to itself.

9. The external reason for the existence of an endless series of dependent beings must be either a dependent being or a self-existent being.

10. The external reason for the existence of an endless series of dependent beings cannot be a dependent being.

11. The external reason for the existence of an endless series of dependent beings must be a self-existent being.

12. If an endless series of dependent beings exists, then a self-existent being exists.

13. This self-existent being must have existed from eternity and be immutable and independent.

Clarke turns next to a lengthy and sophisticated discussion of the nature of this self-existent being. There isn't space to do that here. But I do want to explain each statement in the argument, and the progression of one statement to another.

1. Something must have existed from all eternity. Samuel Clarke has an independent argument for this claim, but I leave it as homework for you to check that out. The statement seems obviously true. But it needs to be noted that what is initially most obvious is that the universe exists. From this it follows that something exists. The present claim is that if something exists, then something—whether or not it is the same thing—has existed from eternity; something has always existed.

Consider the implications if this is denied. The universe exists, but it has not always existed. And neither has anything else. So why is there a universe that has not always existed? This question leads directly to a different kind of argument for the existence of God, namely, a first-cause type of argument. In other words, if someone denies the first premise of Clarke's cosmological argument, we can pursue a different line of argument for the conclusion that God exists as the cause of the beginning of the universe. That sort of argument is developed later in this chapter.

The claim we have started with is not especially controversial. So we proceed to the next premise.

2. If something has existed from all eternity, then either there has always existed one unchangeable and *independent* Being, or there has been an infinite succession of changeable and *dependent* beings. Only two kinds of things can have existed from eternity. The first is an unchangeable and independent Being. The second is an infinite succession of changeable and dependent beings. These are not mutually exclusive. It's possible that both kinds of things have always existed.[3]

In his exposition Clarke expands on both kinds of things that can have existed from eternity. Clearly the universe is not an unchangeable, independent Being. But the universe could be an infinite succession of changeable and dependent beings. The picture here is of a string of changeable and dependent beings that are related to one another in succession (one after the other). Each individual being is changeable

---

[3] Clarke uses the capital letter *B* for an unchangeable and independent Being because of the superior kind of existence it has in comparison with changeable and dependent beings.

(for example, comes to be or ceases to be), and each is dependent on some other individual being in the string.

This string of changeable and dependent beings can have existed from eternity but only on one condition: it must contain infinitely many changeable entities standing in successive dependence relations. Clarke concedes that the universe may be like that. It's possible that the physical universe has always existed. But if it has, it exists, as a whole, as an infinite succession of changeable and dependent entities. These entities, he says, would be "produced one from another in an endless progression, without any original cause at all."

So this argument does not require the assumption that the universe had a beginning.

3. Either there has always existed one unchangeable and *independent* Being, or there has been an infinite succession of changeable and *dependent* beings. This follows directly from premises 1 and 2. By a logical principle called *modus ponens*, if premises 1 and 2 are true, then statement 3 must also be true. Hence, no special argument is needed to establish this point.

4. An endless series of dependent beings either is caused by something external to itself, or it contains within itself the reason for its own existence. Here we come to a premise that makes use of an important principle, called the Principle of Sufficient Reason. There are various formulations of this principle. Clarke holds that *for anything that exists, there must be a reason for its existence.* Only two kinds of *reasons for existence* are possible. Something may contain the reason for its existence within itself. It may, in other words, be *self-existent.*[4] If an entity is not self-existent, then the reason for its existence must lie outside itself.

We are now considering the universe as a possibly endless series of dependent beings. Since the universe exists, it is either self-existent,

---

[4] Clarke's choice of terms here is deliberate. We are not to confuse a *self-existent* being with a *self-caused* being. A self-existent being, while it does contain within itself a reason for its own existence, cannot be caused to exist by itself. For Clarke, a self-existent being is a *necessary* being. Such a being cannot not exist. Hence, it will not have been caused to exist at all. But we can understand why it exists if we understand that it is a necessary being that cannot, given its nature, not exist. This is what it means for such a being to contain the reason for its existence within itself.

or the reason for its existence lies beyond the universe. Now we must consider whether the universe may be self-existent. If it may, then this argument will have entered a cul-de-sac where God cannot be found.

5. If an endless series of dependent beings is self-existent, then at least some one thing in the series must be self-existent. This statement tells us what it would mean for the universe, considered as a possibly endless series of dependent beings, to be self-existent. At least one entity within the series would have to be self-existent, or necessary. No series of dependent things can be self-existent if it has no self-existent parts, even if the series is endless—perhaps *especially* if the series is endless.

Suppose the series is finite and the universe has a beginning after all. Then *perhaps* the first entity in the series is self-existent and therefore supplies the reason for the rest of the series. But on our hypothesis, the universe is an endless series of things (all of them dependent, in virtue of progressing one from the other).

Some complain that premise 5 commits an egregious logical mistake called the *fallacy of composition*. If we're going to make a decent argument for the existence of God, it won't do to have a fallacy buried somewhere in the premises. The accusation here is that one cannot deduce that a whole set of entities has all of the same properties that each of its constituents has.

It's true that often a whole is "greater than the sum of its parts." A sugar cube divided into exactly four parts having exactly the same proportions will weigh more as a whole than any of its four parts weigh individually. So the weights of physical objects vary between parts and wholes. But does this mean that none of the properties of the parts of our sugar cube will be properties of the sugar cube as a whole? Certainly not. For each part of the sugar cube will taste the same as the sugar cube as a whole. Each of the parts, as well as the whole, is sweet.

The question we must consider is whether the part-whole relation we have been considering in this argument is more like the part-whole *difference in weight* or more like the part-whole *similarity in sweetness* in our sugar cube example. The answer depends (here comes an unintentional pun) on what kind of property "being dependent" is. Clarke believed that if all of the parts of our universe are dependent, requiring a reason for their existence that lies outside themselves, then the universe as a whole series must be like that, too. I agree. If there is no internal reason any of the parts of the series should exist, then how can there be an internal reason they all exist as a whole?

Bottom line: if the universe is to be self-existent, it must contain within itself the reason for its own existence.

6. Every being within an endless series of dependent beings depends for its existence on some other being in the series. This is a tautology. It is true by definition. The phrase "an endless series of dependent entities" just means "a series where every entity within the series depends on some other entity in the series." An opponent of this argument has the right to reject the definition, but then the universe will be a different sort of thing. Our argument draws out the implications of thinking about the existence of the universe the way we have been thinking about it.

7. An endless series of dependent beings cannot be self-existent. This follows directly from premises 5 and 6, again, by *modus ponens*: If P, then Q; P. Therefore, Q. Premise 6 says, in effect, that the series we are considering does not include any item that is self-existent. Given conditional statement 5, this means that the series itself cannot be self-existent.

8. An endless series of dependent beings must be caused by something external to itself. This results from following another logical rule, a rule governing *disjunction*. In premise 4 we have a disjunction. It states two possibilities connected by the word *or*. In statements like these, *or* can be interpreted in two ways. If it is construed as *exclusive*, then the statement tells us that exactly one of the two options is true; that is, either one is true, or the other is true, but not both. When the *or* is interpreted in the *inclusive* sense, the statement claims that at least one, and possibly each, of the options is true. In both types of disjunction, however, if one option is ruled out, the other option must be ruled in. That's what is going on here. Statement 4 tells us we have two options. Statement 7 excludes one of the options. Statement 8 just makes explicit the only option that remains. In this case an endless series of dependent beings must be caused by something external to itself. In other words, the series cannot be self-existent.

9. **The external reason for the existence of an endless series of dependent beings must be either a dependent being or a self-existent being.** Now we have another pair of choices. In this case the choices are mutually exclusive. It must be one or the other. If we can rule out one, then we'll know what the right one is. The next statement in the argument tells us which option must be ruled out.

(By the way, in Clarke's own exposition of the argument, he speaks of the need for an "external *cause*" of the endless series of dependent beings. This is because we seek an *external* reason for the existence of this series [i.e., the universe], and an external reason for the existence of such a thing will be causal in nature. For consistency in setting forth the argument in subsequent steps, I've used "external reason" in place of "external cause.")

10. **The external reason for the existence of an endless series of dependent beings cannot be a dependent being.** If it is a dependent being that provides the reason for the existence of an endless series of dependent beings, then this dependent being, while appearing to play a special role, is itself little more than a part of the endless series. In causal terms this special dependent being will be just one more causally dependent being in the whole chain of dependent beings. It is not an external reason for the existence of the series if it is part of the series. (The passage from which this cosmological argument is derived is sketchy at this juncture, and I have developed the point in the way that makes the best sense in context.)

11. **The external reason for the existence of an endless series of dependent beings must be a self-existent being.** This step is the result of exclusive disjunction (statement 9) and the exclusion of one option at step 10. The only possibility is that the external reason we seek is a self-existent being, that is, a necessary being.

12. **If an endless series of dependent beings exists, then a self-existent being exists.** This statement simply makes explicit what follows directly from the assumption that an endless series of dependent be-

ings exists and the conclusion, reached in step 11, that the reason for the existence of such a series must exist.

13. This self-existent being must have existed from eternity and be immutable and independent. A self-existent being will exist from eternity because the reason for its existence is internal, making it necessary. It cannot not exist. For the same reason it will be independent in its existence, not dependent on anything else for its existence. As for its immutability, readers should consult Clarke. He takes pains following this argument to explain what else may be said about this self-existent Being so that it is proper to speak of it as God.

A First-Cause Argument for the Existence of God

So far we have examined one of the more powerful cosmological arguments for the existence of God. We come now to another best of breed, the *kalam* cosmological argument. This argument is one version of a first-cause argument for the existence of God. Like the contingency argument, it has a simple three-step pattern:

1. Establish that the universe had a beginning.
2. Demonstrate that the beginning of the universe had a cause.
3. Show that the cause of the beginning of the universe is God.

The Kalam Cosmological Argument

1. The physical universe exists.
2. The history of the universe is a series of events arrayed in temporal succession.
3. Either the physical universe had a beginning, or it has always existed.
4. If the physical universe has always existed, then the history of the universe is a series of infinitely many events arrayed in temporal succession.
5. The history of the universe cannot be a series of infinitely many events arrayed in temporal succession.
6. The physical universe has not always existed.

7. The physical universe had a beginning.
8. If the physical universe had a beginning, then the beginning of the universe had a cause.
9. The beginning of the physical universe had a cause.
10. If the beginning of the physical universe had a cause, that cause must be either an event or an agent.
11. The beginning of the physical universe was caused either by an event or by an agent.
12. The cause of the beginning of the physical universe could not have been an event.
13. The cause of the beginning of the universe was an agent.

Now for some clarification of each step:

1. The physical universe exists. This is our already familiar starting point.

2. The history of the universe is a series of events arrayed in temporal succession. This statement makes explicit how the events that make up the history of the universe stand in relation to one another. They stand in temporal relations where they occur in succession, one after the other.

3. Either the physical universe had a beginning, or it has always existed. This is an exclusive disjunction. It is a noncontroversial premise in the argument since it conforms to the logical law of excluded middle (*tertium non datur*), which has the form "either P or not-P," where P is any proposition you like.

4. If the physical universe has always existed, then the history of the universe is a series of infinitely many events arrayed in temporal succession. Since the history of the universe is a series of events arrayed in temporal succession, the number of events in the series must be infinite in order for the universe to have no beginning.

5. The history of the universe cannot be a series of infinitely many events arrayed in temporal succession. This is the crucial and most controversial premise of the argument. While sets of infinitely many objects may not be impossible, it does seem that the events that make up the history of the universe could not be infinite in number. This is because they are arrayed in temporal succession, where one event follows another.

Select any event from the history of the universe; call it event E. If the universe did not have a beginning, then infinitely many events must have occurred prior to event E. But if infinitely many events must have occurred before event E could occur, and this would take an infinite amount of time, it seems that event E could never occur. But it has occurred. Since event E could be any event that actually has occurred, it seems that no event in the history of the universe could be preceded by infinitely many events.

6. The physical universe has not always existed. This follows from statements 4 and 5 by a pattern of logical implication called *modus tollens*: If P, then Q; not-Q. Therefore, not-P.

7. The physical universe had a beginning. This is equivalent to the previous statement, stated here in this way for convenient presentation of the premises that follow.

8. If the physical universe had a beginning, then the beginning of the universe had a cause. The rationale for this premise is that for anything to begin to exist is for an event to occur, and every event has a cause.

9. The beginning of the physical universe had a cause. This follows by *modus ponens* from statements 7 and 8.

10. If the beginning of the physical universe had a cause, that cause must be either an event or an agent. The events with which we are familiar are of two kinds. Many events are caused by other events. Many others are caused by agents.

If a baseball strikes a pane of glass at a certain velocity, it may break the glass. The breaking of the glass is an event. What caused the event? That depends on the circumstances. Suppose we wish to know what was the immediate cause of the breaking of the glass. If the baseball was launched by a pitching machine, then the movement of various parts within the machine cause the ball to be launched. That movement is an event. One event, the movement within the machine, has caused the ball to be launched, and another event has occurred, the breaking of the glass. This is an instance of event-event causation. But what caused the movement in the machine? Suppose some person pressed a button that activated the pitching mechanism. Now we have an agent, a personal being with powers and intentions, causing an event. This is an instance of agent-event causation (or simply, agent causation.)

Like any other event, the beginning of the universe must be caused either by an event or by an agent. (This, at least, is what we should think unless and until some other form of causation is discovered.)

11. The beginning of the physical universe was caused either by an event or by an agent. This follows by *modus ponens* from premises 9 and 10.

12. The cause of the beginning of the physical universe could not have been an event. Here we rule out one kind of cause for the beginning of the universe. The reason is simple. The beginning of the universe is, in the nature of the case, the first event in the history of the universe. If that event were caused by a prior event, it would not be the first. So the beginning of the universe could not have been caused by an event. We know now what must be the cause.

13. The cause of the beginning of the universe was an agent. Having excluded one of two available ways that events may be caused, we conclude that the cause of the beginning of the universe must have been an agent. This means that the origin of the universe was caused by a personal being, acting with powers and intentions suitable for such an act.

Is this agent God? As I've written elsewhere, the *kalam* argument allows us to infer that "there must be some personal and timeless being, powerful and intelligent enough to cause the universe to begin to exist. This fully transcendent Agent presumably acted for reasons when creating the universe. Even if that is all that can be said about the most likely cause of the beginning of the universe, it already appears to be a good candidate for the appellation *God*."[5]

[5] R. Douglas Geivett, "The *Kalam* Cosmological Argument," in *To Everyone an Answer: A Case for the Christian Worldview*, ed. Francis J. Beckwith, William Lane Craig, and J. P. Moreland (Downers Grove, Ill.: InterVarsity, 2004), 74. For more detailed exposition and defense of the *kalam* argument, please see the rest of that chapter. *Kalam* is an Arabic term meaning "word/ speech," but it came to mean "natural theology"; it is the classic argument used by Muslims and some Christians in the Middle Ages to defend the existence of God based on the finitude of the past.

Summary

We have sampled two influential cosmological arguments for the existence of God. The first, developed by Samuel Clarke, is an argument from *the contingency of the universe* to the existence of God as a self-existent, necessary Being. The second, known as the *kalam* cosmological argument, reasons from *the beginning of the universe* to the existence of God as the First Cause of the Universe.

Conclusion

There are compelling reasons to conclude that there is a Necessary Being, a self-subsistent Creator and Sustainer of a universe that hangs onto existence by the skin of its teeth.[6] We have good reason to believe that the universe, the theater of human existence, had a beginning and that there must be a First Cause to whom it and we owe our existence. Is this the God of Abraham, Isaac, Jacob, and Jesus? It could be. An argument with such a fantastic conclusion would take dozens of steps. But regardless of where further argument leads, a Necessary Being, a First Cause of everything else we know to exist, is a plausible candidate for the God of Christian theism.[7] If there is but one Necessary Being and it happens that the God of biblical faith does exist, then they must be one and the same. If there is a First Cause of the physical universe, among Christians He goes by the name *Yahweh*, or Jehovah; He is the unique and sovereign God who has expressed Himself more fully in Scripture and in Jesus Christ. That possibility is worth more than a moment's casual reflection.

If the Being upon which our cosmological arguments converge is not the Greatest Conceivable Being, it is surely the greatest being that actually does exist. As such, it is the nemesis of naturalism. Our

---

[6] See Dallas Willard, "The Three-Stage Argument for the Existence of God," in *Contemporary Perspectives on Religious Epistemology*, ed. R. Douglas Geivett and Brendan Sweetman (New York: Oxford University Press, 1993), 215.

[7] For details on how a cumulative case might be made for Christian theism, see my chapter "David Hume and a Cumulative Case Argument," in *In Defense of Natural Theology: A Post-Humean Assessment*, ed. James F. Sennett and Douglas Groothuis (Downers Grove, Ill.: Inter-Varsity, 2005), 297–329.

universe is haunted by a presence that cannot be conveniently contained by the dainty theories of scientific and philosophical naturalists. But that's not all. This greatest of all existing beings is, for all intents and purposes, a god; indeed, it is the only god there is, worthy of capitalization. We are put on notice that there is a *God* with whom we have to do. We ignore this God at our own risk, for this God is our God (see Acts 17:16–31). And we pay our God no compliments with comforting abstractions about some amorphous and remote "spiritual energy force" or the "Religiously Real" common denominator of all world religions. And we should know better than to refer to this God with effete monikers like "a Higher Power" (with or without capital letters).

Chapter 5

THE CONTEMPORARY ARGUMENT FOR DESIGN: AN OVERVIEW

Jay W. Richards

For over fifty years the British philosopher Antony Flew was the English-speaking world's most intellectually serious public atheist. He first engaged Christian apologist C. S. Lewis at Oxford in 1950 and continued to pursue scholarly defenses of atheism for over five decades. His basic argument was always the same: there just wasn't enough evidence to believe in God. Then, at age eighty-one, he changed his mind.

So what did it for Flew? It wasn't a religious conversion. In a 2004 interview with philosopher Gary Habermas, Flew attributes his new view not to any religious text but to *scientific* evidence, in particular, evidence of intelligent design: "I think the argument to Intelligent Design is enormously stronger than it was when I first met it."[1] In an interview with the Associated Press (9 December 2004), Flew said his ideas "have some similarity with American 'intelligent design' theorists."

Flew's change of mind may be the most visible result so far of the work of the intelligent design (ID) movement. It's also a microcosm of the changing state of the debate over the contemporary

---

[1] "My Pilgrimage from Atheism to Theism: A Discussion between Antony Flew and Gary Habermas," *Philosophia Christi* 6/2 (2004): 197–211. See this interview in "Atheist Becomes Theist: Exclusive Interview with Former Atheist Antony Flew," http://www.biola.edu/antony-flew/.

design argument. Hanging in the balance is the status of the materialist worldview that has dominated the commanding heights of culture for over a century. This is good news for anyone interested in Christian apologetics.

The Materialist Legacy

Science left the nineteenth century with a simple view of the universe. Too simple, as it turns out. The official materialistic gloss on natural science went something like this: (1) The universe has always existed, and so we need not address the question of its origin. (2) Everything in the universe, large and small, submits to a few well-understood, deterministic laws. (3) Life initially turned up as a result of luck and chemistry. (4) Cells, for their part, are basically little blobs of Jell-O. (5) Virtually all those complicated adaptations of organisms result from a starkly simple process called natural selection: this almost miraculously creative process merely seizes and passes along those minor, random variations within a population that provide a survival advantage.

The positivist interpretation of science (and of knowledge generally) provided indispensable support to this picture of the world. Positivism, a program designed to purge metaphysics from science, forbade scientists from appealing to an intelligent agency when trying to explain either the features of the natural world or the natural world itself. Such a stricture obviously applied to a divine agent, but it eventually became clear that it applied to agents in general. Everything, at bottom, was thought to be reducible to the impersonal interactions of matter following predictable patterns, and nothing else mattered. In fact, many senior physicists had concluded that physics was basically a complete science. There was little left to do except tidy up here and there.

But almost as soon as this Procrustean bed was made, the real world began to kick out. The startling revelations of the quantum realm suggested that the world was not as submissive as the materialists had expected. Then astronomer Edwin Hubble discovered that the light from distant galaxies was redshifted, indicating that the universe is expanding. This and other details suggested the universe had come into existence in the finite past—that it has an age. This flatly contradicted the earlier picture of an eternal and self-existing cosmos.

Then, in the 1960s and 1970s, physicists began to notice that the universal constants of physics, such as the forces of gravity and electromagnetism, seemed to be "finely-tuned" for the existence of complex life. To astrophysicist and atheist Fred Hoyle, this suggested the activity of a "superintellect."[2]

Then there is the niggling problem of the origin of biological information, which stubbornly transcends its chemical medium in the same way the letters and sentences of a book transcend the chemistry of ink and paper. We see this starkly in molecular biology where the presence of information encoded along the DNA molecule look suspiciously like an extraordinarily sophisticated computer code for producing proteins, the three-dimensional building blocks of all life. Move up a level, and we find complex and functionally integrated machines that look inaccessible to the Darwinian mechanism. Moreover, such structures look much like the systems produced by intelligent agents, who can foresee a future function and bring it into being.

Then there is the three-dimensional complexity of animal body plans, which so outstrips our understanding of the informational systems present at the lower levels. Finally, there are human agents themselves, which are so unexpected in materialist terms, that many actually try to deny their existence—another deliverance of materialist reasoning that has obvious logical problems.

Add to this evidence the philosophical problems with positivism itself. Perhaps the most severe one was this: positivists claimed that only statements that can be verified by the senses are meaningful or at least scientific. That statement, however, cannot itself be verified by the senses. This means that, by its own accounting, it's meaningless or at least unscientific. At the same time any criterion liberal enough to avoid contradiction and accommodate actual scientific practice let

---

[2] Fred Hoyle, "The Universe: Past and Present Reflections," *Engineering and Science* (November 1981): 8–12.

metaphysics in as well. Such problems eventually led to the demise of the entire positivist enterprise. The positivists themselves openly admitted this. For instance, in a BBC radio interview, Brian McGee asked A. J. Ayer, the father of logical positivism, what the main defect of positivism was. Ayer replied that the main problem was that it was "nearly all false."[3]

At the beginning of the twenty-first century, we look out at an utterly different world from that envisioned by the materialistic science of the late nineteenth century. It is a world charged with design, a cosmos that points beyond itself to a transcendent and intelligent cause. But the word is not out! On the contrary, the materialistic definition of science inherited from the nineteenth century still prevents us from considering this new evidence. The problem is so acute that some scientists are willing to posit an infinite panoply of unobservable universes, just to explain away the fine tuning in our universe.

This strange situation led Phillip Johnson in the 1990s to ask a singularly pregnant and subversive question: if the materialistic definition of science and the scientific evidence are in conflict, should we go with the definition or the evidence? To ask the question, as they say, is to answer it. *Scientia* means "knowledge." The essence of natural science is the search for knowledge of the natural world. Knowledge is an intrinsic good. If we are properly scientific, then we will seek to be open to the natural world and not decide beforehand what it's allowed to reveal.

The materialistic definition of science is no mere philosophical trifle. It dictates what may be discussed, funded, and published, at least within official circles. This cultural and institutional power makes materialistic science look like an unyielding structure, extending invincibly into the clouds like Jack's Beanstalk. But if the evidence is as I have described it, then that monolith must surely have its weak spots. So it must and does, just where it doesn't fit the natural world. This suggests that the design argument at the beginning of the twenty-first century has a new set of evidence on which it rests.

[3] B. McGee, ed., *Men of Ideas* (London: BBC, 1978), 131.

The Broadening Case for Intelligent Design

Some of the best-known "signs of design" are information-rich molecules like DNA, and tiny molecular machines, such as the bacterial flagellum, which biochemist Michael Behe immortalized in his best-selling 1996 book, *Darwin's Black Box*.[4] Behe argued that the flagellum and many other molecular machines are "irreducibly complex." They're like a mousetrap. Without all of their fundamental parts, they don't work. Natural selection can only build systems one small step at a time, by traversing a path in which each step provides a present survival advantage. It can't select for a future function. Only intelligent agents possess such foresight.

But not all of the important work is in natural science *per se*. Some of the work is conceptual. Materialism, after all, is a philosophy, even if its contemporary purveyors try to confuse it with science. Thus, the modern design argument has both scientific and philosophical parts. Much of the work involves dismantling the bankrupt philosophy of materialism.

For most of Western history, detecting the activities of intelligent agents has been a mostly intuitive enterprise. Books such as *The Design Inference*[5] by philosopher William Dembski have dramatically strengthened the case for design by bringing it into the publicly accessible realm of objective argument and empirical evidence, and out of the murkier realm of intuition.

A New Design Argument

Still more recently, growing evidence in astronomy has revealed that even in a finely tuned universe many local things have to go right to build a single habitable planet. (And even once you have an environment suitable for life, you don't get life automatically.) Guillermo Gonzalez and I argue in *The Privileged Planet*[6] that, suspiciously, those

---

[4] Michael Behe, *Darwin's Black Box* (New York: Free Press, 1996).
[5] William Dembski, *The Design Inference* (Cambridge: Cambridge University Press, 1998).
[6] Guillermo Gonzalez and Jay Richards, *The Privileged Planet* (Washington, D.C.: Regnery, 2004).

requirements for habitability also provide the best overall conditions for making scientific discoveries. In other words the places compatible with complex observers like us are the same places that provide the best overall conditions for observing. You might expect this if the universe were designed for discovery but not if you were a card-carrying materialist. Let me explain this in a bit more detail.

Read any book on the history of scientific discovery, and you'll find magnificent tales of human ingenuity, persistence, and dumb luck. What you probably won't see is any discussion of the conditions necessary for such feats. A discovery requires a person to do the discovering and a set of circumstances that makes it possible. Without both nothing gets discovered.

Although scientists don't often discuss it, the degree to which we can "measure" the wider universe from our earthly home—and not just our immediate surroundings—is surprising. Few have considered what science would have been like in, say, a different planetary environment. Still fewer have realized that pursuing that question systematically leads to unanticipated evidence for intelligent design.

Think of the following features of our earthly home: the transparency of Earth's atmosphere in the visual region of the spectrum, shifting crustal plates, a large moon, and our particular location in the solar system, and our solar system's location within the Milky Way Galaxy. Without each of these assets, we would have a hard time learning about the universe. It is not idle speculation to ask how our view of the universe would be impaired if, for example, our home world were perpetually covered by thick clouds. After all, our solar system contains several examples of such worlds. Just think of Venus, Jupiter, Saturn, and Saturn's moon, Titan. These would be crummy places to do astronomy.

We can make similar comparisons at the galactic level. If we were closer to our galaxy's center or one of its major, and dustier, spiral arms, for instance—the extra dust would impede our view of the distant universe. In fact, we probably would have missed one of the greatest discoveries in the history of astronomy: the faint cosmic microwave background radiation. That discovery was the linchpin in deciding between the two main cosmological theories of the twentieth century. Underlying this debate was one of the most fundamental questions we can ask about the universe: is it eternal, or did it have a beginning?

The steady state theory posited an eternal universe, while the big bang theory implied a beginning. For a few decades there was no direct evidence to decide between the two. But the big bang theory predicted a remnant radiation left over from the earlier, hotter, and denser period of cosmic history. The steady state theory made no such prediction. As a result, when scientists discovered the cosmic background radiation in 1965, it was the death knell for steady state. But that discovery could not have been made just anywhere. Our special vantage point in the Milky Way Galaxy allowed us to choose between these two profoundly different views of origins.

In *The Privileged Planet* we discuss these and many comparable examples to show that we inhabit a planet privileged for scientific observation and discovery. But there's more to the story. Not only is the Earth a privileged place for discovery; it is also a privileged place for life. It is the *connection* between life and discovery that we think suggests purpose and not dumb luck.

I mentioned above that physicists and cosmologists began realizing decades ago that the values of the constants of physics—features of the universe that are the same everywhere—must be close to their actual values for life to be possible. As a result, they began talking about the universe being fine-tuned for life. And some have even begun to suggest that fine tuning implies a fine-tuner.

It's only more recently that astrobiologists began learning that even in our fine-tuned universe, many other local things must go just right to get a habitable planetary environment.

If you were a cosmic chef, your recipe for cooking up a habitable planet would have many ingredients. You would need a rocky planet large enough to hold on to a substantial atmosphere and oceans of water and to retain internal heat for billions of years. You would need the right kind of atmosphere. You would need a large moon to stabilize the tilt of the planet's rotation on its axis. You would need the planet to have a nearly circular orbit around a main sequence star similar to our sun. You would need to give that planet the right kind of planetary neighbors within its star system. And you would need to put that system far from the center, edges, and spiral arms of a galaxy like the Milky Way. You would need to cook it during a narrow window of time in the history of the universe . . . and so on. This is a partial list, but you get the idea.

This evidence is becoming well-known among scientists interested in the question of life in the universe. Researchers involved in the search for extraterrestrial intelligence (SETI), for instance, are especially interested in knowing what life needs. That knowledge would allow them to determine their chances of finding another communicating civilization. Unfortunately for SETI researchers, the odds are not looking promising. Recent evidence favors the so-called Rare Earth hypothesis (named after a book written by Donald Brownlee and Peter Ward in 2000).[7] The theory posits that planets hosting simple life may be common, but planets with complex life are rare.

We do not yet know if we are alone in the universe. The universe is a big place with vast resources. Astrobiology research has not yet matured to the point where we can assign precise probabilities to all the factors needed to make a planet habitable. We cannot yet state with certainty whether they exhaust all the available resources. Perhaps the universe is big enough that at least one habitable planet would have emerged by chance—or perhaps not. In the meantime, it's difficult to make a strong case for intelligent design based merely on the conclusion that habitable planets are rare.

That said, we do think there is evidence for design in the neighborhood. For, as we argue in *The Privileged Planet*, there is a suspicious pattern between the needs of life and the needs of science. The same narrow conditions that make a planet habitable for complex life also make it the best place overall for making a wide range of scientific discoveries. In other words, if we compare our local environment with other, less hospitable environments, we find a striking coincidence: observers find themselves in the best places overall for observing.

---

[7] Peter Ward and Donald Brownlee, *Rare Earth: Why Complex Life Is Uncommon in the Universe* (New York: Springer, 2000).

For instance, the atmosphere that complex life needs is also an atmosphere that is transparent to the most scientifically useful "light." The geology and planetary system that life needs is also the best overall for allowing that life to reconstruct events from the past. And the most habitable region of the galaxy and the most habitable time in cosmic history are also the best place and time overall for doing astronomy and cosmology. If the universe is merely a blind concatenation of atoms colliding with atoms and nothing else, you wouldn't expect this pattern. You would expect it, on the other hand, if the universe is designed for discovery. By itself, this argument is quite suggestive. But add it to the evidence for design from other fields of science, and you have the ingredients for a powerful and contemporary argument for design.

The Design Argument and Apologetics

Some might think this is all of merely academic interest since at best this is an argument for mere design rather than for Christianity *per se*. Some Christians have argued that intelligent design arguments "don't go far enough." For them the case of Antony Flew might look like exhibit A. When Flew says he believes in "God," he doesn't mean he's put his trust in the God and Father of Jesus Christ. He's referring to the generic "God of the Philosophers"—a First Cause, postulated on the basis of evidence and rational argument. Although he says he remains open to the possibility of a special revelation, he certainly hasn't undergone a full conversion to Christianity. So the critic might ask, what good is the design argument for Christian apologetics?

I think this concern, though understandable, is mistaken. Certainly none of the arguments for intelligent design can establish that God became incarnate in Jesus, died to save us from our sins, and was raised from the dead. That's because we don't learn these things by studying natural science. These are historical claims so evidence for them will have to be drawn from history. But it doesn't follow that design arguments are problematic. Contemporary intelligent design arguments appeal not to the book of Scripture or even historical evidence but simply to the book of nature. They appeal to publicly available evidence from the natural world, especially the natural sciences. The Bible itself tells us that the natural world reveals *some* things about God (Ps 19:1–4, Rom 1:20). That doesn't mean that nature reveals everything.

Nevertheless, the modern design argument still has profound apologetic value, if only as a ground-clearing operation. Success for the design argument would mean defeat for what is surely the chief obstacle to Christian belief in the modern world: scientific materialism. Just imagine how much easier apologetics would be if it were widely taken for granted that the materialist worldview was defunct.

More strongly, I think one can make a cumulative case argument for *theism* based on the evidence for design in biology, astronomy, physics, and cosmology. In fact, it was just such a case that persuaded the world's leading atheist, Antony Flew, that there is a God. And, to state the obvious, to move from atheism to theism is to move *toward* Christianity. For apologetics, that's a move in the right direction. From there the Christian apologist can introduce other lines of argument, such as a historical defense of Christ's resurrection. Surely such a defense is easier to make if God's existence is granted.

The case for intelligent design can't establish everything Christians believe in. But it's a valuable first step. If you're interested in apologetics, then you should recognize the progress made on the design argument for what it is: very good news.

Chapter 6

A MORAL ARGUMENT

Paul Copan

During the Peloponnesian War (431–404 BC, including a six-year truce), the inhabitants of the island of Melos tried to remain neutral in the war between Athens and Sparta. Unfortunately Melos couldn't hold out. Athens demanded tribute payment, offering peace in exchange. The Melians tried to negotiate, appealing to their right to their own empire. The Athenians rejected the Melians' "fine phrases" of duty and morality. The Athenians asked the Melians

> not to imagine that you will influence us by saying . . . that you have never done us any harm . . . since you know as well as we do that, when these matters are discussed by practical people, the standard of justice depends upon the equality of power to compel and that in fact the strong do what they have the power to do and the weak accept what they have to accept.[1]

The Melians replied, claiming the Athenians' interests would best be served by preserving the principles of justice and fair play—after all, *they* too might be attacked one day. The Melians were appealing to the Golden Rule—to do to others as they would have others do

---

[1] Citations from this account are from Jonathan Glover, *Humanity: A Moral History of the Twentieth Century* (London: Jonathan Cape, 1999), 28–30.

to them; they took this moral norm to be transcultural. Alas, Athens replied to Melos:

> It is a general and necessary law of nature to rule wherever one can. This is not a law we made for ourselves, nor were we the first to act upon it when it was made. We found it already in existence, and we shall leave it to exist forever among those who come after us. We are merely acting in accordance with it, and we know that you or anybody else with the same power as ours would be acting in precisely the same way.

In the end the Melians refused to submit to Athens, and Athens besieged the city, killed the military-aged men, and sold the women and children into slavery.

Did the Athenians violate some universal moral law, or does "might make right"? Is the belief in human value or rights nothing more than evolutionary hard-wiring that enhances human survival—comparable to teeth, feet, or opposable thumbs? Do human beings *invent* morality—a social contract perhaps—by which we agree not to harm or steal from one another? If such a transcultural morality exists, can it be explained in natural or supernatural terms?

These are the sorts of questions we'll examine in this brief essay. First, we'll look at the inescapability of objective moral values. Second, we'll address the context of objective moral values, arguing that God's existence and nature make better sense of objective moral values than do naturalistic—and other nontheistic (whether Buddhist, Hindu, Shinto, etc.)—explanations. Third, we'll look at the evolutionary and other subjectivist explanations for morality, which are ultimately inadequate and unsatisfying. Indeed, the existence of an intrinsically good God is needed to ground objective moral values as well as human rights, dignity, and moral responsibility—characteristics which reflect God's making us in His image. Finally, we'll look at the Euthyphro dilemma, which some claim shows that, if God isn't arbitrary in His commands, a moral standard must exist independently of God.

The Inescapability of Objective Moral Values

The eighteenth-century Scottish philosopher Thomas Reid wrote of the fundamental bedrock nature of moral values such as the obligation to treat another person as we would want to be treated. Such moral laws are as inescapable as our conviction that mind-independent objects exist: "The sceptic asks me, Why do you believe the existence of the external object which you perceive? This belief, sir, is none of my manufacture; it came from the mint of Nature; it bears her image and superscription; and, if it is not right, the fault is not mine. I ever took it upon trust, and without suspicion."[2]

The Jewish-Christian Scriptures assume that human beings are morally responsible agents who can generally know what is good and that they ought to do what is good and avoid what is evil. In the Old Testament the prophet Amos (in chapters 1–2) delivers severe warnings from God to surrounding Gentile nations because of their atrocities and crimes against humanity, ripping open pregnant women, breaking treaties, acting treacherously, stifling compassion. The underlying assumption is that these nations, even without God's special revelation, *should have known better*. In the writings of the apostle Paul, the same assumption is expressed more explicitly: "For when Gentiles who do not have the Law [of Moses] do instinctively the things of the Law, these, not having the Law, are a law to themselves, in that they show the work of the Law written in their hearts, their conscience bearing witness and their thoughts alternately accusing or else defending them" (Rom 2:14–15).

Just as we trust our senses and powers of reasoning unless we have good reason to doubt them, we should also assume this "principle of credulity" when it comes to our basic moral sense as well. Even the most radical skeptic takes for granted the reliability of his reasoning powers and the stability of fundamental logical laws so that he can confidently draw skeptical conclusions! And simply because people may be mistaken in their sense perceptions (e.g., the faulty perception

[2] In *Thomas Reid's Inquiry and Essays*, ed. Keith Lehrer and Ronald E. Beanblossom (Indianapolis: Bobbs-Merrill, 1975), 84–85.

that a bird is on the branch, which is in fact being moved by the wind) is not reason to reject their general reliability.

Similarly, while we may make faulty *moral* judgments, there still are certain unmistakable moral truths—what we can't *not* know.[3] Yes, we may suppress our conscience or engage in self-deception. However, when we are functioning properly and aren't stifling our conscience, we can get right the fundamentals of morality. As C. S. Lewis shows in his *Abolition of Man*,[4] people, regardless of time and culture, have *discovered* (not invented) the same sorts of basic moral standards: don't murder, don't take another's property, don't defraud, treat people as you want to be treated. People can know right from wrong apart from special revelation from God. As Amos 1–2 and Romans 2:14–15 indicate, the rightness of basic moral laws and the wrongness of their violation can be known by *anyone* not suppressing his conscience or hardening his heart.

Properly functioning persons generally know when they're being treated cruelly or as a mere object (e.g., child abuse, raping, torturing innocent people for fun) rather than with dignity and respect. Indeed, we possess an in-built "yuck factor"—a basic internal revulsion toward torturing babies for fun and murdering. Humans—God's image-bearers—can, without the Bible, still readily recognize that kindness is a virtue and not a vice, that we ought to treat others as we would want to be treated, and that there is a moral difference between Mother Teresa and Pol Pot or Josef Stalin. Those not recognizing the proper basicality of these truths are simply wrong; they aren't functioning properly. Apart from and prior to any agreed-upon "social contract," we can intuitively recognize that all human beings *already* have certain rights before the law or that racism is immoral. As Nicholas Rescher observes, if members of a particular tribe think that sacrificing firstborn children is acceptable, "then their grasp on the conception of morality is somewhere between inadequate and nonexistent."[5] Such a moral awareness is basic or "bedrock," as Kai Nielsen put it:

[3] See J. Budziszewski, *What We Can't Not Know* (Dallas: Spence, 2003).
[4] C. S. Lewis, *The Abolition of Man* (San Francisco: Harper, 2001), appendix.
[5] Nicholas Rescher, *Moral Absolutes: An Essay on the Nature and Rationale of Morality*, Studies in Moral Philosophy, vol. 2 (New York: Peter Lang, 1989), 43.

> It is more reasonable to believe such elemental things [as wife-beating and child abuse] to be evil than to believe any skeptical theory that tells us we cannot know or reasonably believe any of these things to be evil. . . . I firmly believe that this is bedrock and right and that anyone who does not believe it cannot have probed deeply enough into the grounds of his moral beliefs.[6]

We *just know* the rightness of virtues (kindness, trustworthiness, unselfishness), and *the burden of proof falls on those who deny this*. When the moral skeptic says, "Prove that moral values exist," he doesn't need an *argument*. He really needs psychological and spiritual *help*. There are certain moral intuitions that are immediately apparent—unless there is some serious malfunction.

The philosopher Robert Audi offers a description of these moral intuitions. They are (1) *noninferential* or *directly apprehended*; (2) *firm* (they must be believed as propositions); (3) *comprehensible* (intuitions are formed in the light of an adequate understanding of their propositional objects); (4) *pretheoretical* (they are not dependent on theories, nor are they themselves theoretical hypotheses). Such moral knowledge emerges not from reflection on abstract principles but from reflecting on particular cases (particularism). Moreover, these intuitions are *not* indefeasible. That is, they may be adjusted or refined in light of other considerations or overriding circumstances. For instance, keeping a promise may be overridden by circumstances preventing me from keeping it, but I still have a duty to explain to my friend why I could not keep the promise.[7]

Thus, even if human beings make faulty moral judgments and can be misguided at points, we would be wrong to abandon the quest for goodness or become moral skeptics: "we cannot always or even usually be totally mistaken about goodness."[8] As with our senses or our rational faculties, we are wise to trust our basic moral intuitions even

[6] Kai Nielsen, *Ethics without God*, rev. ed. (Buffalo, N.Y.: Prometheus Books, 1990), 10–11.
[7] Robert Audi, *Moral Knowledge and Ethical Character* (New York: Oxford University Press, 1997), 32–65.
[8] Robert M. Adams, *Finite and Infinite Goods: A Framework for Ethics* (Oxford: Oxford University Press, 1999), 20.

though modification or further reflection may be necessary. As with our sense perception and rational powers, we ought to take our moral intuitions seriously unless there is good reason to doubt them.

Naturalism Versus Theism—Which Is the Better Fit?

The late Carl Sagan confidently affirmed: "The cosmos is all that is or ever was or ever will be."[9] Of course, this is a metaphysical statement, a philosophical assumption, not a scientific observation. This statement, however, nicely summarizes naturalism: nature is all there is—which means no God, no supernatural, no miracles, no immortality. What are the implications of naturalism? They are stark indeed. Philosopher Jaegwon Kim admits that naturalism is "imperialistic; it demands 'full coverage' . . . and exacts a terribly high ontological price."[10] Biologist E. O. Wilson also holds to a naturalistic viewpoint, that all of reality "the Central Idea of the consilience worldview is that all tangible phenomena, from the birth of the stars to the workings of social institutions, are based on material processes that are ultimately reducible, however long and torturous the sequences, to the laws of physics."[11]

What then are the implications for morality if a personal, good God doesn't exist? (Remember that this would apply to nontheistic Eastern religions, not simply to atheism.) Many atheists/nontheists recognize that a naturalistic world doesn't furnish a plausible context for objective moral values (e.g., kindness is virtuous, murder is wrong) as well as human rights and moral responsibility. Philosopher Thomas Nagel points out the implications: "There is no room for agency in a world of neural impulses, chemical reactions, and bone and muscle movements." Given naturalism, it's hard not to conclude that we're "helpless" and "not responsible" for our actions.[12] Likewise, Derk

---

[9] Carl Sagan, *Cosmos* (New York: Random House, 1980), 4.

[10] Jaegwon Kim, "Mental Causation and Two Conceptions of Mental Properties." Paper presented at the American Philosophical Association Eastern Division Meeting (December 1993), 2–23.

[11] Edward O. Wilson, *Consilience: The Unity of Knowledge* (New York: Knopf, 1998), 266.

[12] Thomas Nagel, *The View from Nowhere* (New York: Oxford University Press, 1986), 111, 113.

Pereboom affirms that "our best scientific theories indeed have the consequence that we are not morally responsible for our actions," that we're "more like machines than we ordinarily suppose."[13] Naturalist Simon Blackburn confesses that he prefers dignity over humiliation, but he finds that nature offers no grounds for affirming human dignity or objective moral values: "Nature has no concern for good or bad, right or wrong. . . . We cannot get behind ethics."[14] This is what naturalism leads us to expect—no good God, no objective moral values. Even the noted Oxford atheist J. L. Mackie agreed: "Moral properties constitute so odd a cluster of properties and relations that they are most unlikely to have arisen in the ordinary course of events without an all-powerful god to create them."[15] But he went ahead and denied that objective moral values existed!

Yes, many naturalists deny that objective moral values exist—that our moral impulse is nothing more than the product of a blind evolutionary process that selects out traits that enhance survival and reproduction. In such a case, morality is merely subjective. However, nontheists can and do endorse objective moral values—that rape or child abuse is wrong. These nontheistic moral realists will tell us, "You don't need God to be good." Yet the deeper question is, how did we come to *be* morally responsible, rights-bearing beings? Since all human beings are God's image-bearers, they not surprisingly recognize the same sorts of moral values theists do. The basic issue, though, is this: why think humans have rights and dignity if they're products of valueless, physical processes in a cause-and-effect series from the big bang until now? The more plausible context or scenario is that human value and moral responsibility come from a good God who created us as intrinsically valuable, morally responsible creatures. We function properly when living morally. We glimpse something of a personal God in the world's moral order: without a personal God, no persons would exist at all. If no persons would exist, then no moral properties would be realized

[13] Derk Pereboom, *Living without Free Will* (Cambridge: Cambridge University Press, 2001), xiii–xiv.

[14] Simon Blackburn, *Being Good: A Short Introduction to Ethics* (New York: Oxford University Press, 2001), 133–34.

[15] J. L. Mackie, *The Miracle of Theism* (Oxford: Clarendon, 1982), 115.

in our world. We know that from nothing, nothing comes (*ex nihilo nihil fit*); similarly, *from valuelessness, valuelessness comes*. It's exceedingly difficult to see how we move from a valueless series of causes and effects from the big bang onward, finally arriving at valuable, morally responsible, rights-bearing human beings. If we're just material beings produced by a material universe, then objective value or goodness (not to mention consciousness or reasoning powers or beauty or personhood) can't be accounted for. One will search in vain for any physics textbook describing moral value as one of matter's properties! Perhaps one shouldn't really be surprised when atheists believe that moral values *could* emerge from valueless matter. After all, they tend to believe that the finite, finely tuned, life-producing, consciousness-producing, and value-producing universe could emerge literally from nothing!

We could press the point even further. In the name of simplicity, there seems to be no good reason for naturalists to invoke any independent moral realm. This would seem utterly superfluous and completely out of place given our valueless origins, according to naturalism. The nontheists who say that the moral value "murder is wrong" would hold true even if God didn't exist assume such moral values are just "brute facts."[16] But it's hard to see how love or justice itself could exist, say, during the Jurassic period. Without God, moral properties wouldn't be realized or actualized in this world in the form of human rights or dignity or moral duties: *no God, no moral values*. Since our personhood is rooted in a personal God's specially creating us, a deep connection exists between personhood and objective moral values.[17]

---

[16] E.g., Russ Shafer-Landau, *Moral Realism: A Defence* (New York: Oxford University Press, 2005).

[17] The necessity of moral truths doesn't make God irrelevant; such truths still require grounding in a personal God's good character: He necessarily exists in all possible worlds, is the source of all necessary moral truths, and is explanatorily prior—more basic—to these moral values. They would stand in asymmetrical relation to His necessity—like a pendulum, whose period (completed swing) can be deduced from the pendulum's length but not vice versa (i.e., the pendulum's length explains its period, not the reverse). William E. Mann, "Necessity," in *Companion to Philosophy of Religion*, ed. William Quinn and Charles Taliaferro (Malden, Mass.: Blackwell, 1997). The necessity of moral principles doesn't mean they are analytic. For example, "water is H_2O" is a necessary truth but is certainly not analytic. As Saul Kripke argued, there is a *metaphysical* necessity which, in this case, is discovered *a posteriori*. And, more to the point, "the fact that water is necessarily H_2O by no means rules out the need for an explanation for the existence or structure of

Again, atheists, like believers, can *know* what's good. And why is this? We're all *beings* made in God's image. Who we *are* enables us to *know* right from wrong. This point applies to nontheistic religionists as well—not simply atheistic naturalists. Nontheistic Jains, for example, believe that the soul (*jiva*) in each creature entails strict nonviolence (*ahimsa*). They take this value to be a simple brute given. However, what is the basis of *any value* in this finite world if God doesn't exist?

Furthermore, if nature is all there is, how do we move from the way things *are* (the descriptive) to the way things *ought* to be (the prescriptive)? Why bring in *moral* explanations when bare *scientific* descriptions are all that naturalism requires? Moral categories can be eliminated in the name of scientific simplicity. Rather than saying, "Hitler killed millions of Jews because he was morally depraved," perhaps we can use a nonmoral "scientific" explanation: "Hitler was bitter and angry. He falsely believed that Jews were responsible for Germany's defeat in WWI. His hatred for the Jews helped release his pent-up hostility and anger, and his moral beliefs placed no restraints on his expression of hatred."[18] In a material universe of mindless, valueless origins, scientific explanations are all we need; moral ones are superfluous.

Another problem in assuming moral values as unexplained brute facts is this: a huge cosmic coincidence would exist between (a) these *moral facts* and (b) the eventual evolutionary and highly contingent development of *self-reflective, morally responsible beings* that can actually recognize that moral obligations exist. This connection begs for an explanation. It appears that this realm of moral facts was *anticipating* our emergence—a staggering cosmic coincidence! Even if a moral standard exists independently of God, the question still remains of how morally valuable and responsible beings could emerge from valueless matter. The existence of a good personal God, who created humans in his image, offers a simpler and less-contrived connection, a more plausible context to affirm human value and rights as well as moral obligations.

water" (367). See C. Stephen Evans, "Moral Arguments," in *Companion to Philosophy of Religion*, 346–47.

[18] T. L. Carson, *Value and the Good Life* (Notre Dame: University of Notre Dame Press, 2000), 194.

The Question of Evolutionary Ethics

It's not difficult to find naturalists who consider ethics to be nothing more than a human invention or a biological adaptation that is conducive to our survival and reproduction. Bertrand Russell claimed that "the whole subject of ethics arises from the pressure of the community on the individual."[19] According to Michael Ruse and E. O. Wilson, "Ethics as we understand it is an illusion fobbed off on us by our genes in order to get us to cooperate."[20] Elsewhere Ruse asserts that morality is the "ephemeral product" of evolution—along with our hands, feet, and teeth. It's simply "an aid to survival and reproduction, and has no being beyond this."[21] Morality has biological worth—that's it. Naturalist philosopher Jonathan Glover believes that we are presently in a moral crisis. Given the ethical horrors of the twentieth century, he suggests that morality may survive "when seen to be a human creation."[22] So he advises humans to "re-create ethics" by programming future generations to be repulsed by genocide and concentration camps.[23]

According to many naturalists, to ask why we should be moral is like asking why we should itch or be hungry.[24] We are simply evolutionarily hard-wired with adaptive features that enable survival and reproduction. Morality is one of those features—like our limbs or teeth. We meet the is-ought problem again: how do we move from the *is* of nature and science to the *ought* of moral obligation and value. If our morality is simply evolved, all we can do is *describe* how human beings actually function; we can't *prescribe* how humans ought to behave. There's no difference between whether I *ought* to be moral and whether I *ought* to be hungry since both are functions of evolutionary hardwiring. These states just *are*. Naturalism ultimately can give us a

---

[19] Bertrand Russell, *Human Society in Ethics and Politics* (London: Allen & Unwin, 1954), 124.

[20] Michael Ruse and E. O. Wilson, "The Evolution of Ethics," *New Scientist* 17 (1989): 51.

[21] Michael Ruse, *The Darwinian Paradigm* (London: Routledge, 1989), 268.

[22] Glover, *Humanity*, 41.

[23] Ibid., 42.

[24] Michael Shermer, *The Science of Good and Evil: Why People Cheat, Gossip, Care, Share, and Follow the Golden Rule* (New York: Henry Holt, 2004), 57.

description of human behavior and psychology, but it can't ground genuine moral obligation. Moral obligations in a world of naturalistic scientific descriptions are odd indeed. They fit nicely into a theistic world, however.

We also face the question of why we should even trust our conclusions about truth (or morality) if a truthful Creator doesn't exist? If we're biologically hardwired to form moral beliefs that contribute to our survival and reproduction, then these beliefs simply are what they are. We can have no confidence that they are *true*: Can we trust our minds if we're merely products of naturalistic evolution trying to fight, feed, flee, and reproduce? Darwin himself was deeply troubled by this: "With me the horrid doubt always arises whether the convictions of man's mind, which has been developed from the mind of the lower animals, are of any value or at all trustworthy. Would any one trust in the convictions of a monkey's mind, if there are any convictions in such a mind?"[25]

Naturalistic evolution is interested in fitness and survival—not true belief. Morality then is just a biological adaptation—like the polar bear's thick fur: thick fur isn't more true than thin fur; it just better enhances survival.

So not only is objective morality undermined if naturalism is true; so is rational thought. Our beliefs may help us survive, but there's no reason to think they're true. So we may firmly believe that human beings are intrinsically valuable or that we have moral obligations or that we have free will and our choices really matter. This cluster of beliefs may help the species *homo sapiens* survive, but they may be completely false. So if we're blindly hardwired by nature to form certain beliefs because of their survival-enhancing value, then we can't have confidence about the truth-status of these beliefs.

Again, the existence of a good and truthful God offers a way out: we depend on our rational faculties in pursuit of truth. We trust our sense perceptions as basically reliable; and we tend to assume our general moral intuitions to be trustworthy. A biblical worldview

---

[25] Letter to W. G. Down, 3 July 1881, in *The Life and Letters of Charles Darwin Including an Autobiographical Chapter*, ed. Francis Darwin (London: John Murray, 1887), 1:315–16.

inspires confidence that we can know moral and rational truths even if they do not contribute one whit to our survival. As God's image-bearers, we were designed to seek and find truth. But if we're naturalistically hardwired to reproduce and survive, then we can't trust these faculties. As we've noted, the scandal of such skepticism is this: we're relying on the very cognitive faculties whose unreliability is the conclusion of my skeptical argument; that is, I'm assuming a trustworthy reasoning process to arrive at the conclusion that I can't trust my reasoning! A nontheistic context doesn't inspire confidence in our belief-forming mechanisms.

The Euthyphro Dilemma

In Plato's *Euthyphro* dialogue (10a), Socrates asks: "Is what is holy holy because the gods approve it, or do they approve it because it is holy?"[26] Skeptics like to raise this dilemma: Either (a) God's commands are *arbitrary* (something is good because God commands it—and He could have commanded, "You shall murder/commit adultery"), or (b) there must be some *autonomous moral standard* (which God consults in order to command)?[27] Are we left with divine "caprice," as Bertrand Russell suggested?[28] Or do we have a moral standard completely independent of God? Critic Robin Le Poidevin declares that "we can, apparently, only make sense of these doctrines [that God is good and wills us to do what is good] if we think of goodness as being defined independently of God."[29]

This dilemma ultimately derives from a confusion of *knowing* and *being*. Nontheists can know what is moral, but the question is how they came to be that way. The dilemma is ultimately resolved by rooting objective moral values in the nonarbitrary, essentially good character of God who has made us in His image. We would not know goodness

[26] Plato, "Euthyphro," trans. Lane Cooper, in *The Collected Dialogues of Plato*, ed. Edith Hamilton and Huntington Cairns (Princeton: Princeton University Press, 1961), 178.

[27] These terms are taken from Mark D. Linville, "On Goodness: Human and Divine," *American Philosophical Quarterly* 27 (April 1990): 143–52.

[28] Bertrand Russell, *Human Society in Ethics and Politics* (New York: Simon & Schuster, 1962), 38.

[29] Robin Le Poidevin, *Arguing for Atheism* (London: Routledge, 1996), 85.

without God's endowing us with a moral constitution. We have rights, dignity, freedom, and responsibility because God has designed us this way. In this, we reflect God's moral goodness as His image-bearers.

We should also ponder these further points as well. First, if naturalists are correct, then they themselves cannot escape a similar dilemma: Are these moral values good simply because they are good, or is there an independent standard of goodness to which they conform? Naturalistic moral realism's argument offers no actual advantage. Second, the naturalist's query is pointless since we must eventually arrive at some self-sufficient and self-explanatory stopping point beyond which the discussion can go no further. Third, God, who is essentially perfect, does not have obligations to some external moral standard; God simply acts, and it is good. He naturally does what is good. Fourth, the idea that God could be evil or command evil is utterly contrary to the very definition of God; otherwise, such a being would not be God and would not be worthy of worship. The acceptance of objective values assumes a kind of ultimate goal or cosmic design plan for human beings, which would make no sense given naturalism; such goal-orientedness makes much sense given theism (which presumes a design plan, which favors theism over naturalism).

For the sake of argument, even if some independent moral standard existed, this would hardly make God unnecessary or unimportant. After all, why think that humans—given their valueless, unguided, materialistic origins—evolved into morally valuable, rights-bearing, morally responsible persons who are duty bound to this standard? Even if the Euthyphro dilemma had some punch to it, it would still fail to show why intrinsically valuable, rights-bearing persons should emerge who are duty bound to some eternally preexistent moral standard. Again God makes much better sense of this.

Concluding Remarks

The moral argument for God's existence is vital in two important ways. First, the question of morality cuts to the heart of who we are as human beings. We fail morally; we aren't what we know we should be. Thankfully, recognizing we've fallen short of a moral standard can point us in the direction of God and His grace. How then do we handle our moral deficiency, guilt, and shame? Notice the "moral gap" that exists between (a) our recognition of basic moral values and ideals we know we should live by and (b) our moral failing to live up to these ideals. This gap serves to remind us of the need for (c) divine grace to enable us to live as we ought—grace that can be found in Christ's atoning work and the gift of the Holy Spirit who enables us to live lives that are pleasing to God. So rather than think that "ought implies can," as Kant suggested, we failing humans can recognize our need and cast ourselves on God's readily available mercy and grace. So a more biblical understanding prompts us to conclude: "Ought implies can—with divine assistance."[30]

Second, the moral argument has this important advantage: it offers a ready answer to what philosopher John Rist calls a widely admitted "crisis in contemporary Western debate about ethical foundations."[31] Taking seriously a personal God and Creator, the infinite good and source of all finite goods—including human dignity—helps provide the needed metaphysical foundation for human rights and objective moral values. Apart from such a move, it seems that the crisis will become only more pronounced. If objective moral values exist and if humans have rights and dignity, however, we have good reason for believing in God. Furthermore, a successful moral argument, while enhanced by the doctrine of the mutually loving Trinity, can point us to the need for divine grace and forgiveness through Christ; it can prompt us to ponder our moral and spiritual plight and prayerfully seek assistance through more specific revelation from God. That said, the moral argument does point us to a supreme personal moral Being (1) who is worthy of worship, (2) who has made us with dignity and worth, (3) to whom we are personally accountable, and (4) who may reasonably be called "God."

---

[30] John Hare, *The Moral Gap: Kantian Ethics, Human Limits, and God's Assistance* (Oxford: Clarendon, 1996).
[31] John Rist, *Real Ethics* (Cambridge: Cambridge University Press, 2001), 1.

Part 3

JESUS

Chapter 7

REVISIONIST VIEWS ABOUT JESUS

Charles L. Quarles

I n 2003 Doubleday published the novel *The Da Vinci Code*, which became one of the most popular and best-selling novels of all time. It was listed for months as number one on *The New York Times* best-seller list.[1] At present, more than one hundred million copies of the book have been sold.[2] The novel has been translated into more than forty different languages. The popularity of the novel led to Brown's being named one of the one hundred most influential people in the world by *Time* magazine and to appearances and interviews on CNN, the *Today* show, National Public Radio, and in *Newsweek*, *People*, *GQ*, and *Forbes* magazines. On May 19, 2006, Sony Pictures released a Ron Howard film based on the novel starring Tom Hanks as Robert Langdon. The movie was a box office hit and generated $224 million in ticket sales for its weekend debut, the second highest-grossing debut of all time and just behind the third Star Wars prequel which grossed $253 million.[3] According to a study by the Kagan research group, the film was the most profitable movie of 2006.[4]

[1] As of December 5, 2006, the paperback version of the novel is ranked as the twenty-fifth best seller for nonfiction paperbacks.

[2] According to Daniel Vancini of Amazon.com, more than one hundred million copies of the book had sold at the time of the DVD release on October 16, 2006.

[3] A. J. Hammer, "Showbiz Tonight," May 22, 2006 http://transcripts.cnn.com/TRAN-SCRIPTS/0605/22/sbt.01.html, accessed 5 December 2006.

[4] "Da Vinci Code Year's Most Profitable Movie," http://www.imdb.com/title/tt0382625/news, accessed 5 December 2006.

Even readers who disagree with certain claims of the book generally admit that the novel has a riveting plot and that they found it difficult to put the book down. As the story begins, Robert Langdon, a Harvard symbologist, is in Paris on business. Late in the night, police summon him from his hotel room to assist them in solving the murder of a well-known curator of a famous art museum. Soon after arriving at the crime scene, Langdon discovers that he himself is the prime suspect in the police investigation and that he was summoned by the police in hopes of entrapping him. Langdon, with the help of a beautiful French cryptologist, Sophie, escapes and begins the quest to find the true killer and prove his own innocence.

The novel and, to a lesser extent, the film are a concern to many Christians largely because of a dialogue between Langdon, Sophie, and Sir Leigh Teabing who is described as a "religious historian," "former British Royal historian," and whose life passion is research on the holy grail.[5] In this dialogue Teabing claims that the New Testament Gospels are unreliable accounts that pervert the true story of Jesus. He insists that Jesus was a mere mortal prophet who was deified by Constantine the Great as part of a political ploy for consolidating his own power over the fragmented Roman Empire. He also asserts that Jesus was married to Mary Magdalene and that they conceived and bore children and that this sacred bloodline is the true holy grail.

Since this dialogue is fictional and contained in a novel, Christians might be tempted to ignore Teabing's challenges to their faith. Unfortunately, many readers are taking Teabing's remarks seriously because of page 1 of the novel which is introduced by the title in all caps and bold type, **FACT**. The page affirms the existence of the Priory of Sion, the discovery of the Les Dossiers Secrets, and the existence of Opus Dei, all of which play an important role in the book. The page concludes with the statement: "All descriptions of artwork, architecture, documents, and secret rituals in this novel are accurate." Since Brown claims that all descriptions of documents are accurate, many have concluded that Brown has carefully researched the issues Teabing

---

[5] Dan Brown, *The Da Vinci Code* (New York: Doubleday, 2003), 218. All references to this book in this essay are given in the text.

discusses and that this dialogue on the lips of a Harvard professor and British royal historian must surely be an accurate presentation of the facts about the origins of the Christian faith. This fact page coupled with the enormous popularity of the book and the film require thoughtful believers to prepare to respond intelligently to the claims of the Code. Brown claims that he hopes his work will spark a national conversation about issues of faith.[6] Questions raised by the film provide believers an excellent opportunity to present the historical evidence for the Christian faith.

Several key questions arise for the concerned Christian and for those who wish to explore the historical foundations for the Christian faith.

1. Was Jesus married to Mary Magdalene; and if so, how does this affect our view of Jesus' nature and identity?
   a. What ancient sources describe Jesus as married to Mary Magdalene?
   b. Would Jesus' marriage preclude His deity?
2. How do our earliest sources describe Jesus, as truly God or merely human?
   a. Was the doctrine of Jesus' deity a clever invention of Constantine?
   b. Did the early Christians view Jesus as a mere mortal prophet?
3. Should we trust the Gospels of our New Testament or rely on other ancient sources for our understanding of Jesus?
   a. Which books were recognized by the early church as authoritative and why?
   b. Have these books been preserved adequately to give us reliable information about Jesus?

Providing sound answers to these questions is crucial to fulfilling the biblical mandate that appears in 1 Peter 3:15: "Always be ready to give a defense to anyone who asks you for a reason for the hope that is in you" (HCSB).

---

[6] Dan Brown, "FAQ," http://www.danbrown.com/novels/davinci_code/faqs.html, accessed 5 December 2006.

Jesus' Relationship with Mary Magdalene

One of the claims of *The Da Vinci Code* that has attracted the most attention is the assertion that Jesus was married to Mary Magdalene and that their offspring is the true Holy Grail. In the novel Teabing states: "As I said earlier, the marriage of Jesus and Mary Magdalene is part of the historical record" (245). This shocking claim is patently false. No single extant ancient document states that Jesus was married to anyone. Although some Gnostic gospels refer to a special relationship between Jesus and Mary Magdalene, not even those gospels refer to a marriage of Jesus to Mary or a sexual relationship between them. Although Teabing later claimed that the Gospel of Philip clearly referred to Jesus' marriage to Mary, this chapter will soon demonstrate that Teabing grossly mishandled the evidence.

Teabing also attempted to establish Jesus' marriage to Mary Magdalene by appealing to the cultural norms of first-century Judaism. He claimed: "Moreover, Jesus as a married man makes infinitely more sense than our standard biblical view of Jesus as a bachelor" (245). The novel added:

> "Because Jesus was a Jew," Langdon said, taking over while Teabing searched for his book, "and the social decorum during that time virtually forbid a Jewish man to be unmarried. According to Jewish custom, celibacy was condemned, and the obligation for a Jewish father was to find a suitable wife for his son. If Jesus were not married, at least one of the Bible's gospels would have mentioned it and offered some explanation for His unnatural state of bachelorhood" (245).

Jewish men did normally marry and procreate during the first century. This constitutes the strongest evidence that Jesus may have been married. However, Langdon overstates the evidence. Celibacy was not condemned in Judaism, nor was it unprecedented. Strong evidence suggests that one of the major sects of first-century Judaism was devoted to a celibate lifestyle. Although the Essenes, unlike the Pharisees and Sadducees, are not explicitly mentioned in the New Testament, many people have some knowledge of them due to their association with the Dead Sea Scrolls. However, few know that many of the Essenes remained celibate throughout their entire lives. The celibacy of the Essenes is attested in the writings of Josephus, Philo, and Pliny the Elder (Jos. *Ant.* 18.1.5; *J. W.* 2.120–21; Philo *Hypoth.* 11.14–18; Pliny *Nat.* 5.15.73). Philo was a contemporary of Jesus. Josephus and Pliny wrote about the Essenes later in the first century.

The celibacy of some Essene groups seems to be confirmed by archaeological evidence. In the cemetery at Qumran, the skeletal remains that have been unearthed are mostly male showing that women were in the minority (possibly as much as one-third) and their entrance into the community was the exception to the norm. Some scholars have suggested during one period of the community's history, men who were already married when they joined the community were allowed to bring their wives with them, but single men were expected to remain celibate.[7] Other examples of celibacy among the Jews of this period include Banus, John the Baptist, and the Apostle Paul. Josephus' description of the asceticism of Banus, the wilderness prophet with whom he lived for three years, indicates that he was celibate (Jos. *Vita* 2). Descriptions of John the Baptist and his ascetic and austere lifestyle suggest that he was celibate also. First Corinthians 7 attests to Paul's celibacy.

Langdon argued that celibacy was so unusual for a first-century Jew that one of the Gospels should have mentioned it if Jesus indeed remained unmarried. Although celibacy may not have been so unusual as to demand such a reference, one of the Gospels appears to allude to Jesus' celibacy. Although Jesus clearly held a high view of the institution of marriage, in Matthew 19:12 he affirmed with equal clarity that celibacy was best for some. Jesus said that some were eunuchs for the sake of the kingdom of God. Most scholars recognize the statement as autobiographical (i.e., as explaining the grounds for Jesus' own celibate lifestyle). Paul likewise defended the appropriateness of celibacy for some Christians in 1 Corinthians 7:25–40.

---

[7] C. S. Keener, "Marriage," in *Dictionary of New Testament Background*, ed. C. A. Evans and Stanley Porter (Downers Grove, Ill.: InterVarsity, 2000), 680–93, esp. 682–83.

Teabing claimed that an ancient Christian gospel, the Gospel of Philip, clearly attested to Jesus' marriage to Mary Magdalene. Teabing revealed to Sophie a massive book titled *The Gnostic Gospels* which supposedly contained translations of the Nag Hammadi Codices and the Dead Sea Scrolls.[8] Teabing turned to the Gospel of Philip and had Sophie read the passage:

> And the companion of the Saviour is Mary Magdalene. Christ loved her more than all the disciples and used to kiss her often on the mouth. . . .
>
> The words surprised Sophie, and yet they hardly seemed conclusive. "It says nothing of marriage."
>
> "Au contraire." Teabing smiled, pointing to the first line.
>
> "As any Aramaic scholar will tell you, the word *companion*, in those days, literally meant *spouse*" (246).

Again Teabing (and apparently Brown) betray their ignorance of the facts. Teabing apparently assumed that the Gospel of Philip was written in Aramaic since he refers to Aramaic terms in the gospel. However, the Gospel of Philip, like the rest of the Nag Hammadi texts, was written in Coptic, an Egyptian language inscribed using the Greek alphabet—plus six additional characters. The word *companion* is a Coptic word derived from Greek, not an Aramaic word at all. The Coptic word *companion* (*koinōnos*) means "friend, associate, or companion," not "wife or lover."

The description of Jesus kissing Mary Magdalene on the mouth strongly implies a romantic relationship between Jesus and Mary. However, Teabing failed to acknowledge that we possess only one ancient manuscript of the Gospel of Philip which was discovered in Codex 2 of the Nag Hammadi texts. Unfortunately, in this single surviving manuscript, Gospel of Philip 63:32–64:10 which Teabing quotes is badly damaged, and nearly half of the words that Teabing "quotes" are now missing. In its present form our only surviving manuscript of the Gospel of Philip reads, "And the companion of the . . .

---

[8] The description of the contents of this book is bizarre since the Dead Sea Scrolls contain no Christian Gospels or Gnostic material.

Mary Magdalene . . . her more than . . . the disciples . . . kiss her . . . on her . . ." The fact is that it is merely a guess that the text ever claimed that Jesus kissed Mary on the mouth. Translators of the fragmentary manuscript could just as easily supply the word "cheek" or "forehead." Even if a new manuscript discovery were made which confirmed Teabing's guess that the Gospel of Philip originally described Jesus as kissing Mary on the mouth, this would do little to support Teabing's theory of a marriage to Mary. An earlier discussion in the Gospel of Philip 58:19–59:5 shows that a kiss in Gnostic communities symbolized teaching the secrets of Gnosticism to another person. Such kisses were purely symbolic and did not involve actual physical contact. The fact is that to argue for a romantic relationship between Jesus and Mary based on confused interpretations and missing words in a fragmentary, late, Gnostic text defies all logic and sensitivity to the standards of true history.

At first Teabing's efforts to prove Jesus' marriage to Mary from such scanty and weak evidence are puzzling. However, the motive for his revisionist approach to history soon becomes apparent. Teabing sought to prove such a marriage because he felt that it would disprove the church's claim that Jesus is God: "A child of Jesus would undermine the critical notion of Christ's divinity and therefore the Christian Church, which declared itself the sole vessel through which humanity could access the divine and gain entrance to the kingdom of heaven" (254).

Teabing suggests that many Christian leaders know that Jesus was married but carefully guard that secret as part of some grand conspiracy, fearing that admission of Jesus' marriage would destroy the Christian faith. Most evangelical scholars, however, are convinced that marriage would not necessarily preclude Jesus' deity. Orthodox Christians have always affirmed both Jesus' deity and his humanity. Since Jesus was fully human, he was capable not only of sweating and bleeding; growing hungry, thirsty, or tired; but also of marrying and fathering children. Christian scholars do not deny that Jesus fathered children out of any fear of destroying the church or the faith. They deny that Jesus married and fathered children because no evidence suggests that He did, and much evidence suggests that He did not. The church's insistence on Jesus' celibacy is motivated by a desire to handle the historical data responsibly. It is not a conspiracy driven by a theological agenda.

The Deity and Humanity of Jesus

One of Brown's most shocking claims is his insistence that the Trinitarian theology of the historic Christian church was invented by a pagan emperor as part of a political ploy.

> "At this gathering," Teabing said, "many aspects of Christianity were debated and voted upon—the date of Easter, the role of the bishops, the administration of sacraments, and, of course, the *divinity* of Jesus."
>
> "I don't follow. His divinity?"
>
> "My dear," Teabing declared, "until *that* moment in history, Jesus was viewed by His followers as a mortal prophet . . . a great and powerful man but a *man* nonetheless. A mortal."
>
> "Not the son of God?"
>
> "Right," Teabing said. "Jesus' establishment as 'the Son of God' was officially proposed and voted on by the Council of Nicaea."
>
> "Hold on. You're saying Jesus' divinity was the result of a *vote*?"
>
> "A relatively close vote at that," Teabing added (233).

Teabing argues that before the Council of Nicea in the fourth century, Christians viewed Jesus merely as a man but not as divine, a great mortal prophet but not Deity incarnate, God in the flesh. This claim can be easily tested by examining the writings of the earliest Christians. These earliest Christian writings appear in the New Testament.

The earliest Christian document known today is probably the epistle of James. Internal evidence suggests that the letter was written in the early to mid-forties, within as little as a decade after the death of Jesus.[9] At least three times (Jas 1:1; 2:1; 5:7) the author refers to Jesus using the title *Lord* (*kyrios*). This term served in the LXX (Greek Old Testament) as a title for Deity, translating the Hebrew name *Yahweh*. Since texts like James 1:5 and 1:7 use the terms *Lord* and *God* interchangeably to refer to Yahweh only a few verses after identifying Jesus Christ as Lord, the description of Jesus as Lord strongly implies his Deity.[10]

According to the South Galatian theory, the earliest letter written by Paul was his epistle to the Galatians which was probably written in AD 48–49. This letter refers to Jesus as the "Son of God" no less than three times (Gal 1:16; 2:20; 4:4). Furthermore, the first verse of the letter contrasts Jesus with humanity in such a way as to demonstrate that Jesus is more than a mere mortal man.

Paul's later writings attest to Jesus' deity even more clearly. For example, Romans 10:9 says, "If you confess with your mouth Jesus as Lord, and believe in your heart that God raised Him from the dead, you shall be saved." The context of this statement demonstrates that confessing Jesus as Lord means acknowledging that Jesus is God. Although the title *Lord* may function as either a title of Deity or a title of authority, *Lord* is clearly a divine title here. This is demonstrated by the proof text that Paul quotes four verses later from Joel 2:32, "Whoever calls on the name of the LORD shall be saved" (NKJV). This proof text in Romans 10:13 closely matches the statement in 10:9. "Whoever calls" matches "confess with your mouth"; "name of the Lord" matches "Jesus as Lord"; and "will be saved" (obviously) matches "will be saved." Paul quoted Joel 2:32 to explain and confirm his parallel statement in Romans 10:9. In Paul's Greek translation of Joel 2:32, the name *Lord* is *kyrios*, but in the original Hebrew text the name is *Yahweh* or *Jehovah*. By using a text in which *Lord* means "Yahweh" to explain what it means to confess Jesus as Lord, Paul clearly demonstrates that a sinner must confess Jesus to be Yahweh, God Almighty, in order to be saved. Thus the earliest followers of Jesus not

[9] D. A. Carson, Douglas J. Moo, and Leon Morris, *An Introduction to the New Testament* (Grand Rapids: Zondervan, 1992), 414.

[10] See also James 3:9 in which the title *Lord* refers to the Father and the use in 5:4 in the title *Lord Almighty*.

only affirmed Jesus' deity; they recognized confession of his Deity as necessary for salvation.

Similarly, Philippians 2:9 teaches that because Jesus obeyed the Father by suffering on the cross, "God highly exalted Him and gave Him the name that is above every name." Although the casual reader typically assumes that the name above every other name is the name Jesus (probably due to the influence of traditional Christian songs), the historical and literary context demonstrate otherwise. In the New Testament era, Jews so reverenced the name of God, Yahweh, that they refused to speak this name. Reverent Jews chose instead to refer to God using substitutions for the divine name. The common substitutions were *Adonai* (Lord), the Name (*ha shem*), the Separate name, God's own name, and the name of four letters Y-H-W-H (tetragrammaton). Another clear substitution for the name *Yahweh* is "the Name which is above every other name." When any Jewish Christian at Philippi read the phrase "the Name that is above every name" they automatically recognized it as a reference to the tetragrammaton. Thus, Philippians 2:9 identifies Jesus as God who possesses the very name of God. Paul confirmed this by applying the description of worship of Yahweh in Isaiah 45:23 to Jesus also. Paul's promise that every knee will bow before Jesus and every tongue will confess that Jesus is Lord clearly alludes to the promise, "Turn to me and be saved, all you ends of the earth; for I am God and there is no other. . . . Before me every knee will bow; by me every tongue will swear." Paul's application of a text describing homage to Yahweh to describe worship of Jesus demonstrates that Paul saw Jesus as far more than a mere man or great religious teacher.[11] Evidences of a high Christology which equated Jesus with Yahweh abound throughout the New Testament in even its earliest documents. The claim that Constantine invented the doctrine of Jesus' deity in the fourth century is simply absurd.

The characters of *The Da Vinci Code* appear to misunderstand the purpose of the Council of Nicea and the Nicene Creed which the

---

[11] For a thorough scholarly discussion of the worship of Jesus as God in the early church, see Larry W. Hurtado, *Lord Jesus Christ: Devotion to Jesus in Earliest Christianity* (Grand Rapids: Eerdmans, 2003).

Council produced. Although the Council of Nicea did confirm the church's historic belief in the Deity of Jesus in response to the Arian controversy, the council merely composed a precise articulation of the doctrine. It did not invent it. Although Teabing claims that the vote to approve the confession of Jesus' deity was a split vote, the fact is that the overwhelming majority approved the confession.[12]

Reliable Sources for Understanding Jesus

Teabing claims that if modern truth-seekers want to know the real story about the true Jesus of history, they must jettison the four New Testament Gospels and instead rely on gospels preserved among the Nag Hammadi texts and the Dead Sea Scrolls.

> Understandably, His life was recorded by thousands of followers across the land (231).
> "More than *eighty* gospels were considered for the New Testament, and yet only a relative few were chosen for inclusion—Matthew, Mark, Luke, and John among them.
> "Who chose which gospels to include?" Sophie asked
> "Aha!" Teabing burst with enthusiasm. "The fundamental irony of Christianity! The Bible, as we know it today, was collated by the pagan Roman emperor Constantine the Great" (231).

Teabing's preference for the so-called lost gospels over the New Testament Gospels and his claim that Constantine chose which gospels to include in the New Testament lacks any historical evidence. First, no evidence suggests that thousands of followers recorded Jesus' life. Even including apocryphal gospels written by second- and third-century heretics to promote their perverse theologies, only about twenty gospels offering descriptions of Jesus' life are known to have existed. Although the early church fathers were aware of alternative gospels, the earliest lists of New Testament books consistently include only four

---

[12] Bart D. Ehrman, *Truth and Fiction in* The Da Vinci Code: *A Historian Reveals What We Really Know about Jesus, Mary Magdalene, and Constantine* (Oxford: Oxford University Press, 2004), 23.

Gospels: Matthew, Mark, Luke, and John. Tatian (c. 170), Irenaeus (c. 180), the Muratorian fragment (c. 190), Clement of Alexandria (c. 155–220), Tertullian (c. 160–220), Hippolytus (c. 170–235), and Origen (c. 230) show that the four New Testament Gospels were recognized by the church as inspired and reliable accounts well over a century before the time of Constantine. Early church fathers like Ignatius, Polycarp, and Justin Martyr who wrote from the late first century through the middle of the second century allude to and quote the four Gospels of Matthew, Mark, Luke, and John but never any other gospels.[13]

Although the early church wrestled with questions regarding the authorship and inclusion of some of the general epistles and Revelation, the question of which gospels to include was clearly settled very early. By AD 180, Irenaeus could write: "The Gospels could not possibly be either more or less in number than they are. Since there are four zones of the world in which we live, and four principal winds, while the Church is spread over all the earth, and the pillar and foundation of the Church is the gospel, and the Spirit of life, it fittingly has four pillars, everywhere breathing out incorruption and revivifying men" (*Adv. Haer.* 3.11.8). Christians in the first and second century agreed that the four Gospels were the only inspired and accurate accounts of the life of Jesus.[14]

Teabing also charges that the New Testament Gospels cannot be deemed historically reliable because they have changed so drastically over the last two millennia.

> "The Bible is a product of *man*, my dear. Not of God. The Bible did not fall magically from the clouds. Man created it as a historical record of tumultuous times, and it has evolved through countless translations, additions, and

---

[13] Paul D. Wegner, *The Journey from Texts to Translations: The Origin and Development of the Bible* (Grand Rapids: Baker, 1999), 138.

[14] Although Marcion would challenge the establishment of the four Gospels in the mid-second century, he did not propose alternative gospels but confined the church's testimony about Jesus to a heavily revised edition of the Gospel of Luke. Tertullian appropriately quipped that Marcion critiqued the New Testament with a knife.

revisions. History has never had a definitive version of the book" (231).

Teabing's skepticism regarding the preservation of the Scripture simply does not square with the facts. The New Testament is actually far better preserved than any other book from ancient times. Very few manuscripts (copies of ancient books made by hand before the invention of the printing press) of texts from the New Testament period have survived. One of the most famous and respected Roman historians of the New Testament era was Tacitus, who wrote his *Roman Annals* between AD 115 and 117. No complete manuscripts of this important work have survived. Only two fragmentary ancient manuscript witnesses of Tacitus's book are known to exist, and the oldest manuscript dates to the ninth century, at least seven hundred years after Tacitus wrote his history.[15] By contrast approximately fifty-four hundred manuscripts of the New Testament exist in libraries throughout the world. Many of these date hundreds of years closer to the original document than manuscripts of Tacitus's work. The major uncial manuscripts are Vaticanus and Sinaiticus, which date to AD 325 and 350 respectively. In addition to these complete or nearly complete biblical texts, in the last two hundred years scholars have discovered numerous ancient papyri, texts of the New Testament written on papyrus, an ancient form of paper. Many of the papyri are very early, dating to within a few generations of the original New Testament documents. The earliest of these is P52, a fragment of the Gospel of John which dates to AD 125 plus or minus twenty-five years. Most scholars believe that the Gospel of John was written in the late first century, in which case P52 was produced only a few decades after John first penned the Gospel. P46, which today includes 86 of about 104 leaves of the epistles of Paul, was written around AD 200 and has been dated by some scholars as early as the late first century. By comparing these

---

[15] Michael Grant notes that the end of book 5 is missing, along with the entirety of books 7–10 and the end of book 16. See Michael Grant, *Tacitus: the Annals of Imperial Rome* (London: Penguin, 1996). One manuscript of Books 1–6 is extant which dates to approximately AD 850. The thirty-one late Italian manuscripts of Books 11–16 are all copies from the same medieval exemplar (ms 68.2). See L. D. Reynolds, *Texts and Transmission: A Survey of Latin Classics* (Oxford: Clarendon, 1983), 406-11.

very early and numerous manuscripts, scholars can reconstruct the original New Testament with a high degree of accuracy.[16]

Teabing argues that the New Testament has constantly been evolving and changing and thus casts doubt on whether it can be trusted two thousand years after it was originally written. However, even when questions remain about the original reading of the New Testament after a careful comparison of the ancient manuscripts, the questions are relatively minor, inconsequential for Christian doctrines and understanding the identity of Jesus.

Ironically, after challenging the reliability of the New Testament because of changes that were supposedly introduced into the text over time, Teabing argues that books like the Gospel of Philip and Gospel of Mary can be trusted as reliable documents that tell the real and unaltered story about Jesus. However, we possess only one ancient manuscript of the Gospel of Philip which appears in Codex II of the Nag Hammadi Codices. The books of Nag Hammadi are easy to date since the spines of the leather bindings were strengthened with scrap paper, and some of the scrap paper consisted of discarded business receipts dated to 341, 346, and 348.[17] This demonstrates conclusively that the books were produced in the late fourth century, some time after AD 348 and about one hundred to two hundred years later than several extensive texts of the New Testament Gospels. Furthermore, we have no copy of the Gospel of Philip in its original language, Greek. The single early copy of the Gospel of Philip is a Sahidic Coptic translation. This single extant copy of Philip is a fragmentary text in which about half the text is broken away at its most critical point forcing scholars to fill in the gaps from their own imaginations. To challenge the reliability of copies and translations of the New Testament Gospels and then insist on the reliability of a book for which we have a single

---

[16] For helpful introductions to the science of textual criticism and for summaries of the content and dates of important New Testament manuscripts, see Bruce Metzger, *The Text of the New Testament: Its Transmission, Corruption, and Restoration* (Oxford: Oxford University Press, 1968); and Kurt Aland and Barbara Aland, *The Text of the New Testament: An Introduction to the Critical Editions and to the Theory and Practice of Modern Textual Criticism* (Grand Rapids: Eerdmans, 1989).

[17] James M. Robinson, *The Nag Hammadi Library in English* (San Francisco: Harper, 1990), 16.

copy translated into a secondary language three hundred years after the time of Jesus makes little sense and betrays Teabing's bias against the New Testament.

Finally, most scholars believe that the original Gospel of Philip was written in the early third century, over 150 years after the time of Jesus and long after the eyewitnesses of Jesus' ministry had passed from the scene.[18] The New Testament Gospels were written before the close of the first century while numerous eyewitnesses of Jesus' ministry still lived and could challenge the Gospels if they did not report accurately on Jesus' life.[19] This should show that Teabing's attack on the New Testament Gospels and preference for other documents is prejudicial and illogical.

Conclusion

On page 196 of *The Da Vinci Code*, the albino assassin Silas has lost his confidence that he and his teacher will succeed in their mission. The mysterious teacher assures him by saying, "You lose your faith too quickly." Those whose faith is shaken by Dan Brown's claims lose their faith far too quickly too. If they will take the time to investigate Brown's claims, they will find that his statements about biblical and historical Christianity are a comedy of errors and lack historical evidence. Although Teabing makes the bold assertion that "almost everything our fathers taught us about Christ is *false*" (235), the truth is that almost everything Dan Brown has taught about Christianity, Jesus, and ancient religious documents is wrong. The faith of the fathers of the church, the faith taught by the New Testament, is a faith that has stood the test of time and will withstand Dan Brown's erroneous claims. The evidence shows that readers can trust what the four Gospels report about the life and teachings of Jesus of Nazareth.

---

[18] Ibid., 141.
[19] See especially Richard Bauckham, *Jesus and the Eyewitnesses* (Grand Rapids: Eerdmans, 2006).

Chapter 8

WHAT DO WE KNOW FOR SURE ABOUT JESUS' DEATH?

Craig A. Evans

There are at least five essential questions relating to Jesus' death. Although we cannot know every detail, we can answer these questions with reasonable probability. They are: What were the factors that resulted in Jesus' execution? Who killed Jesus? How was he killed? Was Jesus, after dying, taken down from the cross? Was he buried, and if so, how and by whom? I shall now address these questions in the order that they have been raised.

What Were the Factors That Resulted in Jesus' Execution?

One of the most hotly debated questions, perhaps *the* most hotly debated question, concerns the factors that resulted in the execution of Jesus. What did Jesus do to precipitate His death? One of the reasons this question is so controversial is that it is closely linked to Jesus' ministry—what Jesus proclaimed about God and what Jesus claimed about Himself.

According to the Gospels, Jesus was put to death for having claimed to be the "King of the Jews." Accordingly, a *titulus* was fixed on or near his cross bearing this statement. We know from Roman sources that the *titulus* at the place of execution identified the victim of the execution and/or provided the grounds for punishment (*causa poena*).

The *titulus* in the Gospels, therefore, indicates that Jesus must have claimed, or allowed others to make claims on His behalf, that He was the true ruler of the Jewish people, not Tiberius Caesar.

Most scholars accept the historicity of the *titulus* "King of the Jews" because this epithet does not fit well with either Jewish messianic expectation or with early Christian understanding of the person and work of Jesus. In the case of Judaism of the time of Jesus, the coming one was referred to as "Messiah," "King" or "King Messiah," "Son of David" or "Branch of David," or even "Son of God." These epithets are illustrated in the intertestamental literature, including the Dead Sea Scrolls, and are rooted in the Scriptures of Israel. In the Gospels the ruling priests and scribes mock the dying Jesus as the "Messiah, the King of Israel" (Mark 15:32 HCSB). In the case of early Christianity, Jesus is called "Messiah" (or Christ), "Son of God," "Lord," and "Savior." Christians and religious Jews do not refer to Jesus or the Messiah as "King of the Jews." That was a Roman title, conferred upon Herod the Great by Marc Antony and the Roman Senate.

I am invoking here what I think is an appropriate use of the criterion of dissimilarity. That is, the most likely explanation of the appearance in the Gospels of the *titulus*, bearing the words, "King of the Jews," is that it is historical, that it was public and therefore widely known, and—like it or not—that was what Rome said about Jesus of Nazareth. The language of the *titulus* does not derive from a Jewish commonplace or from Christian confession; it derives from history.

What may we infer from the words of the *titulus*? The epithet "King of the Jews" strongly implies that Jesus regarded Himself—or at least allowed His followers to regard Him—as Israel's anointed King. Accordingly, at the very least we have strong supporting evidence of a messianic self-understanding on the part of Jesus. Had He been no more than an agitator, calling for an end to Roman rule, or for an overthrow of the high priestly administration, it is improbable that Jesus would have been executed as "King of the Jews." The *titulus* could just as easily read "malefactor" or "rebel."

But there is another important factor at play that resulted in Jesus' execution. According to the Gospel accounts, the Jewish temple establishment initiated the action against Jesus. Jesus was not attacked or arrested by troops under the governor's orders; He was seized by officers who answered to the ruling priests.

Some critics have maintained that the role assigned to the ruling priests—from bribing Judas to the hearing before the Jewish court—is part of a largely fictional, anti-Jewish apologetic, perhaps encouraged by the growing anti-Semitism in the Roman Empire thanks to the Jewish revolt in AD 66.

The Gospels' portraits—one Synoptic and one Johannine—receive important corroboration in Josephus, the Jewish aristocrat, who survived the Jewish rebellion and wrote several important works describing Jewish history and especially Israel's relations with Rome. In his famous passage in *Jewish Antiquities*, in which he mentions Jesus, Josephus tells us that it was the "first men among us" that initially took action against Jesus (cf. *Antiquities* 18.3.3 §63–64). By "first men" it is almost certain that Josephus means the ruling priests. These first men present Jesus to Pilate, the Roman governor, who then sentences Him to death. In his account of the *Jewish War*, Josephus tells us of another Jesus, one son of Ananias, who in the year 62 began to proclaim the doom of Jerusalem and her magnificent temple. Like Jesus of Nazareth, Jesus son of Ananias appealed to Jeremiah 7 as the basis of his warning. And, as in the case of Jesus of Nazareth, Jesus son of Ananias was violently opposed by the "first men," who beat him and delivered him up to the Roman governor (this time Albinus), with calls for his execution. Albinus scourged and interrogated the son of Ananias but in the end decided to release him rather than put him to death. The parallels between the two Jesuses in the juridical process, a process involving both Jewish and Roman authorities, are numerous and close.

Why then did the Jewish authorities conspire against Jesus of Nazareth? A satisfying answer is not hard to find. Jesus *entered* the temple precincts amid shouts of the coming kingdom of David, *quoted* part of Isaiah 56—an oracle based on Solomon's prayer of dedication on behalf of the temple—implying that the ruling priests had not lived up to their God-given responsibilities, and then *alluded* to

Jeremiah 7, an oracle foretelling the destruction of the temple. It is no surprise that the ruling priests reacted angrily to Jesus' teaching, not to mention His disruption of the temple trade.

When Jesus is confronted by the temple authorities, He utters a parable (Mark 12) in which He reshapes Isaiah's Song of the Vineyard (Isa 5), implying that the fault does not lie with a fruitless vineyard but a fruit-stealing, oppressive priesthood—a priesthood that will be swept away for having opposed the most important emissary that God sent to His people, His very own Son. The ruling priests clearly and accurately perceive the threat, fearing that Jesus' inflammatory words will incite the crowds against them.

The ruling priests seize Jesus by stealth—that is, late at night and nearly alone. An arrest in broad daylight, in the presence of dozens if not hundreds of supporters, and perhaps hundreds more who were critical of the temple authorities and their Roman overlords, would have precipitated the uprising the ruling priests feared. By taking Jesus into custody quietly and at night, his movement would likely falter and pose a much reduced threat.

The historicity of the betrayal and arrest of Jesus is virtually guaranteed, given the extreme improbability of inventing a story that revolves around a betrayal at the hands of one of the twelve. Here I invoke the criterion of embarrassment. Surely the story of the treachery of Judas is the stuff of history, as embarrassing as it is, and not the stuff of legend or misguided anti-Semitism.

The hearing before the ruling priests also has good grounds for historicity. Indeed, we should assume that the later Jesus, son of Ananias, was also brought before a priestly council for daring to utter prophecies of doom against the temple and city. Such a hearing forms the bridge between priestly reaction in the temple precincts and eventual presentation before the Roman governor.

Jewish law required a hearing that would establish grounds for presenting the accused to Roman authority. One thinks of Gallio, proconsul of Achaia, before whom Paul was presented (Acts 18:12–17). Fellow Jews charged: "This man is persuading people to worship God contrary to the law" (v. 13 ESV). But the proconsul is unimpressed. He retorts: "If it were a matter of wrongdoing or vicious crime, O Jews, I would have reason to accept your complaint. But since it is a matter of questions about words and names and your own law, see to it yourselves. I refuse to be a judge of these things" (vv. 14–15 ESV). The proconsul then drove them away from the tribunal.

Accordingly, the ruling priests cannot simply bring a complaint to the Roman governor, a mere dispute over how God should be worshipped or how sacrifice should be offered, or how much to charge for sacrificial animals, or whatever. What was needed, in the words of Gallio, was evidence of "wrongdoing or vicious crime."

High Priest Caiaphas knows that such evidence should not be too difficult to obtain. Jesus has been proclaiming the kingdom of God; He has been hailed as "Son of David"; some rumor Him to be Israel's Messiah; and He has acted with a messianic authority in the temple precincts. So, after some posturing and fencing, the high priest puts the question to Jesus directly: "Are you the Messiah, the Son of the Blessed?" (Mark 14:61 ESV). And with no equivocation, Jesus replies: "I am; and you will see the Son of Man seated at the right hand of Power, and coming with the clouds of heaven" (v. 62 ESV).

Jesus' bold reply links phrases from Daniel 7 and Psalm 110, two passages that envision judgment upon the enemies of God and of His Messiah. Not only that, but Jesus implies that He—as the mysterious "son of man" figure described in Daniel 7—will sit next to God Himself on His throne. The phrase "coming with the clouds" and the allusion to Daniel 7, where God's throne is said to have wheels of fire (v. 9), indicate that Jesus was speaking of God's chariot throne, the most sacred space in all the universe. That he would share this space and, indeed, share in the divine authority and judgment that issue forth from this space was more than Caiaphas the high priest could tolerate. His cry "blasphemy!" is fully expected. He now has all that he has sought—an utterance utterly offensive to the Jewish council and a charge of treason that the Roman governor must hear.

Who Killed Jesus?

Mel Gibson's movie *The Passion of the Christ* reignited the old controversy surrounding the question concerning those who were responsible for Jesus' death. Thanks to anti-Semitism, which embarrassingly reaches back in some forms as early as the second century, Christians thought that perhaps it was the Jews themselves who executed Jesus, hence the ugly epithet "Christ killers."

But this malignant interpretation does not arise from the New Testament Gospels. While some of the ruling priests and a small number of aristocratic authorities opposed Jesus and called for His death, we should assume that the vast majority of Jews who knew anything of the matter did not.

The actual execution of Jesus was a Roman affair. To be sure, there is compelling evidence that in earlier times Jewish rulers did in fact crucify malefactors and political enemies (the most notorious example being Alexander Jannaeus, who crucified some eight hundred Pharisees). But during the Roman occupation of Judea, capital punishment was carried out by Roman authority, whether the form it took was crucifixion or some other form (such as beheading). Indeed, from the time of Pilate, we have the skeletal remains of one man who was crucified and possibly the skeletal remains of two people who were beheaded. More will be said about this evidence shortly.

The men who beat Jesus and mocked Him with a purple robe, a scepter, and a crown of thorns were Romans, the same men who later that morning scourged Jesus and nailed Him to a cross.

How Was Jesus Killed?

That Jesus was crucified is hardly disputed. The discovery in 1968 of an ossuary at Giv'at ha-Mivtar of one Yehohanan, who had been crucified, provides archaeological evidence and illumination on how Jesus Himself may have been crucified. The ossuary and its contents date to the late AD 20s, that is, during the administration of Pilate. The remains of an iron spike (11.5 cm in length) are plainly seen, piercing the right heel bone (or *calcaneum*). Those who took down the body of Yehohanan apparently were unable to remove the spike, with the result that wood (from an olive tree) remained affixed to the spike. Later the skeletal remains of the body—spike, fragments of wood, and all—were placed in the ossuary. Forensic examination of the rest of the skeletal remains supports the view that Yehohanan was crucified with arms apart, hung from a horizontal beam or tree branch. However, there is no evidence that his arms, or wrists, were nailed to this crossbeam. The lack of nails or spikes in the hands or wrists is consistent with a reference in Pliny Sr., who refers to rope used in crucifixion (cf. *Nat. Hist.* 28.4). However, doubtless many victims of crucifixion did have their hands or wrists nailed to the beam. A third century AD author describes it this way: "Punished with limbs outstretched . . . they are fastened (and) nailed to the stake in the most bitter torment, evil food for birds of prey and grim picking for dogs" (*Apotelesmatica* 4.198–200).

It is significant that in Philippians 2:7–8 Paul cites the ancient hymn that speaks of Jesus "taking the form of a slave" (NRSV) and "being found in human form he humbled himself and became obedient unto death, even death on a cross" (RSV). The hymn probably reflects here the Roman view of death by crucifixion as *servile supplicium*, that is, "slave's punishment."

There can be no doubt that Jesus died the death of a despised criminal, a death usually reserved for a slave. This is hardly the stuff of pious imagination. He was mocked, beaten, scourged, and then led to the place of crucifixion. Although He had warned His disciples to be prepared to take up the cross, when the time comes for Jesus to do so, He is unable, and Simon of Cyrene is compelled. Here again we have grim realism, not fiction.

Was Jesus Taken Down from the Cross?

Yehohanan's leg bones were broken, but there is disagreement over how and when they were broken (i.e., while still on the cross, or after being taken down). If Yehohanan's legs were broken before death, we then know not only that he was taken down and buried (as indicated by the discovery of his remains in an ossuary); we also know that his death was intentionally hastened so that his corpse could be taken down from the cross before nightfall.

In a popular book published a decade ago, John Dominic Crossan argued that Jesus in all probability was not taken down from the cross and given proper burial. He reasoned that because so many Jews who had been crucified had been left to rot in the sun, exposed to birds and animals, in all likelihood Jesus too had been left on the cross, or at best had been cast into a shallow ditch where His body may have been mauled by dogs.

Crossan's novel suggestion should be rejected for two important reasons. First, burial of the dead was a sacred duty in the Jewish world, and our sources tell us that it was accorded to executed criminals. This is an important theme in the book of Tobit. Second, burial of the dead is commanded in Scripture so as to avoid defiling the land (Deut 21:22–23). The Jewish authorities simply had no alternatives: every corpse had to be buried before sundown; the corpse of an executed criminal, as well as the corpse of an honored person.

The evidence suggests that the Romans, during peacetime, did in fact respect Jewish sensitivities in this matter. Indeed, both Philo and Josephus claim that Roman administration in fact did acquiesce to Jewish customs. In his appeal to Caesar, Philo draws attention to the Jews who "appealed to Pilate to redress the infringement of their traditions caused by the shields and not to disturb the customs which throughout all the preceding ages had been safeguarded without disturbance by kings and by emperors" (*De Legatione ad Gaium* 38 §300). A generation later Josephus asserts the same thing. The Romans, he says, do not require "their subjects to violate their national laws" (*Contra Apionem* 2.6 §73). Josephus adds that the Roman procurators who succeeded Agrippa I "by abstaining from all interference with the customs of the country kept the nation at peace" (*J. W.* 2.11.6 §220).

The actions of Herod Antipas, with respect to John the Baptist, are consistent with this policy. Although the Baptist is executed by the tetrarch, his disciples are nonetheless allowed to bury his body (Mark 6:14–29; Josephus, *Ant.* 18.5.2 §119).

Even Roman justice outside the Jewish setting sometimes permitted the crucified to be taken down and buried. We find in the summary of Roman law (a.k.a. *Digesta*) the following concessions:

> The bodies of those who are condemned to death should not be refused their relatives; and the Divine Augustus, in the Tenth Book of his *Life*, said that this rule had been observed. At present, the bodies of those who have been punished are only buried when this has been requested and permission granted; and sometimes it is not permitted, especially where persons have been convicted of high treason (48.24.1).
>
> The bodies of persons who have been punished should be given to whoever requests them for the purpose of burial (48.24.3).

The *Digesta* refers to requests to take down bodies of the crucified. Josephus himself makes this request of Titus (*Life* 75 §420–21). Of course, Roman crucifixion often did not permit burial, request or no request. Nonburial was part of the horror, and the deterrent, of crucifixion. But crucifixion during peacetime, just outside the walls of Jerusalem, was another matter. Burial would have been expected, even demanded.

Was Jesus Buried, and If so, How and by Whom?

If the bodies of executed persons were almost certainly taken down from their crosses during peacetime, then it is equally certain that these bodies would have been properly buried. Of course, the bodies of criminals were not given honorable burial; no public lamentation was permitted. But their bodies were buried properly and were certainly not left exposed.

Again, archaeological evidence provides a measure of support. I have already mentioned the discovery of Yehohanan, the crucified man whose right heel is still transfixed by the iron spike. Also found in the tombs discovered at Giv'at Ha-Mivtar were the remains of a woman who had been decapitated. Although we cannot be sure, she may have been beheaded. If the decapitation of this woman was in fact the result of execution by beheading, then we have another important instance of the proper burial of an executed person.

We may have the skeletal remains of yet another person who, like Yehohanan, was executed and whose remains eventually were placed in the family tomb. These remains were found in a cluster of tombs on Mount Scopus, north of Jerusalem. In Tomb C the skeletal remains of a woman (aged 50–60) give clear evidence of having been attacked. Her right elbow suffered a deep cut that severed the end of the *humerus*. Because there is no sign of regrowth or infection, it is surmised that she died from the attack. In the adjacent Tomb D, which contains the remains of persons related to those interred in Tomb C, were the remains of a man (aged 50), who had been decapitated. It is plausible to speculate that this man too had been beheaded, quite possibly for having murdered the female relative in Tomb C. Physical anthropologist Joe Zias doubts that the man had been executed because his neck had been struck twice. Being struck twice, he reasons, suggests "an act of violence rather than a judicial execution." Zias of course could be correct, but we should not assume that judicial beheadings were always neatly done. One only needs to be reminded of the several badly aimed strokes that finally took off the head of James, Duke of Monmouth, in 1685. (Apparently the executioner was intoxicated. His first stroke buried the axe in the Duke's shoulder!) Accordingly, the man in tomb D may well be another individual who suffered the death penalty—even if it took two strokes to finish the job—and whose skeletal remains, in due course, were placed in the family tomb.

The literary, historical, and archaeological evidence suggests that, contrary to Crossan, Jesus was probably buried. If so, how was He buried and by whom? After all, the body of Jesus might have been buried in a dug grave, or it might have been placed in common burial pit, perhaps along with the other two men who were crucified with Him. The Gospels speak of a rock-hewn tomb belonging to Joseph of Arimathea. Do we have a touch of apologetic here? Or do we have, once again, reliable history?

The story of Joseph of Arimathea, who otherwise is not known, is probably historical. There are apologetic touches, to be sure. In the telling of the story, Joseph grows in sympathy and allegiance to Jesus. But at its core is a story in which Joseph either volunteers or was assigned the task of seeing to the prompt and unceremonious burial of Jesus and, probably, the other two men.

Pilate is accused of accepting bribes, so it has been suggested that Joseph may have bribed the governor. Perhaps. It is more likely that Pilate only required confirmation that the crucified men were indeed dead. Having their bodies taken down and out of public view for the Passover holiday would have been desirable.

The story of the women who witness Jesus' burial and then return early Sunday to anoint his body smacks of historicity. It is hard to see why relatively unknown women would feature so prominently in such an important story if what we have here is fiction. But if the women's intention is to mourn privately, as Jewish law and custom allowed, and, even more importantly, to note the precise location of Jesus' tomb so that the later gathering of His remains for burial in His family tomb is possible, then we have a story that fits Jewish customs on the one hand and stands in tension with resurrection expectations and supporting apologetics on the other.

Carefully observing where Jesus is buried and then returning Sunday morning to confirm and even mark His corpse for identification is in keeping with Jewish burial customs. After all, *m. Sanh.* 6:5–6 implies that bodies are still identifiable long after decomposition of the flesh. How was this done? We don't know, but evidently the Jewish people knew how to mark or in some way identify a corpse so that it could be retrieved some time later. We should not allow our own ignorance of such customs or our condescension to lead us to discount such tradition as implausible.

With the problem of such ignorance in mind, let me digress briefly and review aspects of Jewish burial traditions. Burial normally took place on the day of death. If it occurred too late in the day or during the night, the body remained in the house until the following morning. The body was washed, perfumed, wrapped, and then taken to the family crypt, which could be a natural cave or hewn vault (or combination). Public wailing and lamentation took place during this process. Family and friends gathered at the tomb, weeping, reciting Scripture, and singing. The funeral lasted seven days. A large stone, approximately 80 percent of which were square and only 20 percent were round, would be placed over the opening to the crypt. The opening was usually about one meter square or slightly larger. One year after primary burial, the family reentered the crypt, gathered the bones of the deceased, and placed them in an ossuary, a limestone box slightly longer than the adult femur, slightly wider than the adult hip bones, and slightly deeper than the adult rib cage. The name of the deceased might be incised or written in charcoal on the ossuary, usually on one of the ends or on the back (i.e., the undecorated side). About one quarter of the ossuaries that have been catalogued bear inscriptions.

The skeletons also give us an idea of the size and weight of the people of Palestine in the days of Jesus. Few men were six feet in height. A few men in a family that lived in Jericho were six feet tall. The father was given a nickname. Not surprisingly he was called Goliath. However, most men were five feet five or six inches. Most women were four feet ten or eleven inches. Moreover, the people were lean. We deduce this not only from the coarseness of the bones but also from what we know of their diet. This sheds light on the story of the women who go to the tomb of Jesus, wondering who would assist them in rolling back the stone. Judging by the size of the stones that have been found, even a well-rounded stone in a flat, smooth groove would have been difficult for two women to roll aside if they stood shorter than five feet tall and weighed only about ninety-five pounds. The women would have needed assistance.

According to Jewish tradition, the spirit of the deceased hovered near the body for three days. On the third day the face of the deceased changed, and the spirit departed. In view of this, think of the story of the raising of Lazarus in John 11. He had been dead four days; his corpse now stunk of decay. Jews would have assumed that his spirit had departed and that there was no longer any hope of resuscitation. Lazarus would someday rise again, in the day of the resurrection, but not before. But to everyone's amazement, Jesus raised him up, as proof of His claim that He is indeed the "resurrection and the life." Or think of the panic of the women who on the third day find the tomb of

Jesus empty. This is the last day before His face changes and He is no longer recognizable. His body must be found soon, or there would be no hope of ever identifying it and therefore no hope of gathering His bones one year later and placing them in the family tomb. Finding the tomb empty provoked no thoughts of resurrection, only of a missing corpse and a great sense of urgency.

Outside of the Gospel tradition is Paul's statement that Jesus "was buried [*etaphē*]" (1 Cor 15:4). This pre-Pauline tradition clearly implies an early belief that Jesus was indeed buried in keeping with Jewish customs and that though he was crucified His burial was permitted out of respect for Jewish sensitivities. Elsewhere Paul presupposes the burial of Jesus when he speaks of being "buried with [*sunetaphēmen*] Him" (Rom 6:4; cf. Col 2:12). Usage of forms of *thaptein* ("to bury") can only refer to being properly buried, not left hanging on a cross or thrown into a ditch. To be left on the cross is to be unburied (*ataphos*).

I return to the question of the significance of the archaeological evidence of Yehohanan, the one man known to have been crucified whose properly buried remains have been discovered. It has been argued that in light of the thousands of Jews crucified in the first century in the vicinity of Jerusalem, the discovery of only one properly buried crucifixion victim is evidence that the normal Roman practice of not permitting burial must have obtained even in Jewish Palestine.

At least four objections must be raised against this inference. First, almost all of the bones recovered from the time of Jesus are poorly preserved, especially the smaller bones of the feet and hands, which will normally provide evidence, if any, of crucifixion. The presence of the nail in the right heel of Yehohanan made clear that he had been crucified. The presence of the nail was a fluke. It was due to the sharp end being bent back (like a fishhook), perhaps because the nail struck a knot in the beam. When Yehohanan was taken down from the cross, the nail could not be extracted. Accordingly, no statistics should be inferred from this unusual find.

Second, many crucifixion victims were scourged, beaten, and then tied to the cross, not nailed. Thus, skeletal remains would leave no trace of the trauma of crucifixion. Accordingly, we do not know that Yehohanan is the only crucifixion victim discovered in a tomb.

Third, the best-preserved skeletons are found in the better constructed tombs, within bone pits or in ossuaries. These tombs were mostly those of the rich, not the poor. The poor were usually buried in the ground or in smaller natural caves. Not many of their skeletons have been found. The significance of this point is that the poor are most likely to be crucified, not the wealthy and powerful. Accordingly, those skeletons most likely to provide evidence of crucifixion are the skeletons least likely to survive.

Fourth, the vast majority of the thousands of Jews crucified and left unburied in the first century, in the vicinity of Jerusalem, died during the rebellion of AD 66–70. They were not buried because Rome was at war with the Jewish people and had no wish to accommodate Jewish sensitivities, as Rome did during peacetime. During peacetime—indeed, during the administration of Pontius Pilate—Yehohanan and Jesus of Nazareth were crucified. That both were buried, according to Jewish customs, should hardly occasion surprise. Jewish priestly authorities were expected to defend the purity of Jerusalem (or at least give the appearance of doing so), while Roman authorities acquiesced to Jewish customs and sensitivities.

Conclusion

It is probable that Jesus was buried in keeping with Jewish customs and was not left hanging on his cross or cast into a ditch, exposed to animals. It is probable that some of Jesus' followers (such as the women mentioned in the Gospel accounts) knew where Jesus' body had been placed and intended to mark the location, perfume His body, and mourn, in keeping with Jewish customs. The intention was to take possession of Jesus' remains at some point in the future and transfer them to His family burial place. Discussion of the resurrection of Jesus should assume proper burial and knowledge of the location of the place of burial.

Chapter 9

JESUS' RESURRECTION AND CHRISTIAN ORIGINS[1]

N. T. Wright

Introduction

The question of Jesus' resurrection continues to haunt the think-ing and writing of many scholars. I shall not debate in detail with them here; there are other places for that.[2] I want instead to sketch in broad strokes a historical argument about what happened three days after Jesus' crucifixion.

The question divides into four. First, what did people in the first century, both pagans and Jews, hope for? What did they believe about life after death, and particularly about resurrection? Second, what did the early Christians believe on the same subjects? What did they hope for? Third, what reasons did the early Christians give for their hope and belief, and what did they mean by the key word *resurrection*, which they used of Jesus? Finally, what can the historian say by way of comment on this early Christian claim?

---

[1] This essay is abridged from an article by the same title, originally published in *Gregorianum* 83/4 (2002): 615–35, by permission of the author. Its format has been adapted to the style used in this volume.
[2] Details are given in N. T. Wright, *The Resurrection of the Son of God* (London: SPCK; Minneapolis: Fortress, 2003).

Life after Death in the First Century

1. *Paganism.* Homer was hugely important in the world of late antiquity; and in Homer life after death is pretty bleak. Odysseus's journey to the underworld (in books 10 and 11 of the *Odyssey*) hardly encourages readers to suppose that death will take them into a better world. Hades, the abode of the dead, is a place of shadows and wraiths who can just about remember what life was like but not much more.

Plato held out a different possibility, the chance of a blissful after-life at least for some. He even speculated about reincarnation, though this is not central to his thought, nor is it stressed in later Platonism. His ideas come through into popular first-century culture not least in the mystery religions. Once philosophical speculation began devising alternatives to the Homeric viewpoint, other positions emerged; for instance, that of Stoicism, that the entire world would be destroyed by fire and be reborn, phoenix-like, only for everything to happen again in exactly the same way as before.

> Whenever the question of bodily resurrection is raised in the ancient world the answer is negative. Homer does not imagine that there is a way back; Plato does not suppose anyone in their right mind would want one. There may or may not be various forms of life after death, but the one thing there isn't is resurrection: the word *anastasis* refers to something that everybody knows doesn't happen. The classic statement is in Aeschylus's play *Eumenides* (647–48), in which, during the founding of the Court of the Areopagus, Apollo himself declares that when a man has died, and his blood is spilt on the ground, there is no resurrection. The language of resurrection, or something like it, was used in Egypt in connection with the very full and developed view of the world beyond death. But this new life was something that had, it was believed, already begun, and it did not involve actual bodily return to the present world. Nor was everybody fooled by the idea that the dead were already enjoying a full life beyond the grave. When the eager Egyptians tried to show their

new ruler Augustus their hoard of wonderful mummies, he replied that he wanted to see kings, not corpses.[3]

2. *Judaism.* When we turn to ancient Judaism, the picture is both similar and different. The Hebrew Sheol, the place of the dead, is not very different from Homer's Hades. People are asleep there; they can sometimes be woken up, as with Saul and Samuel, but to do so is dangerous and forbidden.[4] That is the picture we get from most of the Old Testament.

The Psalms begin to explore ways in which YHWH's love will be known after death. It is notoriously difficult to date these passages, and they remain controversial. Psalm 73 is perhaps the clearest statement of a postmortem hope. Unlike Plato, the biblical mentions of a hope beyond the grave are not predicated on the existence of an immortal soul which will automatically have a future life but on the love and faithfulness of YHWH in the present, which must, the poets suppose, continue into the future.

The Jewish hope burst the bounds of ancient paganism altogether by speaking of resurrection. The supposed Zoroastrian origin of this belief is still argued by some but strenuously denied by others who see the metaphors of Isaiah 26 and Ezekiel 37 and the earlier hints in Hosea 6 as opening the way for a new view, generated by Israel's own basic beliefs and contingent circumstances, which comes to full expression in Daniel 12. Despite what is often supposed, this belief, when it arises, is in paradoxical continuity with the ancient Hebrew belief in Sheol. Unlike Platonists, who preferred a disembodied immortality, those who believed in resurrection agreed with the ancient Israelites that real life meant embodied life. The difference is that in the earlier view those in Sheol cannot have it again (as in the book of Job, apart from the controversial passage in chapter 19), whereas in the resurrection passages they can and will.

Postbiblical Judaism offers a range of beliefs about life after death. Resurrection is by no means the only option; and when it is specified, it is not a general word for life after death but a term for one particular

---

[3] Dio Cassius, *Hist.* 51.16.

[4] 1 Sam 28:3–25.

belief. In fact, resurrection is not simply a form of life after death; resurrection hasn't happened yet. People do not pass directly from death to resurrection but go through an interim period after which the death of the body will be reversed in resurrection. Resurrection does not, then, mean "survival"; it is not a way of describing the kind of life one might have immediately following physical death. It is not a redescription of death and/or the state which results from death. In both paganism and Judaism it refers to the reversal, the undoing, the conquest of death and its effects. That is its whole point. That is what Homer, Plato, Aeschylus, and others denied; and it is what some Jews and all early Christians affirmed.

The second point to note about Jewish belief in resurrection is that, where it did occur, it was never a detached belief. It was always part of a larger picture of what God was going to do for the nation and indeed the world. Resurrection is one point on a larger spectrum; it will happen all at once as part of God's future for Israel and the world; and, third, it was fairly unspecific in detail. The rabbis debate whether God will start with the soul and gradually build up to the solid body; or whether, as in Ezekiel, God will begin with the bones and add flesh and sinews, finally adding breath as in Genesis 2. In each case, of course, what you end up with is what we would call a physical body; but there was no agreement as to whether this body would be exactly like the one you had before or significantly different in some way. The belief remains vague and unfocused.

Finally, some at least of those who believed in the resurrection also believed in the coming of the Messiah, though the relation between Messiah and resurrection is not usually clear. The Messiah would defeat YHWH's enemies, rebuild or cleanse the temple, and establish YHWH's rule in the world. Belief in the coming of a Messiah was obviously political as well as theological, as the messianic movements in the period bear witness. Resurrection and Messiah together speak of the time when God will be king and the present rulers (Caesar, Herod, the Sadducees) will be deposed. Together they speak of the coming reign of God.

It was from within one such prophetic and messianic renewal movement that the early Christians emerged, saying two things in particular: Jesus was and is the Messiah, and this is proved because He has been raised from the dead. But before we can look at these claims, we must set the early Christian views about future hope, including life after death, resurrection, and some wider issues like messiahship, in parallel with Judaism and paganism.

The Early Christian Hope: Modified and Realized

Early Christian views about life after death clearly belonged within the Jewish spectrum, not the pagan one, but were also clearly different. This gives us a fresh purchase on the question, why did they reshape the hope in that way?

Almost all early Christians known to us believed that their ultimate hope was the resurrection of the body. There is no spectrum such as in Judaism.

This almost complete absence of a spectrum of belief itself demands explanation, but before we can offer one, we must add two further points. First, the early Christian belief in resurrection had a much more precise shape and content than anything we find in Judaism. In early Christianity, obviously in Paul but not only there, resurrection will be an act of new creation, accomplished by the Holy Spirit, and the body which is to be is already planned by God. This will not be a simple return to the same sort of body as before; nor will it be an abandonment of embodiedness in order to enjoy a disembodied bliss. It will involve transformation, the gift of a new body with different properties.

The other way in which early Christian belief about resurrection is significantly different from that of second-temple Judaism is that, particularly in Paul, "the resurrection" has split into two. Paul still sees the resurrection of the dead as a single theological event,[5] but it takes place in two phases: first the Messiah, then at His coming all His

---

[5] See e.g. Rom 1:4; 1 Cor 15:20–28.

people.[6] This too only makes sense within second-temple Judaism, but it is something no second-temple Jew had said before. Resurrection had been a single all-embracing moment, not a matter of one person's being raised ahead of everybody else.

Finally, the early Christians speak of one major aspect of the Jewish hope as already emphatically realized. Jesus Himself was and is the Messiah, and they looked for no other. This deserves much more elaboration than I can give it here.[7]

Jesus had not done what messiahs were supposed to do. He had neither won a decisive victory over Israel's political enemies nor restored the temple (except in the most ambiguous symbolic fashion). Nor had He brought God's justice and peace to the world; the wolf was not yet lying down with the lamb. But the early gospel traditions are already shaped by the belief that Jesus was Israel's Messiah; Paul regularly calls Him Christos, and if that term had become for him merely a proper name (which I dispute) that only goes to show how firmly Jesus' messianic identity was already established by Paul's day. For Revelation, Jesus is the Lion of the tribe of Judah. The historian is bound to face the question: once Jesus had been crucified, why would anyone say that He was Israel's Messiah?

Nobody said that about Judas the Galilean after his revolt ended in failure in AD 6. Nobody said it of Simon bar-Giora after his death at the end of Titus's triumph in AD 70. Nobody said it about bar-Kochbar after his defeat and death in 135. On the contrary, where messianic movements tried to carry on after the death of their would-be messiah, their most important task was to find another messiah.[8] The fact that the early Christians did not do that but continued against all precedent to regard Jesus Himself as Messiah, despite outstanding alternative candidates such as the righteous, devout, and well-respected James, Jesus' own brother, is evidence that demands an explanation. As with their beliefs about resurrection, they redefined messiahship

[6] 1 Cor 15:23.
[7] See, e.g., N. T. Wright, *Jesus and the Victory of God* (Christian Origins and the Question of God, vol. 2) (London: SPCK; Minneapolis: Fortress, 1996), chapter 11.
[8] See N. T. Wright, *The New Testament and the People of God* (Minneapolis: Fortress, 1992), 175-81 for a description of various movements.

itself and with it their whole view of the problem that Israel and the world faced and the solution they believed God had provided. They remained at one level a classic Jewish messianic movement, owing fierce allegiance to their Messiah and claiming Israel and the whole world in His name. But the mode of that claim and the underlying allegiance itself were drastically redefined.

The rise of early Christianity, and the shape it took in two central and vital respects, thus presses upon the historian the question for an explanation. The early Christians retained the Jewish belief in resurrection, but both modified it and made it more sharp and precise. They retained the Jewish belief in a coming Messiah but redrew it drastically around Jesus Himself. Why?

Reasons for the Development: From Theology to Story

The answer early Christians themselves give for these changes, of course, is that Jesus of Nazareth was bodily raised from the dead on the third day after His crucifixion. Jesus' own resurrection has given force and new shape to the Christian hope.[9] It was, they insist, Jesus' own resurrection which constituted him as Messiah, and, if Messiah, then Lord of the world.[10] But what exactly did they mean by this, and what brought them to such a belief?

We must now come to the third and fourth stages of my argument. First, we must establish, against some rival claims, that they really did intend to say that Jesus had been bodily raised; they were not simply using that language to describe something else, a different belief about Jesus or a different experience they had had. Second, we must enquire as historians what could have caused them to say such a thing.

It is out of the question, for a start, that the disciples were simply extrapolating from the teaching of Jesus Himself. One of the many curious things about Jesus' teaching is that though resurrection was a well-known topic of debate at the time, we only have one short comment of His on the subject, in reply to the question from the

[9] 1 Corinthians 15; 1 Pet 1:3–5; etc.
[10] Acts 2:24–36, etc.; Rom 1:4; 15:12; etc.

Sadducees—a comment which is itself notoriously cryptic, like some of its companion pieces in the synoptic tradition. Apart from that, there are the short repeated predictions of Jesus' passion and resurrection, which many of course assume are *vaticinia ex eventu* and two or three other cryptic references.[11]

These are scarcely enough to suggest that the disciples invented stories of Jesus' resurrection, on the basis of His teaching, after His death. Other Jews had died promising resurrection, the Maccabees being the most obvious example (2 Maccabees 7, etc.); their followers regarded them as heroes and martyrs and believed devoutly that they would be raised from the dead; but nobody said they had been, for the rather obvious reason that they hadn't.[12] And even if, against all probability, we were to suggest that the disciples had indeed invented resurrection stories on the basis of Jesus' sayings, this would still not account for the modifications and new focus they gave to the existing Jewish notions of resurrection.

One regular proposal, which has taken various forms, is that though the early church used the language of resurrection about Jesus, and eventually wrote down stories about how it had happened, this developed originally from something else, a different experience or belief. In particular, some have said, Jesus' followers came first to a belief in His exaltation, and they deduced from this, either by logic or devotion, that He had been raised from the dead.

This needs a little more unpacking. Sometimes it has been argued, or more often assumed, that early Christians believed Jesus had been in some sense exalted (though why they believed this remains uncertain), and they either expressed this belief by saying that He had been

---

[11] The "sign of Jonah," or at least the comments on it which are paralleled in Matthew and Luke (Matt 12:41–42; Luke 11:30–32); the *palingenssia* in Matt 19:28; and the command not to tell about the transfiguration until the Son of Man has been raised (Mark 9:9f.). See further N. T. Wright, "Resurrection in Q?" in *Christology, Controversy & Community: New Testament Essays in Honour of David R. Catchpole*, ed. D. G. Horrell and C. M. Tuckett (Leiden: Brill, 2001), 85–97.

[12] Against S. J. Patterson, *The God of Jesus: The Historical Jesus and the Search for Meaning* (Hamsburg, Pa.: Trinity Press International, 1998), chapter 7, who suggests that Jesus' first followers began by saying He would be raised from the dead in the future and soon changed this into the claim that He already had been.

raised from the dead (misleadingly, because that was never what *resurrection* meant in their world) or deduced from this that He had in fact been raised from the dead (though again why they would make such a deduction in a world where *resurrection* was something to do with bodies, and for that matter something that would happen to all the righteous at once, is not clear). At other times it has been argued that the disciples came to believe in Jesus' actual divinity, perhaps by experiencing Him as a divine presence, and again either expressed this by saying He had been raised or deduced from it the fact that He had been raised. In this case, too, the logic fails at every point when we remind ourselves of how these ideas worked within the historical world of the first century.[13]

Paul sometimes speaks simply of Jesus' death and exaltation without mentioning the resurrection explicitly, as in the poem of Phil 2:6–11, though it is equally true that in the same letter he speaks emphatically of the bodily transformation that Jesus will effect on believers still alive at His return.[14] And when he sums up the traditional gospel announcement in 1 Cor 15:21 a summary, which must have done justice to what Cephas and Apollos said as well, otherwise the Corinthians would have been able to challenge him on it, it is clear that the gospel is about an event which happened at some interval after Jesus' death.[15]

This has not, I think, been sufficiently thought through. If we assume, as is often done, that talking of Jesus' resurrection is simply a flowery, perhaps Jewish, way of talking about His "going to heaven when he died," so that His death and His "exaltation" were actually the same thing, and together constitute Him as divine, where did the notion of an interval come from? I have often heard it said, sometimes by people who should know better, that Jesus died and was "resurrected to heaven," but that is precisely not what the early Christians said. Raised from the dead, yes; exalted to heaven, yes; but resurrection never did mean "going to heaven when you die," and it certainly

---

[13] Similarly with attempts along the lines of "they experienced the Spirit." Other people did this—e.g., Qumran—without deducing that their leader had been raised from the dead.
[14] Phil 3:20f.
[15] Verses 3–9; see too 1 Thess 4:14a.

did not mean that when people used it to talk about Jesus. No: if the early Christians had been merely deducing Jesus' resurrection from some other belief about something He had become through dying, the talk of an interval between death and resurrection would never have arisen, unless we are to postulate yet another cycle of improbable development of tradition, moving from exaltation to resurrection to a three-day gap.[16] Jews, after all, had well-developed ways of talking about martyrs being honored and respected, and they believed they would be raised in the future. If the early Christians thought Jesus, upon His death, had gone to a special place of honor with God, that would have been the obvious language for them to use.

The key questions here are the following: (1) whether Jesus' death would by itself have precipitated the language of exaltation or vindication; (2) if not, whether any subsequent experience (other than resurrection itself) would have done so; and (3) what reason there is, even if we were to grant that people had begun to speak of Jesus being exalted, being glorified, or even perhaps being seen as divine, to suppose that they would deduce from that that He had been raised from the dead? The answers are all obviously negative. One can understand why, if they believed that Jesus had indeed been raised from the dead, they came to believe, after He had ceased to appear to them, that He had now been exalted to heaven. But when you think about the options open to first-century Jews faced with a dead Messiah, there is simply no route in the opposite direction.

In any case, with all of these accounts which suppose that the disciples deduced Jesus' resurrection from something else, or expressed some other belief in the (misleading) fashion of "He's been raised from the dead," we are still faced with the major problem: why would resurrection itself, and the hope for a Messiah, have been so drastically adjusted as we find them to have been in early Christianity?

We are forced to conclude that when the early Christians said that Jesus had been raised from the dead, and gave that as their reason for

---

[16] Here belongs also, properly, an account of Paul's conversion and the ways in which it was, and he and the others knew it was, peculiar; in other words we cannot assimilate all encounters with the risen Christ to the blinding light on the Damascus Road.

reshaping their beliefs about resurrection itself on the one hand and messiahship on the other, they were using the language in its normal sense. That which Aeschylus said couldn't happen to anyone, and Daniel said would, to all God's people at once, had happened to Jesus, all by Himself. That was what they intended to say. And this brings us, at last, to the resurrection narratives themselves.

The first point to make here is vital. I have argued that the early Christians looked forward to a resurrection which was not a mere resuscitation, nor yet the abandonment of the body and the liberation of the soul, but a transformation, a new type of body living within a new type of world. This belief is embroidered with biblical motifs, articulated in rich theology.

Were the four Gospels, then, all derived from this developed theology? Are they all later narratival adaptations of a doctrinal and exegetical basis, from which of course all traces of dogma and exegesis have, in each case, been carefully extracted? Hardly. It is far easier to say that the stories, or something like them, came first and that Paul and the other later theologians have reflected deeply upon them, have indeed reshaped and rethought one branch of mainstream Jewish theology around them, but have not substantially modified them.

A few more remarks about the narratives themselves. Matthew's story is often seen as anti-Jewish apologetic—not surprisingly because he tells us that he is countering a story current among non-Christian Jews of his day. But even if Matthew does represent a later polemic, the debate itself—that some say Jesus' body was stolen, and others say it wasn't—bears witness to my more fundamental point, that in the first century resurrection wasn't about exaltation, spiritual presence, a sense of forgiveness, or divinization; it was about bodies and tombs. If someone had been able to say, "Oh, don't you understand? When I say 'resurrection,' all I mean is that Jesus is in heaven and He is my Lord, that I've had a new sense of God's love and forgiveness," the dangerous debate about tombs, guards, angels, and bodies could have been abandoned with a sigh of relief all round.[17]

---

[17] I have in mind here not least the treatment of E. Schillebeeckx, *Jesus: An Experiment in Christology* (London: Collins, 1979), e.g. 390ff.

Second, a word about Mark. When Mark says that the women "said nothing to anyone because they were afraid," he does not mean they never said anything to anyone. I do not think, in any case, that Mark finished his Gospel at chapter 16 verse 8. I think he wrote more, which is now lost. But I think his emphatic denial that the women said anything to anyone is meant to counter the charge, actual or possible, that if the women really had seen something remarkable—an empty tomb, a rolled-away stone, an angel—they would have been bound to tell everyone they met. This they had not done; so (the charge would run) maybe they had not seen anything after all? Certainly not, replies Mark: the reason they said nothing to anyone (until, we presume, they got to the disciples) is because they were scared stiff.

Third, a word about Luke and John. They tell, of course, much fuller stories than Matthew and Mark, and it is they who are normally accused of having developed, or invented, these stories to combat the danger of docetic views within the early church, beliefs that Jesus in His risen body wasn't really a physical human being but only seemed to be. Leave aside the fact that that is not what mainstream docetism wanted to say anyway—it was a belief about Jesus' precrucifixion humanity more than about His risen body—and concentrate on what Luke and John actually say. Yes, they have Him eating food. Yes, He invites them to touch Him, to inspect Him, to make sure He is a real human being. But these are the same accounts, in the same passages, which have Jesus appearing and disappearing, sometimes through locked doors. If Luke or John wanted to invent antidocetic, no-nonsense, real-body stories, they surely could have done better than this.

I suggest, in fact, that the gospel stories themselves, though no doubt written down a good deal later than Paul, go back with minimal editorial addition to the early stories told by the first disciples in the earliest days of Christianity. They are not the later narratival adaptation of early Christian theology; they are its foundation.

This does not mean, of course, that they are photographic descriptions of "what happened." No historical narrative is ever quite that. But they challenge today's historian, as they challenged their first hearers, either to accept them or to come up with a better explanation for why Christianity began and why it took the shape it did.

From Story to Event

This brings us, finally, to our fourth question. What can the historian say that will account for the early Christians' claim that Jesus of Nazareth had been raised from the dead, the explanation they themselves offer for their drastic modification of the Jewish hope?

There has been no shortage of hypotheses designed to explain why the early Christians really did believe that Jesus had been raised from the dead. These come in many shapes and sizes, but most of them feature one of three types of explanation. (1) Jesus did not really die; He somehow survived. (2) The tomb was empty but nothing else happened. (3) The disciples had visions of Jesus but without there being an empty tomb.

1. The first can be disposed of swiftly. Roman soldiers knew how to kill people, especially rebel kings. First-century Jews knew the difference between a survivor and someone newly alive.

2. The second is only a little more complicated. Faced with an empty tomb but with no other evidence, the disciples would have known the answer; the body had been stolen by someone. These things happened. They were not expecting Jesus to rise again; by itself an empty tomb would prove as little to them as it would to us.

3. Visions were frequent and well-known, including visions of someone recently dead. We did not have to wait for modern medicine, psychology, and pastoral records to tell us that these things happen. Faced with Peter knocking on the door when they thought he was about to be killed, the praying church assumed he had died and was paying them a post-mortem visit; "it must be his angel," they said.[18] Even lifelike visions would not prevent people conducting a funeral, continuing to mourn, and venerating the tomb.

To cut a long story short, to explain why early Christians really did believe that Jesus really had been raised from the dead, we must

[18] Acts 12:15.

postulate three things: Jesus really had been dead; the tomb really was empty, and it really was His tomb; they really did see, meet, and talk with a figure who was not only demonstrably the crucified Jesus but who seemed to be in some ways different—though not in the ways one would have imagined from reading Isaiah, Ezekiel, or Daniel.

Can we go beyond this? What then can and must be said?

Historical investigation, I propose, brings us to the point where we must say that the tomb previously housing a thoroughly dead Jesus was empty and that His followers saw and met someone they were convinced was this same Jesus, bodily alive though in a new, transformed fashion. The empty tomb on the one hand and the convincing appearances of Jesus on the other are the two conclusions the historian must draw. I do not think history can force us to draw any particular further deductions beyond these two phenomena; the conclusion the disciples drew is there for the taking, but it is open to us, as it was to them, to remain cautious. Thomas waited a week before believing what he had been told. On Matthew's mountain some had their doubts.

However, the elegance and simplicity of explaining the two outstanding phenomena, the empty tomb and the visions, by means of one another, ought to be obvious. Were it not for the astounding and worldview-challenging claim that is thereby made, I think everyone would long since have concluded that this was the correct historical result. If some other account explained the rise of Christianity as naturally, completely, and satisfyingly as does the early Christians' belief, while leaving normal worldviews intact, it would be accepted without demur.

That, I believe, is the result of the investigation I have conducted. There are many other things to say about Jesus' resurrection. But as far as I am concerned, the historian may and must say that all other explanations for why Christianity arose and why it took the shape it did are far less convincing as historical explanations than the one the early Christians themselves offer: that Jesus really did rise from the dead on Easter morning, leaving an empty tomb behind Him. The origins of Christianity, the reason this new movement came into being and took the unexpected form it did, and particularly the strange mutations it produced within the Jewish hope for resurrection and the Jewish hope for a Messiah, are best explained by saying that something happened two or three days after Jesus' death for which the accounts in the four Gospels are the least inadequate expression we have.

Of course, there are several reasons people may not want, and often refuse, to believe this. But the historian must weigh, as well, the alternative accounts they themselves offer. And to date none of them have anything like the explanatory power of the simple but utterly challenging Christian one. The historian's task is not to force people to believe. It is to make clear that the sort of reasoning historians characteristically employ—inference to the best explanation, tested rigorously in terms of the explanatory power of the hypothesis thus generated—points strongly toward the bodily resurrection of Jesus, and to make clear, too, that from that point on the historian alone cannot help. When you're dealing with worldviews, every community and every person must make their choices in the dark, even if there is a persistent rumor of light around the next corner.

Part 4

COMPARATIVE RELIGIONS

Chapter 10

CHRISTIANITY IN A WORLD OF RELIGIONS

Craig J. Hazen

One afternoon I received a call in my office at Biola University from a teaching assistant at a local community college. He was contacting me on behalf of a professor of a religious studies course who was looking for representatives from various spiritual traditions to come and speak in his classroom. The professor wanted the students to hear firsthand from a wide range of religious thinkers and devotees—an admirable idea in my view. I was free on the morning they were asking about, so I was delighted to go and address the group.

A couple of days later I found myself in the classroom, and after a few announcements the professor began to introduce me as the morning's speaker. "This is Craig Hazen, and he will be interacting with us this morning from the standpoint of his religious tradition, fundamentalist Christianity."

The label caught me off guard. I thought I was coming in to talk about a much broader category such as Christianity in general, or maybe Protestant Christianity, or Evangelical Protestant Christianity—all of which I could claim as my tradition. The term *fundamentalist* used to carry a noble meaning along with it but had lost its cachet long ago.

In the brief introduction the professor did not mention that I had earned a Ph.D. in religious studies at the University of California, that I had studied at the International Institute for Human Rights in Strasbourg, France, or that I had run a biology research laboratory. Perhaps he didn't mention these because they do not fit the stereotype of a fundamentalist which has come to mean, among other things, a kind of anti-intellectualism and separation from mainstream society. He knew that I was a professor of some kind myself but probably assumed that my graduate education consisted of memorizing obscure verses from the King James Bible at Grover's Bible College and Feed Lot.

In order to paint a more positive picture as quickly as possible, I reintroduced myself and gave them a little bit of background about my interest in the study of religions from around the world, human rights, and science. This caused the students a little bit of confusion because they did not connect fundamentalists with serious academic work, especially in these kinds of subjects.

I made a snap decision to turn the tables on them that morning by doing something much different from a standard presentation about biblical Christianity. I told them that given my background in religious, scientific, and cultural studies, I wanted to impart to them something valuable, some practical knowledge that would help them in tangible ways.

I assumed something about the students that turned out to be correct. Many of them were taking the popular religious studies survey class because they were curious about various traditions. In some respects they were using the class to take some of these religions out for a kind of nonthreatening test drive.

What I proposed to do that morning was to give them an expert guided tour on just how a clear-thinking person would go about a religious quest. Here you are at college, I told them, attempting to use analytic skills and careful reasoning to gain knowledge and insight into subjects ranging from music appreciation to organic chemistry. Why shouldn't we use those same cognitive tools to help us make sense of the seemingly crazy world of religion, especially since many of you are doing some careful evaluation about which religion you might embrace yourself one day? In other words, how would a thoughtful person go about a religious quest?

The students were genuinely interested in this idea. It did not dawn on me until later why they were so fascinated at this prospect. As it turned out, in their experience no one had ever linked the ideas of clear thinking or rational assessment with the pursuit of religion—as if they were separate categories (rationality and religion) and "never the twain shall meet." Nevertheless, they really thought this was a novel idea and a great gesture. It was already toward the end of the term, and the professor had never offered anything along these lines, and neither had any of his guest speakers. The students were enthusiastic, but the whole topic had the added side bonus of helping the students forget all about fundamentalism. So with a willing nod from the professor of the class, who later told me he too wanted to hear what I had to say about such a novel topic, I started.

The first point I made in my impromptu presentation was actually a setback for my hope of shedding the fundamentalist label the professor had pinned on me. The students recoiled at the first proposition to come out of my mouth. In all honesty looking back, I probably said it without much in the way of nuance in order to stir things up a bit. Maybe deep down I wanted to get the students to a full and verifiable state of consciousness before I got onto the details of my talk. It worked. In fact, one sleepy surfer in the back of the room came alive after my statement and was even waving a skateboard with one hand to emphasize certain points when he joined the discussion.

What was this unsettling statement I made that attracted the momentary ire of the college class and caused the bags under their eyes to disappear? It was this: I made the unabashed claim that any thoughtful person who was on a religious quest would obviously start that quest by exploring Christianity first. In other words, a person eventually has to make a choice about where to start any kind of journey. If one is looking to buy a new car, one needs to decide if he should first visit the Daewoo or the BMW dealership. There must be some rational, objective criteria that a person uses to decide where to go first to kick the tires—price, proximity, status, reputation, quality, and a whole range of personal preferences. To at least some extent, the same should be true with religious traditions if you are intentionally setting out to explore them. Remember, I'm not trying to decide which tradition is *true* at this point but rather with which tradition it makes the most sense to start the quest. A person has to start somewhere. I think Christianity is, by any rational measure, the obvious place for a thinking person to start the exploration.

After a few moments of mostly good-hearted heckling from the students, I told the class that I would give them four reasons a thoughtful person on a religious quest would obviously start that exploration with Christianity. I spent the rest of my time with them that morning presenting this case with a lot of spirited interaction.

What follows is the case I made to the class. Of course, I've done a lot of thinking about my off-the-cuff lecture and have fleshed it out a bit in these pages. But the basic four points are the same.

Four Reasons a Thoughtful Person on a Religious Quest Should Start That Quest with Christianity

1. Christianity Is Testable

I told the students that morning that at the heart of the Christian tradition are some claims about Jesus—His life, His teaching, His death, and His resurrection—that are testable. What I mean by this is that these claims are such that any thinking person can examine the evidence and reasonably determine whether the claims are historically accurate or justified. I think this is one of the primary reasons a thoughtful person sorting through the various religious traditions would obviously start with Christianity. Christianity is unique in that it actually *invites* people to investigate carefully its claims about God, humankind, the universe, and the meaning of life.

A passage in the Bible supports this notion, and I consider it to be one of the strangest passages in all of religious literature. In the New Testament the apostle Paul writes something that is a bit shocking given the way we normally think about religion and faith in the modern world. In this passage Paul is giving a discourse on the Christian view of life after death. But then in the midst of this, he says something that seems startling to our common sensibilities about religion. He says, "If Christ has not been raised [from the dead], our preaching is useless and so is your *faith*." Maybe just to make sure we would not be confused about what he is saying here, he repeats the idea several verses later. "And if Christ has not been raised, your *faith* is futile" (1 Cor 15:12–19 ESV, emphasis mine).

Now why would I consider this to be one of the strangest passages in all of religious literature? For this reason: I have not been able to find a passage in the Scriptures and teachings of the other great religious traditions that so tightly links the truth of an entire system of belief to a single, testable historical event. Real "faith" in these statements seems to be invariably linked to the truth of a real-world occurrence. What the apostle Paul said here was radical in the context of most religious traditions. He was saying, in essence, that if Jesus did not come back from the dead (in his own transformed but still physical body, as the witnesses and Scriptures declared), if this did not really take place in time and space, then Christianity is bunk; our Christian faith is worthless, useless, or futile.

This idea that the truth of Christianity is linked to the resurrection of Jesus in a testable way does set Christianity apart from the other great world religious traditions in a dramatic fashion. Historic Asian religions by and large don't even argue with this point. When you boil it all down, Hinduism, Buddhism, and the like are about inner, personal experience and not about objective public knowledge. Other traditions *seem* to be about objective knowledge until you probe a little more deeply. Mormonism, for instance, seems to be about hidden gold plates, Jesus' ancient visit to the Western hemisphere, and latter-day prophets—things that could certainly, in principle, be evaluated in an objective way. However, when facing evidence contrary to these claims, the Mormon missionary, scholar, or apostle steps back and begins to talk about the special inner knowledge, a "burning in the bosom," that is the only confirmation that really counts about these unusual stories. At the end of the day, the Mormon is no different from the Buddhist in that they both rely on inner experience as their ultimate source and warrant for religious knowledge.

This is why Christianity is unique and why a thoughtful person on a religious quest would be wise to start the quest with Christianity; it really is testable. If Jesus did not come back from the dead after being executed by a Roman crucifixion team in first-century Jerusalem, then, according to the apostle Paul, Christianity is simply not true. It openly invites people to investigate its claims objectively.

2. In Christianity, Salvation Is a Free Gift from God

Almost every time I speak on a college campus about why a thoughtful person would start her religious quest with Christianity, I wonder if I really need all four reasons. The first two reasons are so powerful that in my mind they can carry the day without much help from the other two that I present.

This isn't a hard conclusion to come to. Think about it. What if someone were to come up to you on a street corner and present to you a new path to God? During the presentation it becomes clear that the ideas being offered are in no way testable so you can never in principle objectively know whether they are true. In addition, the picture painted of God is that He requires a great deal from you. You must strive heroically to change the way you think, feel, and behave in every corner of your life in order to please the Deity and move forward on the path of salvation or enlightenment. Indeed, it might be the case that you will need to strive heroically for many lifetimes in order to reach the mark. Of course, there is a final logical twist here. If you have no way to gauge whether the basic religious system is true, you could also never know whether your intense striving to please the Deity was enough or if you were doing the right things in the right way. Even if at the end of the day a religious system like this *is* true, it doesn't make a whole lot of sense for someone exploring the various religious options to start the exploration with such a system.

By way of contrast, what if someone were to come up to you on the same street corner and present to you a religious system that was testable, hence opening the door for you to do a vigorous investigation of its claims. In addition, the system set forth a picture of God as a loving Father who wants to give the free gift of salvation to anyone who will receive it. Do I need to say more? If this testable and free system accurately describes Christianity and if the untestable and arduous system accurately describes the other religious options, then I don't see how reasonable persons would not start their search with Christianity. It seems like a no-brainer of Olympic proportions.

Christianity is unique in its offer of salvation by grace alone, a free gift from God to anyone who will receive it. In the history of religion, there have only been a couple of instances of a religious movement that considered salvation or enlightenment to be a free gift from a deity. But even in those cases (such as in *Amida* Buddhism or a certain form of *Bhakti* Hinduism), it is not a no-strings-attached kind of gift. There is still work to be done on the part of the devotees.

Hence, the Christian tradition stands in a solitary spot in the spectrum of world religions when the apostle Paul writes in Ephesians 2:8–9, "For it is by grace you have been saved, through faith—and this not from yourselves, it is the gift of God—not by works, so that no one can boast" (NIV).

Salvation in Christianity is a free gift, and hence it is equally available to anyone. You don't need to be a spiritual superstar, of noble birth, or highly educated. Anyone can come, as they sometimes sing at revival meetings, "just as I am." This is an attractive and unique feature and makes Christianity an obvious choice as a starting place for a religious quest.

3. In Christianity You Get an Amazing Worldview Fit

If you are trying to prioritize a group of religions in order to know which one you ought to check out first, it would be extremely helpful to know which of the religions painted a picture of the world that seemed to be a tight match with the way the world really is. If such a match could be determined, I know it would give reasonable people a lot of confidence that they were making a good choice about their starting point.

Let me come at this from the other direction. It seems reasonable to me that a thoughtful person would not want to start his religious quest with a religion that seemed to have tremendous difficulty making sense of the world we encounter. The problem here is that the world we bump into on a daily basis is one of the only sources of data we have to work with in evaluating all kinds of claims, including religious claims.

So if you have a choice to study under a guru whose mission is to reveal to the world that the moon's surface is made of spumoni ice cream, or under one who thinks the moon's outer layer is primarily anorthosite rock, a reasonable person would go with the one whose teaching seems to have the closest match to the way the universe really is. That is the general principle I am trying to communicate with this third reason.

To say that the Christian view of the world is the best fit with the way the world really is is a bold claim simply because there is so much that would need to be examined to find out if this assertion is justified. After all, the list of things to compare seems endless. But from my perspective, what I have learned about the various religions and about the world in general makes this claim totally plausible. Since I obviously cannot explore every aspect of the world (from cosmology to cosmetology) to demonstrate in just a few pages that this is reasonable, I shall use one profound example to illustrate the point: the problem of evil, pain, and suffering.

Every human being observes evil and experiences pain and suffering on almost a daily basis. It seems obvious that any religion that does not do justice to these common human experiences should probably not be at the top of the list for a thoughtful religious seeker. How do the various religious traditions explain these phenomena or make sense of them?

Devotees of Eastern religious traditions, such as Buddhism and Hinduism, certainly encounter the same kinds of evil, pain, and suffering that other people around the globe experience. But teachers, thinkers, and leaders in these movements have a different way of dealing with the experience than we normally do in the Western world. Eastern traditions normally put evil, pain, and suffering in the category of *illusion*. Suffering can therefore be overcome through the understanding of its true nature. Evil and pain will fade away as the

devotee gains enlightenment about the illusory nature of the phenomenal world. As a famous Tibetan lama wrote to me in a letter one time
after I had given a lecture on Buddhism, "Evil and suffering are real
only as long as the ego believes them to be real." The lama put it in
the simplest words possible for practical purposes. His solution to evil
and suffering was to change the way we believe about them. They will
then cease to be real.

It's finally time to ask the big question. If we are in search of a
worldview that matches the way the world really is, then how do we
evaluate these approaches to evil? After having some dialogue with the
students for a short time on this question, I gave them the following
illustration.

I have twin boys, and when they were babies, they played a character on a highly rated television sitcom. My wife and I would be on the
set quite often taking care of our kids when they were not rehearsing
or filming. Several of the writers and cast members heard that I was
some sort of religion professor and found it interesting to discuss some
of their religious ideas with me. One time over dinner before an evening filming, I remember listening at length to one of them describing
in great detail the teachings of a new guru she was following. Although
some of it sounded a bit off kilter to me, it was easy to sit and listen
because it was so interesting to see how Eastern religious concepts were
being enfolded into a Hollywood mind-set. One of the points this
woman was making was that her guru thought that good and evil were
ultimately not real and could be transcended through "right views."
After I'd had several plates of food (the catered cuisine was outstanding on the day of the performance) and a couple of cappuccinos, the
woman finally asked me for my reaction to all of this, and she had
covered a range of topics. I only asked one question, and I didn't ask it
to be provocative or cheeky. I was genuinely curious about the answer.
I thought it would simply keep the conversation going. I asked, "What
would your guru say about the Holocaust?"

Several things happened the moment I asked the question. I hadn't
realized that a number of people sitting nearby had already been tuned
into our conversation for some time. But now they weren't pretend-

ing to pick at their food any more. They lifted their heads and turned them in our direction. It turns out that a good number of the cast, crew, and production staff were Jewish. As you can imagine, they were also interested in the answer to the question. The woman I was dialoguing with didn't notice an audience had subtly grown around us. She was busy thinking through the implications of the question. She had a bit of a blank stare; and from the look on her face, it seemed as if her whole worldview was imploding inside her head. You see, she too came from a Jewish family. And although she was far too young to be involved in the horror herself and did not even practice her family's faith, she knew very well from her family, extended family, and her Jewish cultural connections that the Holocaust was a defining chapter in her own identity and approach to life. The Holocaust was real and could not be denied in any sense—not historically, not emotionally, not morally.

Somehow (and I've seen this happen often) this woman had been completely blind to a gaping hole in her view of things as she was learning from her new guru. How could she so thoroughly buy into her guru's teaching about evil being an illusion and still take seriously the unthinkable suffering the Jews of Europe endured? She couldn't. And it certainly wasn't anything I said. I just happened to be there when she had a moment of enlightenment of a different kind: a realization that a worldview that attempts to dismiss such profound evil, pain, and suffering as illusion is simply not a viable guide to life.

Every religion has to attempt to make sense of evil because it is such a pervasive and serious phenomenon. And every religion struggles in the task. The Scriptures of Christianity confront the issue of evil head-on starting with the first pages of Genesis. There is a whole section of the Bible, the book of Job, dedicated to the unanswerable questions involved in personal suffering. Although the Bible never provides an answer to the *why* question in the cases of individual instances of suffering (such as, why did the drunk driver crash into *me?*), it does provide the most satisfactory context for coming to terms with the existence of evil.

Although I believe the biblical approach to the problem of evil to be true, I am not arguing that point here (there are many persuasive books that argue the point effectively). I am trying to make the more modest claim that if given the choice between a worldview that simply dismisses pain and suffering as ultimately not real and a worldview that admits they do indeed exist, which would you start with if you were shopping for a religion? This really is tightly analogous to the question I asked at the beginning of this section. Would you be more inclined to follow a guru who taught that the surface of the moon was made of spumoni ice cream or one who taught that it was made of anorthosite rock? Saying that evil is an illusion is like saying that the moon's surface is made of spumoni. We can rightly claim to have knowledge that both claims are not true. A good worldview deals with the obvious; it does not dismiss it.

My bold assertion at the outset was that the picture Christianity paints of the world actually matches, better than any other option available, the way the world really is. Of course, as I predicted at the beginning, I didn't even come close to proving this point because I would have had to explore so many issues in great depth. But I (and, more importantly, a whole host of people much smarter than me in our own day and throughout history) have come to the conclusion that the basic Christian view of the world is the only game in town if one is looking for the best fit.

4. Christianity Has Jesus at the Center

The time I had in my guest lecture to the college students was almost over. I was talking fast all morning to try to pack in all of my reasons as to why a thoughtful person on a religious quest would start that quest with Christianity. I thought I had made a pretty good case. The students were attentive and, hence, I assumed, interested in what I had to say. However, when I presented my fourth reason, things turned unexpectedly sour for a moment. I claimed that a good reason to start with Christianity was that it had Jesus as the indisputable center point in the tradition. The student with the skateboard immediately chimed in. He remarked that it was interesting I waited until the end to slip in such a loaded reason, a reason that sounded a lot more like straightforward evangelism than anything else.

I looked at the professor for the class who was sitting at the far end of the first row. I asked him if he had a chance during the semester to go over the views about Jesus among the religions of the world. He said he hadn't and gave me permission to address it if I wanted to. I took him up on the offer.

I could understand why "skateboard guy" and others in the class had an initial problem with my point about Jesus. They were missing some crucial information, so they were misunderstanding where I was going with my remarks. Jesus is without doubt the closest thing the world has to a universal religious figure. Almost every religious tradition wants to claim Him as its own in one way or another. My comment that "Christianity has Jesus at the center" is not a raw assertion of my own religious position. Rather it is an argument that if Jesus is such an attractive figure that the religious people of the world want to co-opt Him for their own traditions, then it makes perfect sense to give special attention to Christianity—the tradition that has Jesus firmly planted at the center and claims Jesus as its founder.

This is certainly not a raw assertion of religious favoritism—just the opposite. It is another strong reason for a thoughtful person to start a religious exploration with Christianity. Many religious perspectives want to claim Jesus as their own.

Take Hinduism for example. Many teachers and scholars have proclaimed Jesus to be one of the ten *avatars* of Vishnu alongside Rama and Krishna. Vishnu is one of the major deities in the Hindu pantheon of gods, and an *avatar* is "one who descends." Hence it is not uncommon to find Jesus set forth as a kind of incarnation of Lord Vishnu. This is certainly not the documented historical picture of Jesus, but it does demonstrate the respect and influence he commands among many faithful Hindus. It is not unusual for a Hindu to revere Jesus to the point of veneration because He is such an impressive figure.

Likewise, it is not at all unusual for Buddhists of the later Mahayana traditions to see Jesus as a preeminent spiritual figure. Often He is considered to be a great *bodhisattva*—that is, one who is motivated by compassion to step back from the brink of nirvana in order to help others along the path to awakening. Buddhists often believe that during His day Jesus offered all of the Buddhist teaching (*dharma*) to which His generation was open. A few even see Him as the *maitreya bodhisattva*, an enlightened messianic being in the *Tusita* heaven awaiting His last reincarnation. The Tibetan Buddhist leader, the Dalai Lama, has said on several occasions that he is not worthy to be compared with Jesus, believing that Jesus is a "fully enlightened being."

Islam is an especially interesting case. One would not glean from popular treatments of Islam that Jesus even enters into the religious picture. But knowledgeable Muslims and their texts give the fuller view. If the Muslim prophet, Muhammad, and Jesus went head-to-head in a simple contest where their special attributes were tallied up, Jesus would win by at least six to one. Muhammad was a prophet. According the *Qur'an* and Islamic tradition, Jesus was also a prophet. However, unlike Muhammad, Jesus was also born of a virgin, was a worker of miracles, was carried to heaven by Allah without tasting death, was called the Word of God, and will return to appear to all before the final judgment—all according to the *Qur'an*. Now clearly Muhammad is considered the greatest prophet because he carried the final message of Allah to humankind. But Jesus is a revered figure who is second only to Muhammad in honor and respect. He is certainly not considered to be divine by Muslims but is considered a pinnacle of righteousness and a nonnegotiable object of Muslim belief.

Of course the parade of Jesus enthusiasts does not end there. It is hard to find a major tradition or a minor movement that does not give Him a special place of honor and find a significant way to enfold Him into their system of beliefs. The Baha'i, the Sikhs, the Mormons, the New Age Movement, the Unitarians, Religious Science, the Jehovah's Witnesses, the Jains, the Deists, and many more find a way to put their "hand in the hand of the man from Galilee."

Since Jesus is by any measure the only universal religious person, a figure so towering that almost every religious body has to find a way to bring Him aboard in some capacity, it makes perfect sense to me that anyone on a religious quest would know just where to start.

My official time in front of the class of college students had ended, but the discussion certainly did not. At least a dozen students followed me out the door, and we sat at some tables outside and discussed big religious issues for several more hours. Even though my talk ended up being quite a Christocentric presentation, the students were not put off by that. These are difficult issues, and they seemed to appreciate not just that I took a position but that I invited careful scrutiny of my own conclusions. As one young woman said at the end of our time together, "What are we so afraid of? We ought to be asking the toughest questions, and religious leaders and teachers should be prepared with honest answers. If there is a God, one thing is certain: He made us thinking people. As long as we are kind to one another, we should be able to discuss these things openly."

She was right: we shouldn't be afraid. Her comment reminded me of a famous saying of the apostle Peter from the New Testament—really a command to all Christian believers. "Always be prepared to give an answer to everyone who asks you to give the reason for the hope that you have. But do this with gentleness and respect" (1 Pet 3:15 NIV).

Chapter 11

THE EAST COMES WEST
(OR WHY JESUS INSTEAD OF THE BUDDHA?)

Harold Netland

The past century has produced dramatic changes in the religious landscape of the West. Whereas at the beginning of the twentieth century the majority of Christians were in Europe and North America, most Christians today are in Asia, Latin America, and Africa.[1] As a result of the phenomenal growth of the church worldwide during the twentieth century, Christianity is today a genuinely global religion.

Growth in the number of Christians worldwide, however, has been combined with the declining significance of Christianity in much of the West. Not only has the church lost much of its cultural and social influence in Europe, but the numbers of Christians there is in serious decline. Although Christianity remains the dominant religion in the United States and retains greater cultural influence there than in Europe, the religious demographics of both North America and Europe are being transformed as growing numbers of Muslims, Hindus, Buddhists, Sikhs, and Jains reside in the West. The presence of adherents of other religions has become so pronounced that Diana Eck of Harvard states, "The United States has become the religiously most diverse nation on earth. . . . Nowhere, even in today's world of

---

[1] On the changing demographics of Christianity worldwide, see Philip Jenkins, *The Next Christendom: The Coming of Global Christianity*, 2nd ed. (New York: Oxford University Press, 2006); and Lamin Sanneh, *Whose Religion Is Christianity? The Gospel beyond the West* (Grand Rapids: Eerdmans, 2003).

mass migrations, is the sheer range of religious faith as wide as it is in the United States."[2] Changing immigration patterns, along with globalization and new telecommunications technologies which bring the world into our living rooms, have produced an unprecedented awareness of other religious traditions.

Western Fascination with Eastern Religions

The West has long had a fascination with Eastern religions. Europeans were captivated by the exotic reports from seventeenth-century Jesuit missionaries to China. The Chinese thinker Confucius was idealized as a rational theist who had arrived at belief in God and sophisticated moral teachings apart from any divine special revelation.[3] Increased British contact with India, culminating in the colonization of the Indian subcontinent in the nineteenth century, had a significant impact on European intellectuals. The Hindu sacred text *Bhagavad Gita* was translated into English in 1785, and translations of other Hindu and Buddhist texts soon followed. Philosophers and literary figures in Great Britain and Germany such as Shelley, Byron, Coleridge, Herder, Schelling, and Schopenhauer were well acquainted with Hindu and Buddhist thought and helped to popularize concepts from Eastern religious traditions.

In the United States during the 1840s, transcendentalists such as Ralph Waldo Emerson and Henry David Thoreau were fascinated by the Vedanta philosophy of Hinduism and the *Bhagavad Gita*. Later in the nineteenth century Buddhism became sufficiently attractive to American intellectuals that prominent Christians began to speak of Buddhism as a threat to Christianity. The remarkable popular appeal of Buddhism is illustrated in the phenomenal success of *The Light of Asia*, a poem about the life of Gautama the Buddha published in 1879

---

[2] Diana Eck, *A New Religious America: How a "Christian Country" Has Become the World's Most Religiously Diverse Nation* (New York: HarperCollins, 2001), 4–5.
[3] See, for example, P. J. Marshall and Glyndwr Williams, *The Great Map of Mankind: British Perceptions of the World in the Age of Enlightenment* (London: J. M. Dent, 1982), chapters 3–4; J. J. Clarke, *Oriental Enlightenment: The Encounter between Asian and Western Thought* (London: Routledge, 1997), chapter 3.

by Sir Edwin Arnold. The book went through sixty English and eighty American editions, selling between half a million and one million copies in the United States and England.[4]

The 1893 World Parliament of Religions in Chicago was a major event which greatly increased popular awareness of Eastern religions and helped to legitimize them as alternatives to Christianity.[5] The eloquent Hindu Swami Vivekananda had an electrifying effect upon the conference and quickly became a symbol of reasoned, enlightened tolerance, in contrast to the alleged intolerance of Christian missionaries. One of the most significant results of the parliament was setting in motion the first Buddhist mission to the United States. Japanese Buddhists returned home convinced that America was decadent and spiritually bankrupt. A Buddhist participant at the parliament, Shaku Soen, recruited his disciple D. T. Suzuki as a Buddhist missionary to the West. Suzuki arrived in the U.S. in 1897, and during the next five decades he split his time between Japan and America, lecturing and writing on Buddhism for Westerners.[6] Suzuki became the most influential spokesman for Buddhism in the West.

During the 1960s and 1970s Eastern religious traditions became especially prominent in American culture. In part, this was due to greatly increased immigration of Asians, as a result of the immigration law reforms of 1965. Among the new immigrants were Hindus, Buddhists, Sihks, Jains, Confucianists, and Daoists. At the same time, growing numbers of Americans were traveling and studying abroad, bringing back with them greater appreciation of Asian cultures and religions. Disillusionment with Western social and cultural patterns found expression in the countercultural movements of the 1960s, which

---

[4] Edwin Arnold, *The Light of Asia, or the Great Renunciation* (New York: A. L. Burt, 1879). See also Carl T. Jackson, *The Oriental Religions and American Thought: Nineteenth Century Explorations* (Westport, Conn.: Greenwood, 1981), 143.

[5] On the 1893 Parliament and its effects, see *The Dawn of Religious Pluralism: Voices from the World's Parliament of Religions, 1893*, ed. Richard Hughes Seager (La Salle, Ill.: Open Court, 1993); and Joseph Kitagawa, "The 1893 World's Parliament and Its Legacy," in Joseph Kitagawa, *The History of Religions: Understanding Human Experience* (Atlanta: Scholar's Press, 1987).

[6] Among Suzuki's many writings are *An Introduction to Zen Buddhism* (London: Rider and Company, 1948); *Zen Buddhism* (New York: Doubleday, 1956); and *Mysticism: Christian and Buddhist* (New York: Harper & Brothers, 1957).

incorporated many Eastern religious symbols and spiritual practices. The attraction of Eastern mysticism was enhanced by the 1968 visit by the Beatles to India and their public identification with the Maharishi Mahesh Yogi of Transcendental Meditation fame. During the 1970s a steady stream of self-proclaimed holy men and gurus found their way to America, spreading their *dharma* of enlightenment and peace.

By the 1980s and 1990s, what had been countercultural and exotic was mainstream and chic in the form of the New Age movement. Hindu, Buddhist, and Daoist terms became part of the cultural lexicon and were reflected in movies and popular music. Buddhism, especially Tibetan Buddhism, became popular within the entertainment industry and the academy, due in no small part to the enormously attractive figure of the Dalai Lama. But in some ways the forms of Hinduism and Buddhism now found in the West are different from those which developed in Asia. The elaborate metaphysical frameworks and cosmologies of these ancient traditions (especially assumptions about rebirth as nonhuman forms of life and multiple, ghoulish hells) receive little attention in the West, where the focus tends to be on the practical "this worldly" benefits of meditation.

Growing awareness of other religions—and especially personal interaction with intelligent, morally respectable and deeply committed Hindus and Buddhists—raises troubling questions for Christians. How can Christians claim that Jesus alone is the one Savior for all peoples? Does it make sense to believe that so many sincere, intelligent, and good people are simply wrong in their religious convictions? How do we know that Christianity is distinctively true? Why should one be a Christian rather than a Hindu or Buddhist?[7] The church in the West must be intentional in preparing people to understand and respond appropriately to questions prompted by exposure to Eastern religions. Although we cannot explore these questions further here, I will summarize briefly the perspectives of some Asian religions, highlight some

---

[7] See Robert Wuthnow, *America and the Challenges of Religious Diversity* (Princeton: Princeton University Press, 2005). I have addressed some of these issues in Harold Netland, *Encountering Religious Pluralism* (Downers Grove, Ill.: InterVarsity, 2001).

challenges they present to the Christian faith, and conclude with some contrasts between Gautama the Buddha and Jesus Christ.

Some Asian Religious Traditions

Many in the West assume that all Eastern religious traditions are basically the same: they offer variations on the same basic theme, usually characterized as a vague monism which maintains that "all is one." But this is misleading. There is enormous variety, both among various Asian religions and within a single religion such as Hinduism or Buddhism.

Indian traditions include Hinduism, Buddhism, and Jainism. Although Hinduism includes a bewildering variety of religious and philosophical movements which have developed over the past thirty-five hundred years, all accept in some sense the authority of the Vedas as sacred literature, belief in reincarnation of the soul (*atman*) in accordance with *karma*, and, at least until modern times, the importance of caste.

According to the doctrine of reincarnation, persons (and other living things) are continually being reborn as the *atman* passes from one life to another. The endless cycle of rebirths is regulated by *karma*, a metaphysical principle which determines current and future states on the basis of past actions and dispositions. The entire process of birth, death, and rebirth is *samsara*, and the soteriological goal of Hinduism is *moksha*, or liberation from rebirth through breaking the causal conditions of *karma*. Traditionally, there are three ways in which *moksha* can be attained: the way of knowledge or correct insight, the way of works or duty, or the way of devotion to a personal deity.

Many, but not all, Hindu traditions accept the idea of Brahman as the ultimate reality and sustaining power of the cosmos. But there is disagreement over the nature of Brahman and its relation to the human person. Advaita Vedanta claims that the sole reality is Brahman, a nonpersonal reality utterly beyond human concepts and categories, and that *moksha* comes only through an existential awareness of one's essential identity with Brahman. More theistic forms of Hinduism regard Brahman (or Shiva or Vishnu) as a personal deity and insist that liberation comes not through knowledge alone but through devotion to the deity.

Buddhism, based on the teachings of Siddhartha Gautama (c. fifth century BC), accepts assumptions about *samsara* but differs from Hinduism in its rejection of the authority of the Vedas. Gautama was born into the home of a local chieftan or ruler. But, determined to discover the cause of suffering, he rejected the comfortable lifestyle of a prince and entered the ascetic life. In his enlightenment experience he discerned the causes of suffering and its cure. The Buddha, as Gautama was known after his enlightenment, traveled around India for over forty years teaching the way to enlightenment and attracting a large following.

The heart of the Buddha's teaching is expressed concisely in the Four Noble Truths: (1) All of existence is characterized by *dukkha* (suffering, pain, dissatisfaction). That is, *dukkha* is found in every aspect of existence. (2) The root cause of suffering is *tanha* (literally "thirst," but often translated "craving" or "desire"). (3) The disease of *dukkha* is curable, and when *tanha* ceases, then *dukkha* ceases as well. (4) The cessation of *dukkha* is achieved through following the Noble Eightfold Path.

The Buddha held that everything that exists is characterized by *anitya* or impermanence and is continually coming into being and passing out of being. He rejected contemporary Hindu and Jain views on the reality of a substantial soul which passes from one life to another. What we normally think of as a person is no more than the ever-changing combination of psychophysical forces—the Five Aggregates of matter, sensations, perceptions, mental formations, and consciousness. What passes from this life to the next is merely the cumulative *karmic* effects of actions, which form in the next life the (mistaken) perception of an enduring person. Only *nirvana* is permanent and unconditioned. *Nirvana* is not annihilation or extinction; it is the ultimate reality which is realized when the conditions producing rebirth are eliminated.

Jainism, founded by Mahavira (d. 527 BC), also rejects the authority of the Vedas. It accepts belief in *karma* and rebirth but maintains
that the soul (*jiva*) is eternal, self-conscious, and indestructible. *Karma*
is composed of fine particles of matter which cling to the soul and
weigh it down, resulting in rebirth. Final liberation comes from the release of the soul from all matter, resulting in the bliss of *nirvana*. Strict
asceticism and adherence to *ahimsa* (nonviolence to all living things)
are necessary for liberation. Jainism traditionally has been atheistic,
denying the reality of a supreme being.

We should note briefly the major Chinese religions Confucianism
and Daoism. Confucianism, deriving from the teachings of Confucius
(d. 479 BC), is primarily a system of moral, social, and political teachings. At a time of great social and political turmoil, Confucius sought
principles and virtues which, when manifest in the ruler, society at
large, and the family would ensure social harmony and human flourishing. The obligations of filial piety and ancestral veneration reinforce
the importance of family and strict social roles for social harmony.
Confucianism holds that social and ethical patterns should reflect the
cosmic moral order of heaven (*Tian*). Confucianism eventually came
to maintain that human nature is originally good and is corrupted by
external influences. Rigorous education, strict enforcement of laws,
and careful observation of the rites for ancestral spirits all work together to sustain human flourishing.

Philosophical Daoism (or Taoism) is in many ways a response to
Confucianism. Daoism maintains that the cosmos is a manifestation
of the eternal Dao (the Way) and that our lives are to be ordered in
accordance with the Dao. As the metaphysical ultimate, the Dao is
the source of everything. It is mysterious and cannot be captured in
words or concepts. Individuals flourish when external constraints are
removed, and they follow the natural Way. Paradoxically, it is through
wu-wei (nonaction) and reverting back to the Dao, not through for-
mal education and strict laws, that social harmony is realized.

Even this cursory survey reveals that Asian religions are not all the
same. The diversity can be seen in the ways they answer two questions. First, is there a Supreme Being who has personal attributes (is

good, merciful, an agent who can act, etc.)? Buddhism and Jainism both deny the existence of a Supreme Being or Creator. Although Buddhism acknowledges the reality of many *buddhas* and *bodhisattavas*, and Mahayana Buddhism teaches the ultimacy of the *Dharmakaya* or universal Buddha-essence, Buddhist metaphysics rules out the possibility of an eternal creator God. Some Hindu traditions, for example those following the Advaita Vedanta of Shankara (d. 820), claim that the religious ultimate is Nirguna Brahman, a nonpersonal absolute. By contrast, the Vishist Advaita Vedanta tradition of Ramanuja (d. 1137) insists that the religious ultimate is a Supreme Being with personal attributes, Saguna Brahman. In the case of Daoism, the Dao is generally regarded not as a personal being but as a nonpersonal, metaphysical ultimate.

Second, are there real, enduring persons or souls? This issue was hotly debated by the three major Indian religions. Buddhism emphatically denies the reality of an enduring substantial soul, whereas this is affirmed by both Hindu and Jain traditions.

Diversity in Eastern religions is also found in their respective views on reason and rationality. Eastern traditions are widely understood in the West as rejecting reason in favor of an antirational mysticism. It is true that some forms of Buddhism, Zen in particular, do reject rigorous rational analysis as an obstacle to attaining enlightenment. And certainly meditation and various forms of mystical experience are integral to Hinduism, Buddhism, and Jainism.

But some major forms of these religions also value rigorous rational activity. Theravada Buddhists typically stress the highly rational nature of the Buddha's teaching. The Four Noble Truths exhibit a rational structure that proceeds logically from diagnosis of the problem to a prescription for the cure of suffering. Many Buddhists insist that Buddhism is based solely on reason and experience and has no place for faith. The Japanese Buddhist scholar Hajime Nakamura states, "According to Buddhism, faith becomes superstition when it is not examined by reason. Gotama was described as one who has reasoned according to the truth rather than on the basis of the authority of the Vedas or tradition."[8]

Christian Theism and Eastern Perspectives

While there are some similarities between Christian faith and Eastern religious traditions, the differences are clear and significant. Hindu, Buddhist, and Daoist perspectives challenge Christian theism at several critical points.

1. *What is the nature of ultimate reality? Is the religious ultimate a personal being or a nonpersonal reality?* Christian theism maintains that an eternal Creator God exists and that God is a personal being. God is a moral being—good, holy, and merciful. God acts in time and history and reveals himself in an intelligible manner to human beings.

Many, but not all, Hindu, Buddhist, and Taoist traditions regard the religious ultimate as a nonpersonal reality. And yet, as we have seen, there is disagreement among them over the nature of this nonpersonal reality. Advaita Vedantin Hindus claim the religious ultimate is Nirguna Braham, a nonpersonal absolute. Theravada Buddhists ascribe religious ultimacy to *nirvana*. For Mahayana Buddhists the ultimate is the Dharmakaya or *sunyata* (emptiness), and Daoists hold that the ultimate is the Dao.

2. *How do we attain religious truth? Do we do so through divine revelation or through introspective mystical experience?* Christian faith maintains that the one eternal God has spoken and revealed Himself to humankind, preeminently through the incarnation (Heb 1:1–3). God's self-revelation to the patriarchs, prophets, apostles, and in the incarnation is preserved in recorded form for us in the Old and New Testaments.

Hindus also regard their scriptures as divinely inspired, but the Hindu understanding of inspiration is different from that of Christianity.[9] The Vedas are records of what the *rishis* or seers "saw" or inwardly "heard" through special mystical experiences. Buddhist

---

[8] Hajime Nakamura, "Unity and Diversity in Buddhism," in *The Path of the Buddha: Buddhism Interpreted by Buddhists*, ed. Kenneth W. Morgan (New York: Ronald, 1956), 372.

[9] On the views of the religions regarding their sacred texts, see *The Holy Book in Comparative*

texts, by contrast, are not said to be divinely inspired since there is no God/gods to reveal the texts.

In attaining religious truth, Hinduism, Buddhism, and Jainism give priority to mystical or introspective experiences based on rigorous psychophysical meditative disciplines, which are said to provide direct, unmediated access to ultimate reality. Enlightenment and liberation from rebirth come from a correct understanding of ultimate reality, an insight gained not from divine revelation but through intense introspective experiences which transcend the ordinary world of experience.

3. *Can religious truth be expressed adequately in words? Or is "ultimate truth" something that eludes conceptual and linguistic categories and must be directly experienced?* Christian faith maintains that God has spoken and revealed Himself to humankind in an intelligible manner. It is significant that the preincarnate Christ is referred to in John 1 as "the Logos," a term which includes within its range of meanings notions of rationality and intelligibility. Christian faith maintains that, although God cannot be exhaustively or comprehensively known by finite human beings, He can be adequately understood through His self-revelation.

Many Hindu, Buddhist, and Daoist traditions, however, are deeply suspicious of words and doctrines and stress the importance of direct intuitive experiences which cannot be expressed in words. The enigmatic *Dao de Jing*, a major text of Daoism, begins with this cryptic statement: "The Dao that can be told of is not the eternal Dao; the name that can be named is not the eternal name." Suspicion of words is evident in statements such as, "The one who knows does not speak; the one who speaks does not know."[10] Zen Buddhism, heavily influenced by Daoism, similarly rejects the idea that the *dharma*, or Buddhist truth, can be expressed adequately in language; it is passed on directly from *roshi* (master) to disciple. Buddhists frequently say that words and doctrines are like a finger pointing to the moon; the

Perspective, ed. Frederick M. Denny and Rodney L. Taylor (Columbia, S.C.: University of South Carolina Press, 1985).
[10] *Lao Tzu: Tao te Ching*, trans. D. C. Lau (New York: Viking Penguin, 1963), 57, 117.

finger helps one to focus on the moon, but one must not mistake the finger for the moon.

4. *Has God revealed Himself uniquely in the incarnation in Jesus? Was Jesus really God become man, God incarnate; or was He simply one of many great religious figures?* Christians claim that the incarnation in Jesus Christ was a one-time, utterly unique event. The astonishing claim of the New Testament is that in Jesus of Nazareth the one eternal God has become man. "The Word became flesh, and dwelt among us" (John 1:14). Understood within the context of strict Jewish monotheism, this is an amazing assertion, without parallel in other religions. And it is precisely this that makes the question of Jesus so controversial today. As Sri Lankan theologian Vinoth Ramachandra remarks, "It is this traditional claim—that in the human person of Jesus, God himself has come amongst us in a decisive and unrepeatable way—that constitutes an offence to pluralist society."[11]

The biblical teaching on the incarnation is sometimes said to resemble the Hindu notion of *avatar*, according to which a deity takes on human or animal form. In the *Bhagavad Gita*, for example, Krishna is depicted as an *avatar* of Vishnu who is born into the world repeatedly in evil times to revive true doctrine, to destroy the wicked, and to restore righteousness.

But the biblical teaching of incarnation is different from that of *avatar* in Hinduism. First, the *avatars* in Hinduism take the form not only of humans but also of various animals and mythological figures. Furthermore, there are multiple Hindu *avatars*; indeed, many Hindus include religious figures from other religions—such as Jesus or Gautama the Buddha—as *avatars*. Thus there is nothing definitive about any one *avatar*. Finally, to the philosophical Hindu, belief in such *avatars* represents a lower level of spiritual insight and is an accommodation for the less sophisticated. As one matures in theological and philosophical insight, one moves beyond the need for such beliefs.

---

[11] Vinoth Ramachandra, *The Recovery of Mission: Beyond the Pluralist Paradigm* (Grand Rapids: Eerdmans, 1996), 181.

But the New Testament picture of Jesus is different. Jesus was a historical figure; and His life, death, and resurrection are firmly rooted in first-century Palestine. According to the New Testament, in a unique one-time event the eternal Creator became man, lived a sinless life as a man, took upon Himself the punishment for the sins of the world in His sacrificial death on the cross, and then rose victorious over death. And through this one-time event sinful humankind can be reconciled to God.

Why Jesus Instead of the Buddha?

In considering a Christian response to challenges from Eastern religions, two questions are especially significant: Does God exist? Who is Jesus Christ? Although we cannot pursue either question here, we will conclude by pointing out several respects in which Jesus is different from the Buddha.

1. *The relation between Jesus and history in Christianity is different from the relation between history and Gautama in Buddhism.* In 1960 the Protestant theologian Paul Tillich visited Japan, and in conversation with Buddhist scholars in Kyoto, he asked the following question: "If some historian should make it probable that a man of the name Gautama never lived, what would be the consequence for Buddhism?" The Buddhist scholars responded by saying that the question of the historicity of Gautama Buddha had never been an issue for Buddhism. "According to the doctrine of Buddhism, the *dharma kaya* [the body of truth] is eternal, and so it does not depend upon the historicity of Gautama."[12] Whether Gautama actually said and did what is ascribed to him does not affect the truth of Buddhist teaching, which transcends historical events.

The same cannot be said about Jesus Christ. Christian faith is inextricably rooted in the historical person of Jesus of Nazareth. The apostle Paul unambiguously states that if in fact Jesus was not raised from the dead, then our faith is futile and useless, and we are still in

---

[12] See "Tillich Encounters Japan," ed. Robert W. Wood, *Japanese Religions* 2 (May 1961): 48–71.

our sins (1 Cor 15:14–19). Christianity is not merely a collection of religious teachings. At the center of Christian faith is God's active intervention in history, revealing His purposes for the redemption of sinful humanity and then the provision of the means for our redemption through the incarnation in Jesus of Nazareth. What Jesus did on the cross and through the resurrection, and not simply what He taught, makes reconciliation with God possible.

Moreover, we have much greater access to the historical Jesus and the early Christian community than we do to Gautama and the early Buddhist community. Although we cannot treat here the issue of the historical Jesus, we should note that the gap in time between the death of Jesus and the earliest New Testament writings is much smaller than the time between the death of Gautama and the earliest written Buddhist texts.[13] Jesus was crucified in either AD 30 or 33. The earliest New Testament writings were written about AD 50 or 51, leaving a gap of only seventeen to twenty-one years from the time of His death to the first writings. Furthermore, we can be confident that the text of the New Testament today is the same text the early Christians accepted. New Testament scholar Paul Barnett states, "There still exist more than five thousand early manuscript copies of part or all of the New Testament in Greek. In addition, there are numerous early translations into Coptic, Latin, Syriac, Armenian, Georgian, etc."[14]

By contrast, although there is little question that Gautama actually existed, there is considerable uncertainty about his life. Scholars are not certain even about the century in which he lived. The dates for his life are given as either 566–486 BC or 448–368 BC. The earliest Buddhist scriptures, which were primarily concerned with monastic

[13] There is much discussion over questions about the historical Jesus. Helpful introductions to the issues can be found in Ben Witherington III, *The Jesus Quest: The Third Search for the Jew of Nazareth*, 2nd ed. (Downers Grove, Ill.: InterVarsity, 1997); C. Stephen Evans, *The Historical Christ and the Jesus of Faith: The Incarnational Narrative as History* (Oxford: Oxford University Press, 1996); Paul Barnett, *Is the New Testament Reliable?* 2nd ed. (Downers Grove, Ill.: InterVarsity, 2003). On historical issues concerning Gautama the Buddha, see Donald W. Mitchell, *Buddhism: Introducing the Buddhist Experience* (New York: Oxford University Press, 2002); Hajime Nakamura, *Gotama Buddha: A Biography Based on the Most Reliable Texts*, vol. 1, trans. Gaynor Sekimori (Tokyo: Kosei, 2000); and David Edward Shaner, "Biographies of the Buddha," *Philosophy East and West* 37 (1987): 306–22.

[14] Paul Barnett, *Is The New Testament Reliable?* 44.

practice, were not put into writing until sometime near the end of the first century BC.[15] Extant versions of the life of the Buddha did not appear until much later; the influential *Buddhacarita* (*The Acts of the Buddha*) was written around the second century AD. So, depending on the dates of Gautama's death, there is a gap of roughly three or four hundred years between the Buddha's death and the first Buddhist scriptures being written, with the versions of the Buddha's life coming even later.

2. *Jesus and the Buddha disagree on the question of God's existence.* The teaching of the Buddha is usually understood as ruling out the possibility of God's existence. The Buddhist scholar Jayatilleke observes that if by "God" we mean a Supreme Being and Creator, then "the Buddha is an atheist and Buddhism in both its Theravada and Mahayana forms is atheistic. . . . In denying that the universe is a product of a Personal God, who creates it in time and plans a consummation at the end of time, Buddhism is a form of atheism."[16] The Buddha made no claim to special inspiration or revelation from any divine source. If he was concerned about the question of the existence of God, this was a matter on which the Buddha remained silent.

By contrast, Jesus Christ was a strict monotheist who accepted the Old Testament understanding of Yahweh as the one eternal God, Creator of all that exists. Not only that, but Jesus identified Himself in a unique manner with the one eternal Creator God, resulting in the Christian understanding of the divine incarnation.[17]

3. *Jesus and the Buddha disagree on what is the root problem plaguing humankind.* The Buddha diagnosed the root problem as ignorance—ignorance about the true nature of reality and the impermanence of all things, which results in craving and attachment and thus the suffering of rebirth. Although he has much to say about the importance of doing what is right and avoiding evil, nothing in his teaching resembles

---

[15] See Donald Mitchell, *Buddhism*, 65.

[16] K. N. Jayatilleke, *The Message of the Buddha*, ed. Ninian Smart (New York: Free Press, 1974), 105. On Buddhist critiques of the idea of God, see Paul Williams, "Aquinas Meets the Buddhists," in *Aquinas in Dialogue: Thomas for the Twenty-first Century*, ed. Jim Fodor and Frederick Christian Bauerschmidt (Oxford: Blackwell, 2004), 87–117.

[17] On the New Testament understanding of Jesus and Jesus' own self-understanding, see James R. Edwards, *Is Jesus the Only Savior?* (Grand Rapids: Eerdmans, 2005).

the biblical understanding of sin. Nor is this surprising. For sin, according to Christian Scripture, is always an offense against a holy and righteous God, something conspicuously absent in Buddhism.

The difference here with Jesus is striking. According to Jesus our root problem is not ignorance but rather sin, the deliberate rejection of God's righteous ways (Mark 7:1–22). Furthermore, although Jesus consistently called others to repentance, He never repented for any sin. He challenged others to point out any sin in His own life and claimed to have the authority to forgive sin (John 8:46; Mark 2:1–12).

4. *Early Buddhism teaches that we are each responsible for attaining our own liberation, whereas the New Testament teaches that we cannot save ourselves.* There is within the early teachings attributed to the Buddha a strong sense of the human individual being responsible for his or her own liberation. The Buddha proclaimed the *dharma* (true teaching) which results in liberation, and in this way he can be said to assist all sentient beings. But it is up to the individual to grasp the truth, to appropriate it, and thereby attain *nirvana*. Although later Buddhism did develop the idea of the *bodhisattva* who assists others on the way to *nirvana*, the Buddha himself seems to have regarded each person as responsible for his own destiny. The Buddhist scholar Walpola Rahula puts it this way: "If the Buddha is to be called a 'saviour' at all, it is only in the sense that he discovered and showed the Path to Liberation, *Nirvana*. But we must tread the Path ourselves."[18]

The difference here with Jesus is unmistakable. According to the Bible, human beings cannot save themselves; we are utterly helpless and hopeless apart from the grace of God and the atoning work of Jesus Christ on the cross for us. What we cannot do for ourselves, God in Christ has done for us (Eph 2:1–10). Jesus thus called on others to believe in Him and to find salvation only in Him. Jesus does not merely teach the way; He claims to *be* the way (John 14:6). It is not simply that Jesus has discovered the way and the truth and that if we follow His teachings we too can find the way for ourselves. The Buddha, in effect, says, "Follow me and my teachings, and you too can experience the way leading to enlightenment." But Jesus says more than that He

---

[18] Walpola Rahula, *What the Buddha Taught*, 2nd ed. (New York: Grove, 1974), 1–2.

has discovered the way to the Father and that if we follow Him and His teachings we too can find the way. Jesus makes the much stronger claim that in Himself He embodies the way, the truth, and the life. The truth of Jesus' teachings cannot be separated from the grounding of this truth in the person of Christ as the incarnate Word of God. It is because of who He is and what He has done for us on the cross that He is Himself the way, the one Savior for all people in all cultures.

5. *The Buddha, like Jesus and other great religious leaders, died, but there is no reliable historical record of any others—apart from Jesus—being resurrected after death.* With the resurrection we come to the foundation of the Christian faith. Death—the ultimate symbol of sin, evil, and suffering—has been conquered through the resurrection of Jesus Christ. Because of Christ's resurrection, "death has been swallowed up in victory" (1 Cor 15:54 NIV). Both Jesus and Gautama were concerned with the causes of suffering. Gautama pointed to eliminating the causes of suffering by breaking the causal chain resulting in rebirth through eliminating desire (*tanha*). Jesus, by contrast, accepted upon Himself the causes of suffering, namely the effects and penalty of sin, in His death on the cross on behalf of sinful humanity. And in His victorious resurrection from the dead, Jesus Christ broke the power of sin and death, providing hope for our own resurrection (1 Cor 15:20–22). While Jesus' resurrection from the dead is central to Christian faith, it is not something that is to be blindly accepted apart from corroborating evidence. Significantly, the apostle Paul reminded King Agrippa that Jesus' death and resurrection was publicly accessible, for "it was not done in a corner" (Acts 26:26 NIV). A recurring theme in early Christian preaching is the fact that the apostles and other Christians were witnesses to Christ's being raised from the dead (cf. Acts 2:22–24,32; 1 Cor 15:3–8). The resurrection of Jesus of Nazareth sets Jesus Christ apart from Gautama and puts the Christian faith in a different category from Eastern religions.

Chapter 12

CHRIST IN THE NEW AGE

L. Russ Bush

"**A**ge" usually refers to the years of someone's life or to an era in history. What is the distinctive meaning, then, of the term "New Age"? It would not be enlightening to speak of every moment or day or year as a "new" moment, day, or year, though of course it is. New Age has come to refer to a supposed new consciousness about time, our place in the universe, and the nature of reality. The claim is that we humans have just recently begun to realize that things are not what they have seemed to be over the centuries. We the people of the world are supposedly gaining a new consciousness, a deep spiritual awareness, and a divine identity that rivals that possessed by Christ Himself.

That is a big leap intellectually; so we need to go back and review a little history so as to make this leap meaningful. New Age implies an old age, does it not? So what and when was the "old age"?

The Old Age

This can be misleading, but for the sake of discussion, let's characterize the ancient world (superficial though my characterization may be) as a world of two groups—those who were materialists and those who were spiritualists. That is, some believed that ultimate reality was matter alone. Life was a natural phenomenon. It had no source other than the constant interaction of earth, air, fire, and water. These same four "elements" also produced animals and spirits in addition to people. Animals were controlled by people, and people were controlled by spirits, but everything was a continuum of life forms.

Thales was the first, but there were also other pre-Socratic Greeks who proposed a scientific materialism to explain the movements of the stars and planets (including the sun and moon). The sun was no god, just a large, hot object without awareness or intelligence. The moon was cold and also stood without intelligence.

Many in the pre-Christian world worshipped idols, but they did so by believing in a universal life force that supposedly permeated all things to different degrees. Most people, however, saw this universal life force in all other things, but they did not identify themselves as merely being a manifestation of the same inner life as that of the animals. Some idols looked like people, but most looked like animals or monsters. People were unique and distinct. Animals do not have human consciousness or intelligence.

The Greeks developed idealistic and materialistic philosophies. Jews believed in creation—that God had made real things, including people, but that these real things were not to be worshipped. The idea that a person should carve from wood or stone an image and then worship it was considered to be ludicrous. Such an idol cannot speak or hear or act in any way. If it could, it would have no more knowledge or power than its manufacturer; but of course it would not really have any such power since we have no ability to transfer our knowledge to anything that has no consciousness or intelligence.

The Middle Age

Greek thinking continued to influence the Roman world throughout the years from around AD 500 to 1500. But the rise of Islam, the growth of Christianity, and the increasing intellectual sophistication of European society led most in the old Roman Empire to abandon the notion of idolatry as a viable option for cultural advance. Those who remained superstitious and involved in astrology announced that European culture had recently come through the age of Aries (the "age of the Father" [c. 2000–0 BC]). From the birth of Christ until recent times, we supposedly experienced the age of Pisces (the "age of the Son"). Then in the late twentieth century, from the 1960s onward, the terms changed again, and the new age was announced in the popular culture as the "age of Aquarius," a time of transformation characterized as the "age of the Spirit."

These titles are essentially meaningless, but most of us realize that something unusual is happening in culture. The war culture of the twentieth century, and the explosion in the real world of that bomb that melted the elements with a fervent heat, was overwhelming in its impact. The countercultural youth who went to college in the 1960s sought a new kind of spirituality. Hallucinogenic drugs quickly became a part of that culture. The church seemingly did not address their needs in any significant way. The church was seen as the bastion of tradition, and yet everything seemed to demand a new level of emotion, a new kind of music, a new openness to alternative traditions (based on a new awareness of Eastern religious styles) and a new openness to alternative lifestyles (previously unimaginable within the spiritual lifestyles of Christian faith).

Notice that this is not tied to an intellectual, philosophical teaching spread through postmodern philosopher Jacques Derrida's classroom. The change is a product of human experience, and it is widespread. People were and are attempting to explain their experiences in ordinary life. No one can deny that the world they live in today is not much like the world they grew up in, and certainly it is vastly different from the world and life experiences of their parents: biotechnological and medical advances (yet horrible new diseases); technological tools and developments, such as telecommunication satellites; instant information flow; computers and industrial automation; the Internet itself; mass media; the deception of naturalism; globalization; climate change; and a hundred more.

The Modern Age

By the 1960s young people in particular were aware that the weapons in the hands of the U.S. military (and other less trustworthy nations) had the potential of destroying Earth's ecosystem. Governments seemed reckless and untrustworthy. After all, they were being run by the older folks who did not support peace movements and who wanted to send the young people into wars that were not "their" wars. The emotions sought by the moderns could be produced by rock music and drugs. Aldous Huxley suggested that drugs should be given to healthy people in order to find the reality that was inside their own heads.

Rock music (primarily through the Beatles and Elvis Presley) swept the world. Drug usage soared. Law enforcement was overwhelmed in trying to deal with the existing laws, much less the new laws fearful politicians were passing in efforts to resist and restrict the loss of order that seemed inevitable. For many 9/11 is simply the latest example of the kind of world that technology without boundaries will inevitably bring. Most of us are afraid of the growing AIDS crisis (no longer just sub-Saharan Africa), the return of malaria, and our growing dependence on oil at the very time, for good reason, Western politicians have an increasing distrust of Islam and its impact on the Arab states of the oil-rich Middle East.

With insight, J. W. Drane comments:

> The influence of a dualistic world-view, which validated all this by distinguishing spirit from matter, body from soul, people from nature, men from women, and Westerners from the rest of the world, guaranteed that any discussion of these matters would have an overtly spiritual dimension. This is where the holistic approach of the New Spirituality comes in, by highlighting what look like valuable insights from other cultures and reinstating aspects of Western spirituality that have either been marginalized or forgotten.[1]

[1] Drane adds: "In the past, people looked to the church as their spiritual guardian, but that is no longer the case in Britain, and northern Europe generally. Although the situation in the USA is different, the same signs of impatience with traditional Christian churches can

David Clark and Norman Geisler simply identify New Age thought as Pantheism.[2] They then proceed to examine the work of Suzuki, Shankara, Radhakrishnan, Plotinus, and Spinoza. On the other hand, Russell Chandler, religion writer for the *Los Angeles Times*, provides one of the best descriptions of the nature and impact of New Age thinking without reference to any of these philosophers.

New Age is a hybrid mix of spiritual, social, and political forces, and it encompasses sociology, theology, the physical sciences, medicine, anthropology, history, the human potential movement, sports, and science fiction.

New Age is not a sect or a cult, per se. There is no organization one must join, no creed one must confess. . . . The New Age influence touches virtually every area of life, and thousands of New Age activists seek to transform society through New Age precepts. Millions more have adopted the movement's view of reality, though they may simply think of it as a pragmatic, humanistic philosophy of life. . . .

The insidious danger of the New Age is its view of the nature of reality, which admits to no absolutes. History provides evidence that relative standards of morality breed chaos and—ultimately—the downfall of society.[3]

Supposedly the old, limited, and finite order is giving way; and the glorious new order of peace, prosperity, and perfection is on its way. The New Age is full of mixes. We have the health and wealth gospel proclaimed under the banner of a suffering Savior. New Age healing ministries are almost always conducted at some distance from medical facilities. The wages of sin is death, but eat right and remain healthy. Live long to prove how faithful to God you have been!

---

be documented there too." J. W. Drane, "New Age" in the *New Dictionary of Christian Apologetics*, ed. W. C. Campbell-Jack and Gavin McGrath (Downers Grove, Ill.: InterVarsity, 2006), 483.

[2] See David K. Clark and Norman L. Geisler, *Apologetics in the New Age: A Christian Critique of Pantheism* (Grand Rapids, Mich.: Baker, 1990).

[3] Russell Chandler, *Understanding the New Age* (Dallas: Word, 1988), 17–18.

Try "Christian yoga" since the use of two religions should increase the value. Worry not that the word *yoga* has no precedent in Christian vocabulary. It feels good to stretch those muscles, and it opens the mind to avoid the "mental suppression" required when we think only on those things above and not on earthly things. Are not all the passionate things earthly things? Have you been baptized? They say it is a refreshing experience. (You did notice tongue planted firmly in cheek, did you not?)

The New Age

One can see certain common elements in most instances of New Age thinking. *First is the claim of the ultimate unity of all things.* Reality is said to be fundamentally one. By whatever name, "God" is ultimately that one reality. This means that nature is a manifestation of this one reality, for there are not and cannot be two ultimate realities. God is all there is, and everything else that makes things appear to be separate realities must therefore be an illusion. This is the essence of New Age thinking.

One can see the parallel here between New Age pantheism and naturalism. The philosophical naturalist believes there is only the natural order, that everything is matter and energy (two sides of the same coin). Nature is all that exists. A pantheist may deny that nature is real and claim that it is all a manifestation of the divine mind, but in either case, both naturalist and New Age pantheist believe in only one kind of reality. The New Ager sees ultimate reality as divine. Thus human beings have the divine essence within them, sustaining them. All people have a divine consciousness. In fact, God is the All. Nothing exists that is not divine, nothing that is not a part of God. So whatever is real is a part of God.

The second element concerns the blurring of goodness and evil. Most of us experience and thus believe in suffering, and we believe some things are evil (like brutal torture and murder). Thus, the pantheist, the committed New Ager, is faced with an acute problem regarding the goodness of God. The New Age usually pushes this aside and says that God is so great that we must think of "It" as transcending these earthly opposites (good and evil). In the same way the New Age often says that God is both personal and impersonal, finite and infinite. In other words, no one can say anything definitive about God. God is everything, and as bearing the God consciousness, the New Age follower is also slowly getting in touch with himself by growing in his own divine nature.

Third, the New Age view of creation is different from theism's creation out of nothing. Christians and other theists believe in creation *ex nihilo* (out of nothing). The pantheist speaks more of creation "out of God." Mystical consciousness is the necessary means of knowing. This is how Yoda teaches the young Jedi to learn and know the world around him: "You must reach out with your feelings, Master Luke." The "Force" is, of course, that all-pervading divine reality that gives power to those who seek it and depend mystically upon it. *Star Wars* is the most perfect expression in modern cinema of New Age beliefs (though the New Age does not require belief in ancient empires and prehistoric wars between opposing ideological forces).

Fourth, the New Age movement emphasizes the human problem as ignorance, with salvation coming through enlightenment and self-effort. In New Age philosophy, knowledge is salvation; ignorance and/or the grasp for power is a source of evil; and salvation comes by human effort. Many church leaders have so moved away from confessionalism that they cannot see that this New Age perspective is not a view within the bounds of Christian orthodoxy.[4]

Fifth, the cycle of birth, death, and rebirth (reincarnation) is commonly held by New Agers. The New Age movement typically emphasizes that we were in touch with our divine nature in the past (perhaps in a former life, from which this one is a reincarnation—though not everyone accepts traditional reincarnation beliefs). Supposedly we have fallen from that previous understanding, and we cannot get back to it. We need to restore our lost knowledge of our own divine nature, and

---

[4] Cf. Thomas J. Nettles, *Ready for Reformation* (Nashville: Broadman & Holman, 2005). Written to Southern Baptists, this book is relevant to most evangelicals. In a day of anticonfessionalism, such as today, this should be required reading for pastors and church leaders.

thus we need to reclimb the ladder, so to speak. This can supposedly be done through various programs, retreats, training sessions, conferences, and contact with powerful occult forces or psychic teachers.

The Way of the World

Strangely, the twenty-first century has not been so good for the optimism of New Age thinking. The crises have been too great, the battles too vicious, the stress too intense. But behind the scenes in business and in the corporate world, seminars in Transcendental Meditation continue to be conducted regularly; the yoga classes are filled; the search for just the right nonthreatening (so-called "seeker") churches goes on. Virtually every church either is or has gone through a debate over music and worship styles. Biblical content for many preachers seems trivial, boring, or irrelevant; and it is mostly ignored in modern sermons. It is a confusing time for the church. New Age spiritualism and pop psychology are often substituted because they are popular, easy to work with, and seemingly helpful at first for many. But such content leads nowhere, helps no one, and utterly fails to communicate the teachings of Christ to believers, much less to the unsaved world.

The television has shows about UFOs and aliens almost every day (a typical New Age theme). Any number of communes and groups meet to promote New Age ideas. Bookstores, such as Barnes & Noble and Borders, have entire sections labeled "New Age Spirituality." Channeling (i.e., letting a departed guru or "spirit guide" speak through a mystical medium using occult techniques) is still popular with some. One seldom hears of "harmonic convergence" anymore, but the term remains in the literature. Crystal consciousness and pyramid power still have their followers. Today we have seen a return to goddess worship and neopaganism.

Holistic health continues right alongside pop psychology as health consciousness rises, especially among the upper middle class. In science the New Age catchphrase is "mind over matter." Science fiction has its own cable TV channel; and, other than the news channels, it is one of the most popular. We have to admit that the stories are more varied, the dialogue is more interesting, and the special effects demonstrate the almost unlimited human imagination. Most people eventually get tired of the murder and mayhem that characterizes the typical detective or law enforcement show today. We grow dull to it all, and the producers simply move to more graphic images and even more horrible plots.

By contrast, New Age thinking has given us the following:

- *X-Men* (three films of great energy and fun, hopefully a fourth one on the way, where it is "perfectly normal and understandable" to walk through walls, create and calm storms, shoot fire from the eyes, and read minds)
- *Star Trek* (five television series plus several clean, high-quality films, where we accept without question or misunderstanding the existence and function of a transporter, a holodeck, and warp speeds)
- *Star Wars* (six incredible special-effects films following New Age motifs)
- *Stargate* (where we travel with the SG1 team via worm holes accessed through thousands of round, powerful, dial-up Stargates that we walk through in order to get to distant civilizations for high adventures and dangers that the SG1 team can always overcome in the end).

It is a fantasy world, but it all seems so real. The characters all play their roles with seriousness. Many of us love it if it is well-done, even if we are fully aware of the illusion that is being constructed. The moral context of these stories is not in the gutter; the language is clean; and right is ultimately victorious; but clearly these are not stories portraying an explicitly Christian worldview. They are essentially setting forth New Age ideas.

Chinese herbs, acupuncture, Korean massage, UFOs entering our space with impunity to deliver warnings about nuclear weapons (or to colonize Earth), and the ubiquity of life (a belief that results from our uncritical acceptance of evolutionary theory): these are a few of our "favorite" things. If we can imagine it, we can tell a story about it or at least incorporate our more interesting fantasies into our entertainment world. New Age thinkers, however, do not see all these things as imaginary or fantasy items. What we see on science fiction shows may not be real today in the way that football is real, but the Star Trek idea of a life-filled universe of intelligence and advanced technology simply has its attraction to many. Most people know that sci-fi is fiction and fantasy, but they accept the premise (after all, with a universe this large, there must be others like ourselves somewhere out there), and they believe we will always be smart enough or powerful enough or lucky enough to survive any hostile attacks from these "others."

If God is within us, God is in other life forms as well, and thus in our stories we are encountering other "divine sparks" throughout the universe. Their weapons are almost invincible. The human victory usually comes from good fortune, courage, and intelligence. (Interestingly, the human hero in the story is often laid back; and his luck and skills, which are necessary for victory, do not show up until they are required at the end.) Universal peace is assumed to be a universal goal—except for the really bad guys, of which there are plenty, whose goal is domination through cruelty and power. Consider the inevitable and irresistible advance of the Borg and the horrible practices of the Wraith; but remember also the Vulcans (Spock and Topal), the Klingons (Warf and Balana), and 7-of-9. The common element is the divine nature that dwells in each life-form from the nanoprobes to the Force.

Not everyone would agree, but it seems to many that the superheroes of the comics/movies fit well in the world of the New Age. They have "divine" powers; they defend the right; and they live in a world of the supernatural. But the best way really to conceptionalize the New Age is not through popular culture icons but through following the loss of absolutes. New Age thought in its purest form is relativism. Secularism has led the way to a loss of significance. New Age thought is postmodern in it essence. It has roots in the ancient world, in the occult, and in the paganism of the ancients. It draws its power from the passion its ideas generate.

Identifying the New Age

Woulter J. Hanegraaff has produced perhaps the most scholarly analysis of New Age religion to date.[5] According to Hanegraaff, *five basic elements* constitute New Age religion:

- *"This-worldliness."* This is opposed to an other-worldly view; the new age is focused on the here and now; it is not a pie-in-the-sky sort of faith; it is a belief that the New Age itself is for the here and now and for this world and its people; it looks forward to an earthly transformation, not a heavenly one; new age faith is not eschatological.

- *Holism.* This term is often applied to holistic medicine; the idea is that you must treat the entire person in that person's unique context in every case. We are not forbidden from using medicine, but medicine should never be used alone; there must be "treatment" of one's entire physical and spiritual condition, one's associations, one's place in life. The idea is not to divide up any part of our life but to see ourselves and our weaknesses as part of a whole; this often leads to the use of natural substances in place of medicine, the so-called herbal approach to medicine in place of traditional drugs; this goes beyond herbal medicine, but it is the use of food and special plants and certain practices to ward off disease and keep oneself healthy. This includes yoga, acupuncture, massage, and similar practices.

- *Evolutionism.* The explanation of life, cultural patterns, disease, relationships with other nationalities, language development, and so forth is a result of evolution, not providence; thus our life's context is accidental, not purposeful.

- *Psychologization of religion and sacralization of psychology.* Religion is not a response to divine revelation but is simply a psychological response to experiences we have that are mystical or spiritual. We then take the psychological responses we have and consider them to be sacred moments to be treasured

[5] See Woulter J. Hanegraaff, *New Age Religion and Western Culture: Esotericism in the Mirror of Secular Thought* (Albany, N.Y.: State University of New York Press, 1998).

as personal encounters with the divine spirit that infuses all reality, making our life and our experiences sacred, even though we are not encountering the biblical God. The idea is that we are turning our personal psychology into our religion; there is no objective revelation in the New Age.

- *Eschatological realization.* The literal expectation of the soon-arrival of a new, open-minded, nonexclusive era where freedom of thought is mixed in with political correctness and nonjudgmental relativism.

Things simply are not what or how they used to be. World population is exploding. Technology is changing our lives before our very eyes. In a fifteen-year time span the Internet literally changed the way we do business, entertainment, shopping, and socializing. What will be next? Even youth (under twenty) hardly recognize the world in which we live today compared to the world in which they lived as a child. Today is in a literal sense a new world in which we have to worry about oil, globalization, nuclear fallout, global warming, pollution, environmental disasters, and ethnic wars. Put a "no absolutes" message into a framework of "self-centered relativism," add a "seek happiness" slogan, avoid parental discipline, find pleasure in mystical hypotheses, and you too can have a personal New Age religion, ministry, or secular view that draws fellow travelers. Study the ancient Egyptians (a popular avocation for New Agers), and compare their pyramid architecture with that of the Mexican and South American Indian architectures. Did these ancient people predict the end of the world in our lifetime? How likely would it be that they could do that? Even with all of our modern computer processing power, can we predict events that will occur in France in the year 2437? Have we in the past been visited by extraterrestrials? (Are you aware that for many this is not a silly question at all but one that could just as easily be answered by yes as by no? But, of course, in reality it remains a silly question.)

Clearly there is no standard creed that defines the banner of New Age beliefs. Yet we get the clear impression of unity within New Age circles. How could that be the case? Hanegraaff suggests that it is because almost all of the New Age emphases are intended as alternatives to current, dominant, cultural trends in the West.[6] Unity, as opposed to dualism, characterizes the central emphasis of the New Age. Thus, *new* is an appropriate term because the New Age is in every way a rejection and a cultural criticism of the old way that has characterized the West in previous decades and centuries. Some of the traditional dualisms rejected by New Age thought are Creator/creation, man/nature, and spirit/matter. New Age rhetoric also strongly opposes reductionism (aiming in this case primarily at scientific rationalism). The New Age opposes all dualisms in favor of holism.

In the final analysis the New Age is a rejection of Christian faith. To resist it and overcome the negative effects it imposes, there must be a defense of the faith that is heard and examined by church people first and by the religious culture second and the secular culture third. We probably have the capability to get people to hear, but can we get them to listen and consider?

A New and Enduring Way

As you are going throughout the world, make disciples. With God's help, make people into students of the teachings of Christ. When you tell them who Jesus really is, and as initial responses come, we must ask them for commitments to the truth, at which time we should seal these commitments through the act of water baptism in the name of the triune God. Then the task is to teach them all the things Christ has taught us (Matt 28:18–20).

What is that specifically? For starters, there is a metaphysical or real distinction between God as the Creator and the world as the creation. Naturalistic evolution has no creator other than the reality that is supposedly evolving by blind chance; it attempts to explain everything as a result of time plus chance plus matter (which is not designed for any purpose). Without creation, however, there is nothing of value in existence. Naturalistic evolution is an illusion, however. Something capable of great diversity must already be there in order for there to be

---

[6] Ibid., 515.

anything that could evolve. Evolution cannot bring into being something that is not already there in prototype. Out of the void nothing comes. But a personal God can bring something absolutely new into being, and from that initial reality He can shape and mold His creation in any way He wishes. And He has the right to tell us exactly how He did it, and we have the obligation to listen and believe what He tells us and learn from that by rational and experimental extensions that apply the truth to other areas of thought. But we do not have the right to take revealed truth and then develop irrational and impossible extensions that conflict with that which God has clearly revealed to us about creation.

Apparently God considered a creation (that is, He thought about it), and then He spoke it into being according to His own plan. Christ, the Word of God, was the agent of creation, the One by whom all things were made that were made (John 1:3). This Word, by which all things were created, became flesh (i.e., took on a human body and persona, and was born of a virgin to live as one of us, yet without sin). The phrase "yet without sin" is crucial. Only a sinless man could hope to deal with sin with integrity. All of us have sinned. All are worthy of death except Jesus. Thus only Jesus has the credentials to stand before God to offer Himself as a substitute, a final sacrifice for sin.

Buddhists are not immediately convinced of their sinfulness, so our witness must focus on what it means to sin. Muslims know about sin but usually do not admit it openly, for Allah is not as tolerant as we might have hoped.

This man Jesus is not well-known among the Buddhists, so in some ways there is more work to be done with a Buddhist. Muslims generally know Jesus as a prophet, usually thought to be second in greatness only to Muhammad. So we can talk about Jesus, but we will be told that the New Testament has been corrupted and cannot be trusted. The evidence for such corruption is virtually nonexistent. The textual variants are not the point at issue here, generally speaking. We can simply compare the thousands of independent manuscripts that we have access to from ancient times to show that it is relatively easy to recognize such variants and determine the authentic readings.

Textual criticism reveals that we have an authentic text, and archeological research and comparative historical studies will demonstrate that the text we have is historically reliable. The level of reliability is exceedingly high compared to other ancient and comparable manuscripts. This is (or should be) acknowledged even by those scholars who are not believers.

What do these manuscripts say? *First, we learn that the claim is made that Jesus had a unique and symbolic birth that revealed His divine nature.* By contrast, Muhammad did not have a symbolic birth. Jesus also lived a sinless life. Muhammad did not claim that for himself, nor did his followers claim it for him.

Second, we learn that Jesus taught a message of righteous living. Allah also gave some similar messages and warned of hell, but those messages seldom had elements of forgiveness and grace. The nonviolent, healing messages of Jesus were proclaimed as the divine will for mankind. In Islam, only after standing before the judgment is someone's eternal destiny to be sealed. Jesus claimed to do only what His Father did, taught only what His Father taught, and in every way was the servant of the faithful. Thus it becomes more and more difficult to understand how God could speak so clearly through Jesus against violence (turning the other cheek) and then (supposedly the same God speaking through a later prophet) set up Sharia law, call for death for converts from Islam to any other religion (but especially to Christianity), or call for ritual death for anyone who might criticize or in any way portray an image of the prophet Muhammad.

Third, Jesus lived out His teachings, going so far as to offer Himself as a sacrifice on the cross, fulfilling the requirements of Scripture for the forgiveness of sin. God raised Him from the dead to indicate His acceptance of that sacrifice. Muslims know that there is a theological problem with the horrible form of the death of this good man, but they do not realize that God's plan is bigger than they have yet understood, and they have not yet understood that grace rather than works is the basis for salvation.

Fourth, Muslims extend this misunderstanding to make the claim that there was a substitute for Jesus on the cross, that God would not allow His great prophet to die such a death. It is speculative to decide what God would and would not allow, but clearly God did not prevent the death of Muhammad (though, admittedly, it was not a crucifixion).

Fifth, it is certain that Jesus was the man on that central cross. Roman soldiers would not have made the mistake of substituting another prisoner in the place of Jesus (as the Muslims claim), when coming directly from that prisoner's encounter with Pilate, the governor. Pilate thought it was Jesus on the cross; thus he made a sign, which he posted on the cross, identifying Jesus; and he later checked the situation to reconfirm that it was Jesus on the cross, expressing surprise that He had died so soon and did not need His legs to be broken. Mary the mother of Jesus was there. Moms can usually recognize their firstborn. The man on the cross is not protesting His punishment. Rather He is speaking words of forgiveness and compassion. He offered hope to one of the criminals also being crucified. He made a great impression on the Roman soldier standing by. He called upon John to take His "mother" into his custody to care for her for the rest of her life (she would have been nearly fifty at this time). Joseph of Arimathea and Nicodemus would have recognized a substitute. Suggesting that these are examples of the corrupted text is just too much. These are historical references, validly preserved; and it was Jesus who was crucified and Jesus who was raised from the dead.

Sixth, the tomb was observed to be empty all day on the first day of the week and thus into the next weeks; the possibility of historically investigating the first Easter extends to the present day. Anyone could go to see the tomb. We could see the tomb today if we knew the location with confidence. Some look to the garden tomb; some to the Church of the Holy Sepulcher; some a location on the Mount of Olives. Blood stains likely remained on the linen strips of cloth with which Jesus had been wrapped that first day. The blood must have been that of Jesus since the tomb had no other occupants. Mix-ups were simply not possible. The tomb had been guarded by Roman soldiers who were there for the sole purpose of preventing an empty tomb following that first weekend.

Seventh, after Jesus rose to life from the dead, He appeared to His disciples and others who could have exposed the fraud. No efforts were made to expose anything. Jerusalem literally had become the location of the empty tomb of Christ. Though diligently searched for, the corpse was never found because for the next forty days after the purported resurrection, Jerusalem was where one could encounter the living, resurrected Christ. In this resurrected body Christ appeared to many; and soon, from the Mount of Olives, He ascended back into heaven from where He was also seen as He located Himself at the right hand of the Father, one day to return in that same body to receive the faithful unto Himself, conduct the final judgment, and initiate the eternal kingdom.

So What?

The Christian gospel outlined above means everything. But what does the outline of New Age beliefs mean? I hope it will not disappoint the reader to find that the New Age movement has made virtually no substantial impact on Western society. Nothing sticks! Many people dabble in New Age esotericism. Some actually believe in the rise of a "new" consciousness (a relativistic, personal, worldwide transformation of values and relationships). Some claim to have lived before (reincarnation and past lives are favorite tales that, of course, cannot be proved but provide a lot of excitement for the ones who convince themselves that they have lived before and will live again, just as they are living now). Many try the various New Age communal practices for a while. Many are attracted to spirits or to outer space, the so-called final frontier.

Many seek to find meaning in their lives through New Age teachings, but there is nothing there. It is a dead end that deceives many, but what do deceived people do except deceive themselves further regarding the meaninglessness of the false claims of New Age philosophy. In Christ all the wisdom of God dwells bodily. In Him alone we find the way, the truth, and the life.

Chapter 13

ISLAM AND CHRISTIANITY[1]

Emir Fethi Caner

D uring the season ten premiere of the hit reality show *Amazing Race*, a program that pits couples from vastly different backgrounds against one another in a race that literally spans the globe, viewers watched an interaction between two devout Muslims, Bilal and Sa'eed, and two cheerleaders, Kellie and Jamie. This interaction sadly, yet accurately, demonstrates the lack of knowledge most Americans have of Islam. When Kellie attempts to introduce herself to Bilal by offering to shake his hand, Bilal cordially refuses the gesture, acknowledging that he is a Muslim and that it is not proper for him to touch her. A few moments later Kellie quietly inquires to her partner, Jamie, "Do Muslims believe in Buddha?" Jamie curiously responds, "I don't know."

The vacuity of general religious knowledge by this generation is arguably unparalleled in American history. Things are much different now than when Alexis de Tocqueville (1805–1859), the nineteenth-century French social scientist and political thinker, documented his travels throughout America in his classic *Democracy in America*. Indeed, one can say with some certainty that if he were to visit America today, he would not conclude regarding American religiosity as he did 175 years ago: "Men thus have an enormous interest in forming for themselves well-settled ideas about God, their soul, their general duties

[1] References from the Qur'an are from *The Presidency of Islamic Researches*, Ifta, Call, and Guidance, ed., The Holy Qur'an (Medina: King Fahd Holy Qur'an Printing Complex, n.d.).

toward their Creator, and their fellow men." In fact, this generation should also heed the stern and prophetic warning Tocqueville asserted a few paragraphs later regarding a religiously illiterate society:

> When religion is destroyed among a people, doubt takes over the highest regions of the intellect, and it halfway paralyzes all the others. Everyone becomes used to having only confused and unstable notions about the matters that most interest his fellow men and himself; men defend their opinions badly or abandon them, and since they despair of being able, by themselves alone, to resolve the greatest problems that human fate presents, they are reduced in cowardly fashion to not give them any thought.[2]

The past two generations have grown up functionally illiterate in the realm of religion, and they mirror much of Tocqueville's above conclusion. With religion successfully removed from the public square, most Americans are either confused about religion or cower from any discussion of it. Most today are theologically bewildered and suffer from historical amnesia.

Evangelicals do not seem to have fared much better regarding a general knowledge of the major world religions. Since the onslaught of modernity within the United States, evangelicals, for the most part, have chosen to cocoon themselves into their own subculture, refusing to engage the culture at large in any intellectual or apologetic manner. Fearing that the mind of our children will be corrupted by perverted texts and ideas, the vast majority of evangelicals have created nothing less than our own virtual monasteries and index of prohibited books. Not only are Darwin, Freud, and Marx off-limits from our bookshelves; other religious texts such as the Qur'an, Talmud, and *Analects* of Confucius are forbidden as well.[3] In the end we have mis-

---

[2] Alexis de Tocqueville, *Democracy in America*, ed. Sanford Kessler (Indianapolis: Hackett, 2000), 179.

[3] Ibid., 180. Tocqueville also denounced Islam as antithetical to democracy. He states: "Mohammed brought down from Heaven and placed in the Koran not only religious doctrines, but political maxims, civil and criminal laws, and scientific theories. The Gospel, on the contrary, speaks only about the general relations of men with God and among themselves. Beyond that, it teaches nothing and does not oblige belief about anything. That alone, among a thousand

taken engaging culture in conversation with converging with culture through compromise. In an attempt to secure theological purity, we have instead secluded theological persuasion.

But 9/11 has changed our world, forcing Americans and American Christians to engage and understand Islam, a cradle-to-the-grave religion which does not divorce any aspect of life from its foundational roots in the Islamic faith. In the aftermath of the attacks, television personalities such as Dan Rather became pseudo-theological experts on Islam. Instantly, Americans sought out familiar voices such as Oprah Winfrey, arguably the most powerful voice of pop religion in America. The cultural chatter became nearly deafening for a few months, but thereafter many Americans went back into religious hibernation, once again immersing themselves into the self-help religion that has become American Christianity.[4]

Thankfully, a segment of Christianity, albeit small by most standards, is emerging which wishes to engage Islam, its theology and history. A plethora of books has been published which illustrate a varied landscape of how to view the second largest faith in the world. Among traditional evangelicals, illustrated by books such as *Answering Islam* by Norman Geisler and Abdul Saleeb, biblical apologetics and argumentation take center stage in the discussion. Theological distinctives are emphasized, and Islam is recognized as a repudiation of Christianity.[5] Yet neo-Evangelicals, represented at least in part by J. Dudley Woodberry, highlight the similarities between the two faiths such as supposedly worshipping the same god.[6]

We have thus come to a theological crossroads. Will we go the route of traditional Christianity, which has rejected Islam as a false religion and emphasizes the role of apologetics in defending our faith? Or shall

---

other reasons, suffices to show that the first of these two religions cannot rule for long during times of enlightenment and democracy, whereas the second is destined to reign during these times as in all others" (181).

[4] See John W. Whitehead, "An Empty Shell of Faith," *Fort Worth Star-Telegram*, 13 November 2006, www.dfw.com/mld/dfw/news/opinion/15988200.htm.

[5] See as well Ergun and Emir Caner, *Unveiling Islam* (Grand Rapids: Kregel Publications, 2002).

[6] Thomas S. Kidd, "Islam in American Protestant Thought," *Christianity Today* (September/October 2006), 39. Kidd also references Woodberry's article, "Do Christians and Muslims Worship the Same God?" *Christian Century*, 18 May 2004, 36–37.

we take the road of progressive Christianity, which attempts to affirm certain truths within Islam, find common ground between the two faiths, and reject the role of all but soft apologetics?[7] The author's central premise is clear: *We cannot have an authentic witness to the world without having an authentic apologetic of Christianity*. Hence, the use of reasonable apologetics and biblical distinctives cannot be sacrificed at the altar of political correctness and cultural contextualization.

Two Preliminary Misconceptions About Christianity

Imagine if your view of Christianity was dependent upon mainstream media outlets, Islamic media, or televangelists. For many Muslims the portrait that is drawn of Christianity comes from Islamic television networks such as Al-Jazeera, American television shows like *The Gilmore Girls* or *The Simpsons*, and from the prosperity preachers of our day.[8] Moreover, the Qur'an, the holiest book of Islam, misunderstands key tenets of the Christian faith such as the Trinity. Thus, Christians must recognize how they are viewed by Muslims across the world.

First, the majority of Muslims believe that *all Americans are Christians*. Indeed, America is seen as a Christian nation; and, consequently, the woes of America are blamed on Christians. Freedom, to a traditional Muslim, results in perversion and licentiousness and is therefore inferior to Shari'a law, the Islamic law code which finds its ba-

---

[7] The traditional view is seen through notables such as John Calvin who asserted that Muhammad "allowed to men the brutal liberty of chastising their wives and thus he corrupted that conjugal love and fidelity which binds the husband to the wife. . . . Mohamet allowed full scope to various lusts—by permitting a man to have a number of wives. . . . Mohamet invented a new form of religion." (*Commentaries on the Book of the Prophet Daniel*). Jonathan Edwards asserted that there were "two great works of the devil . . . his Anti-Christian (Romish or Papal) and Mahometan (Muslim or Islamic) kingdoms . . . which have been, and still are, two kingdoms of great extent and strength. Both together swallow . . . up the Ancient Roman Empire. . . . In the Book of Revelation . . . it is the destruction of these that the glorious victory of Christ at the introduction of the glorious times of the Church, will mainly consist" (*A History of the Work of Redemption*).

[8] In an article entitled "Poll shows divide between Muslims, West," Susan Page of *USA Today* exposed the "chasm of suspicion" between Islam and the West. For example, a majority of Muslims in Indonesia, Jordan, Egypt, and Turkey do not believe Arabs carried out the attacks of 9/11. The article can be found at www.usatoday.com/news/washington/2006-06-22-muslim-west-divide_x.htm?POE=click-refer.

sis in the Qur'an and the Hadith. The basis for freedom is Christianity, which Muslims perceive to argue that one can do whatever one wants as long as he says the words of salvation.

Second, *all Christians are Catholic*. Though some Muslims may realize the divide between Catholics, Orthodox, Protestants, and Evangelicals, many merely see all Christians as followers of the Pope. Furthermore, Christians are thought to worship Mary, a perception that finds credence in the Qur'an. In surah 5:116, Allah supposedly asks Jesus this question: "Did you say unto men, 'Take me and my mother for two gods beside Allah'?"[9] This misconception is further resolved through Catholic reverence to Mary as well as the Eastern Orthodox belief in Mary as the "Mother of God" (Gk., *theotokos*).[10]

A Christian Quadrivium: Understanding Four Key Doctrines in Islamic Apologetics

During the emergence of the university in Europe, educators emphasized the importance of building upon the foundation of the seven liberal arts first popularized by the Romans. First, the student was required to study the Trivium, a curriculum in the arts which consisted

[9] Muslim scholars, recognizing the error of such a statement if it is referring to the Trinity, reject the notion that Muhammad is referring to the practice of worshipping Mary as part of the Trinity. Instead, they note that it was commonplace among Eastern and Western Christians by the time of Muhammad to kneel in front of images of Mary and pray to her as the "Mother of God." Additionally, some historians believe Muhammad was referring to an obscure heretical sect which actually implemented Mary as part of the Trinity. This theory has some plausibility since the rejected fourth-century work, "Gospel of the Hebrews," identifies Mary with the Holy Spirit. The context of the chapter, though, seems to indicate an implied connection to the Trinity. Surah 5:73 states, "They disbelieve who say: Allah is one of three." Furthermore, the main Christian denomination of the day, the Nestorians, denied that Mary was divine. It should also be pointed out that the word Arabic Christians use for the Trinity (*thaluth*) is not mentioned in the Qur'an. In the end, such scholarly arguments give way to a large number of Muslims who merely assume surah 5:116 points out a false Trinity in Christianity and equate a sexual relationship between the Father and Mary in giving birth to Jesus. The Web site, Answering Islam (www.answering-islam.org/Index/index.html), provides valuable introductory information on the topic as well as links to articles which explain and defend the doctrine.

[10] Surah 19, "Maryam," is devoted to honor Mary as a devout and chaste Muslim who is given "the gift of a pure son" (v. 19). During the pains of childbirth, Mary is said to have cried out, "Ah! would that I had died before this!" (v. 23). In this chapter Jesus speaks from the cradle (v. 28), and He also speaks about the coming judgment of those who are not Muslim (unbelievers; vv. 37-40).

of grammar, rhetoric, and logic. He was obliged to master these elementary studies before moving on to the next course of study known as the Quadrivium, which included arithmetic, music, geometry, and astronomy. The latter, the equivalent of a master's degree today, prepared the student for study in philosophy and theology.[11]

When entering the arena of Islamic apologetics, the Christian similarly must master four crucial doctrines—a Christian Quadrivium—fortifying the distinctive nature of Christian doctrine in comparison to Islam. The course of study the author proposes includes theology proper (doctrine of God), Christology (doctrine of Christ), soteriology (doctrine of salvation), and epistemology (the study of knowledge with particular reference to the doctrine of revelation). If these doctrines are not astutely discerned, the Christian will either walk the path of theological compromise or the path of theological confusion.

Theology Proper: Discerning the Doctrine of God

> And Elijah came to all the people, and said, "How long will you falter between two opinions? If the LORD is God, follow Him; but if Baal, follow him." But the people answered him not a word.
>
> 1 Kings 18:21 NKJV

Simply put, the God of Muhammad is not the Father of Jesus. The subject in its essence is not a linguistic issue but a theological matter with eternal ramifications. To say that since *Allah* is Arabic for God and *YHWH* is Hebrew for God, Christians and Muslims worship the same God is beyond naive; it is blasphemous. When Elijah challenged his fellow Jews to follow the one true God, he did so without regard to linguistics. In the verse cited above, Elijah reprimands his kinsmen for committing idolatry. Yet the etymology of Baal is derived from the root word for *lord* or *master*. If the matter at hand were only about

---

[11] See Fred Hutchison, "A cure for the educational crisis: Learn from the extraordinary education heritage of the West," *Renew America*, 1 June 2006, at www.renewamerica.us/analyses/060601hutchison.htm.

words, Elijah's statement would make absolutely no sense.[12] Would the Israelites not be worshipping the same god as their forefathers since they have a title similar to that of their forefathers? Would Elijah not owe an unqualified apology to the prophets of Baal for assuming their worship was inadequate and their god nonexistent?[13]

This is not an argument which denies that God is sovereign over Muhammad and all followers of Islam. But as Timothy George noted in a *Christianity Today* article:

> Muslim theology rejects the divinity of Christ and the personhood of the Holy Spirit—both essential components of the Christian understanding of God. No devout Muslim can call the God of Muhammad "Father," for this, to their mind, would compromise divine transcendence. But no faithful Christian can refuse to confess, with joy and confidence, "I believe in God the Father . . . Almighty!" Apart from the Incarnation and the Trinity, it is possible to know that God is, but not who God is.[14]

Popular Muslim apologetics acknowledge the difficulties in saying Christians and Muslims worship the same God. In a recent abrasive editorial in the *Pak Tribune*, Ahmer Muzammil, after attempting to prove his respect for Jesus, asserted:

> The haters can spew venom but as far as I am concerned, I believe that whoever believes in one Allah (GOD) without any partners, sons, daughters or incarnations, whether they are Christians, Jews, Muslims or whoever they might be, they all believe in the same Allah (GOD) that we do and that Jesus, Moses, Adam, Noah and Mohammad called masses to the same GOD.[15]

---

[12] The passage, if we assume that language is primary to the argument, would thus read: "If the Lord is God, follow Him, but if Lord (Baal) follow him."

[13] This is, indeed, the concept which then leads the text to conclude regarding Baal's power, "There was no voice; no one answered; no one paid attention" (v. 29).

[14] Timothy George, "Is the God of Muhammad the Father of Jesus," *Christianity Today*, 4 February 2002, cited in Emir and Ergun Caner, *More Than a Prophet* (Grand Rapids: Kregel, 2003), 28.

[15] Ahmer Muzammil, "Answering Tough Questions and Misconceptions about Islam," *Pak-Tribune*, 20 June 2006, at www.paktribune.com/news/index.shtml?147414. The article also deals with difficult issues including jihad and women.

Like the traditional Christian who points to the doctrine of Christ's divinity as nonnegotiable, the traditional Muslim concedes that no one is permitted to partner anyone (or anything) with God and still be considered to worship the God of Islam. Furthermore, Muzammil, following the revisionist history of the Qur'an, claims that Jesus, Noah, and others were worshippers of Allah, not the Christian God.

The Qur'an further substantiates the claim that Christians do not worship the same God as Muslims. Surah 5:72 denounces partnering "other gods with Allah," and warns those who do so, "Allah will forbid him the Garden, and the Fire will be his abode." Surah 112 divorces Allah from the Christian God, explaining:

> Say: He is Allah
> The One and Only,
> Allah, the Eternal, Absolute;
> He begets not,
> Nor is He begotten;
> And there is none
> Like unto Him.

Finally, surah 4:116 poignantly concludes, "Allah forgives not (the sin of) joining other gods with Him." Commenting on this verse, noted Islamic commentator Yusuf Ali maintains:

> Just as in an earthly kingdom the worst crime is that of treason, as it cuts at the very existence of the State, so in the spiritual kingdom, the unforgivable sin is that of contumacious treason against Allah by putting up Allah's creatures in rivalry against Him. This is rebellion against the essence and source of spiritual Life. It is what Plato would call the "lie of the soul." But even here, if the rebellion is through ignorance, and is followed by sincere repentance and amendment, Allah's Mercy is always open.[16]

Ali's implication is that Peter, for example, committed this heinous sin when he publicly proclaimed, "You are the Christ, the Son of the

---

[16] Abdullah Yusuf Ali, *The Meaning of the Holy Qur'an* (Brentwood, Md.: Amana, 1992), n. 569. See surah 5:48 as well.

living God" (Matt 16:16). The church itself is built on this confession of faith in the Lord Jesus Christ, indeed, in the very character of Jesus Christ as the Son of God. To remove Him from the Godhead would be the death knell of the church, the end of Christianity. "For no other foundation can anyone lay than that which is laid, which is Jesus Christ" (1 Cor 3:11 NKJV). Ultimately, Muslims reject the fatherhood of God, the deity of Christ, and the person of the Holy Spirit. The triune God is replaced by a figment of Muhammad's imagination, a god that is beyond the characteristics of monotheism and transcendence resembles only remotely the God of the Scriptures.

Christology: Discerning the Person and Work of Christ

Let this mind be in you which was also in Christ Jesus, who, being in the form of God, did not consider it robbery to be equal with God, but made Himself of no reputation, taking the form of a bondservant, and coming in the likeness of men. And being found in appearance as a man, He humbled Himself and became obedient to the point of death, even the death of the cross.

Philippians 2:5–8 NKJV[17]

Muslims are quick to point out that they have a great respect for Jesus and that no one can rightly be called a Muslim who does not honor Christ. Yet Muslims, like all other people, must realize that one cannot merely respect Jesus; one either worships Him or rejects Him. Jesus, pointing out His eternality in stating, "Before Abraham was," (John 8:58a), identifies Himself as "I AM," the term for the sacred name of God Himself, YHWH (Exod 3:14).[18] Jesus not only uttered the unutterable word YHWH, but He ascribed it to Himself on the temple grounds. The Jews then picked up stones, a logical response

---

[17] Christians should be intimately familiar with the four great Christological passages of the New Testament: John 1:1–18, Phil 2:5–11, Col 1:15–23, and Heb 1:1–8.

[18] In commenting on this verse, John Calvin elucidates, "Some think that this applies simply to the eternal Divinity of Christ, and compare it with that passage in the writings of Moses, *I am what I am* (Exod. iii. 14.) But I extend it much farther, because the power and grace of Christ, so far as he is the Redeemer of the world, was common to all ages. It agrees therefore with that saying of the apostle, *Christ yesterday, and to-day, and for ever* (Heb. xiii.8.)"

for someone charged with blasphemy. Commenting on this passage with regards to Muslims, Erwin Lutzer, in *Christ among Other Gods*, stated:

> The divinity of Christ sharply divides Christianity from all of the other religions of the world. This is the great divide, the unbridgeable chasm, a gulf that extends from here to eternity. If it is false, it is worthy of great tribulation and a curse; if it is true, it is the best news—perhaps the only really good news—available on planet earth.[19]

The Qur'an identifies Jesus with many of the same terms Christians use, but these words are given vastly different definitions than those found in the Bible. Jesus is said to be the "Word" (surah 3:45), meaning He simply communicated the work of Allah. Jesus is viewed as "Messiah" (surah 9:30–31), referring to Him as an anointed prophet empowered to proclaim Allah's truth. Furthermore, Muslims believe Jesus was born of a virgin (surah 3:47)[20] and performed many miracles including raising people from the dead (surah 3:49).[21]

However, Jesus is declared to be fully man, a "messenger" (surah 5:75) who adamantly refuses any form of worship (surah 5:77). Moreover, He was created from dust (surah 3:59) and was not ordained to die the cruel death of the cross (surah 4:157).[22] Paramount is this diversion from Christianity, as the Qur'an articulates:

---

[19] Erwin W. Lutzer, *Christ among Other Gods* (Chicago: Moody Press, 1994), 103. Amazingly, Muslims believe Jesus spoke from the cradle, defending Mary's purity. Yet why did Jesus remain silent when the magi came to worship Him (Matt 2:11)?

[20] It is ironic that Muslims extend more respect to Jesus as a high prophet than do most liberal Christians. Muslims believe Jesus was born of a virgin; rejection of the virgin birth is a foundation stone of modern theologies. Muslims believe Jesus actually lived in space and time. Liberal Christians proclaim that we cannot know anything substantive about the man Jesus of Nazareth; they scoff at miracles and the supernatural in general. The sad truth is that Jesus is held in higher esteem in mosques around the world than in the lectures from purportedly Christian pulpits.

[21] To understand the Islamic perspective of Christ, Christians should especially familiarize themselves with chapters 3–5 in the Qur'an.

[22] The Hadith also weighs in on the character of Jesus. For example, to illustrate Jesus' pure birth it asserts, "The Prophet said, 'When any human being is born, Satan touches him at both sides of the body with his two fingers, except Jesus, the son of Mary, whom Satan tried to touch but failed, for he touched the placenta-cover instead'" (Bukhari 4.506). To substantiate that Christ was only human, it reiterates, "The Prophet said, 'If anyone testifies that None has the

That they said (in boast), "We killed Christ Jesus the son
of Mary, the Messenger of Allah"; but they killed him not,
nor crucified him. Only a likeness of that was shown to them.
And those who differ therein are full of doubts, with no (certain) knowledge. But only conjecture to follow, for of a surety
they killed him not: Nay, Allah raised him up unto Himself;
and Allah is Exalted in Power, Wise (surah 4:157-158).[23]

Though Muslims believe the end of Jesus' life remains a mystery,
it is certainly legitimate to ask what happened on that Friday of the
crucifixion. Who replaced Christ? When was He replaced?[24] Were the
disciples deceived by Allah on purpose? Did the mother of Christ not
recognize that her Son was not removed from the punishment of the
cross? Did Allah leave her to weep for her Son even though He had
not died in such a criminal manner?[25] Who cried out on the cross, "It
is finished!" and why was He allowed to deceive the people that they
were no longer left in their sin?[26]

Ultimately, Muslims believe that Jesus is coming back. Surah 43:61
stipulates, "And (Jesus) shall be a sign (for the coming of) the Hour
(of Judgment): Therefore have no doubt about the (Hour), but follow
you Me: this is a Straight Way." The main purpose of Jesus' return is
to prepare the way for universal acceptance of Islam and thereby bring
peace to the earth. Though Muslim theologians disagree here, many

right to be worshiped but Allah Alone Who has no partners, and that Muhammad is His Slave
and His Apostle, and that Jesus is Allah's Slave and His Apostle and His Word which He be-
stowed on Mary and a Spirit created by Him, and that Paradise is true, and Hell is true, Allah
will admit him into Paradise with the deeds which he had done even if those deeds were few.'"
(Junada, the sub-narrator said, "'Ubada added, 'Such a person can enter Paradise through any
of its eight gates he likes'" [Bukhari 4.644].)

[23] Yusuf Ali states, "It is not profitable to discuss the many doubts and conjectures among the
early Christian sects and among Muslim theologians" (n. 663). In an attempt to legitimize the
Qur'an and put into question the historicity of the crucifixion, Ali argues that many Christian
sects denied the death of Christ (Basilidans, Docetae, and pseudepigraphal gospels).

[24] If Jesus was replaced after the scourging, did not others recognize that His replacement was
without wounds? Or did Allah somehow deceive the people by placing artificial wounds upon
Christ's replacement?

[25] In fact, if Allah took Christ without tasting death, would it not be better for Mary to know
this fact which would inevitably lead to her rejoicing at the privileged status of her Son?

[26] Other questions include, What did the replacement do to deserve such a painful end?
Because of such inquiries, many Muslims believe it was Judas who replaced Christ because he
betrayed Christ and thereby betrayed Allah.

believe the verse which states, "The People of the Book but must believe in Him before his death," (surah 4:159) elucidates the fact that Christians will revert to the one true path of Islam at Christ's return. Other traditions note that Jesus will descend to the earth, instruct others on the Qur'an and Hadith, lead people in prayer, bring peace and prosperity, end the use of unclean animals, and remove idolatrous images including crosses.[27]

Thus, Christians must be prepared to discuss the person and work of Christ on the cross as well as the imminent return of Christ. Christ is the soon-coming King who will indeed bring peace and prosperity while also establishing His kingdom on Earth. He brings with Him rewards for the righteous and judgment for the wicked. The power of this certain promise is described well by Charles Haddon Spurgeon (1834–1892), who wrote:

> Beloved, we must preach the coming of the Lord, and preach it more than we have done; because it is the driving power of the Gospel. Too many have kept back these truths, and thus the bone has been taken out of the arm of the Gospel. Its point has been broken; its edge has been blunted. The doctrine of judgment to come is the power by which men are to be aroused. There is another life, the Lord will come a second time, judgment will arrive, and the wrath of God will be revealed. Where this is not preached, I am bold to say, the Gospel is not preached.[28]

Soteriology: Discerning the Doctrine of Salvation

> But these are written that you may believe that Jesus is the Christ, the Son of God, and that believing you may have life in His name.
>
> John 20:31

---

[27] The last two facts are referenced in Sahih Muslim Hadith while the previous facts are defended by Muslim scholars including Mufti A. H. Elias. See Caner and Caner, *More Than a Prophet*, 139–60.

[28] Charles Spurgeon, *The Second Coming of Christ* (New Kensington, Pa.: Whitaker House, 1996), 113.

The centrality of salvation in Islam is found in its first pillar, the creed (*shahada*) which states, "There is no god but Allah, and Muhammad is the messenger of Allah" (surah 47:19; 48:29). Indeed, it is the faithful recitation of this statement by a non-Muslim which then converts him to Islam.[29]

It can be persuasively argued that Islam demands more work to gain heaven than all of the other major religions in the world. Consider the strenuous obedience that is required of a Muslim even to hope to obtain Paradise. He must recite the creed of Islam thousands of times throughout his life. He must pray (*salat*) five times a day, hoping that Allah will see his faithfulness and give him mercy (surah 2:3–4; 20:14–15). These prayers must be preceded by ablution, a ritual of cleansing the head, hands, mouth, nostrils, ears, face, forearms, and feet. Without such cleansing, Allah will not hear the prayers uttered by Muslim believers (Bukari Hadith 3.57).

Furthermore, Muslims are required to give 2.5 percent of their income to the poor and destitute (*zakat*), a demonstration of care for the community as well as a renunciation of greed (surah 2:277).[30] The consequences of withholding the almsgiving will inevitably be hell (Bukhari 2.498). Fasting (*sawm*), the fourth pillar of Islam, is mandatory throughout the lifetime of a Muslim (surah 2:183). Honoring the month in which Muhammad received his first revelations from Allah, Muslims, from sunrise to sunset, replace daily activities such as eating and drinking with the reading of the Qur'an and worship. Finally, the pilgrimage to Mecca (*hajj*), the fifth pillar, is in many ways the climax of the Muslim faith. Each year three million Muslims converge upon Islam's holiest sites in Mecca to celebrate the oneness of Allah. The ritual is meticulously planned as pilgrims follow specific stages beginning with circling the Ka'aba, a building which holds the black stone that Muslims believe was built by Abraham and Ishmael. Other parts of the pilgrimage include running seven times between two hills of

---

[29] The term *convert* is used loosely as Muslims argue they believe in "reversion" not "conversion." Islamic theology argues that all are born Muslims and thus, after reciting the creed, return to their original faith.

[30] Obviously, poor Muslims are not required to fulfill this obligation. Also, the amount given varies according to detailed calculations of income, expenses, and taxes.

Mecca reenacting Hagar's frantic search for water for her son Ishmael, traveling thirteen miles to the plains of Arafat to honor the place of Muhammad's last sermon, throwing stones at the devil, and sacrificing an animal in remembrance of a ram offered in place of Ishmael.

Yet all of the laborious exercise cannot give any guarantee of heaven. The Muslim believes that he will stand before Allah one day and that his works will be weighed accordingly. "Those whose balance (of good deeds) is heavy, they will be successful. But those whose balance is light, will be those who have lost their souls; in hell will they abide" (surah 23:101–102). Since salvation is based on his actions, a Muslim cannot know his fate until he is finished working, that is, when he is dead. Additionally, the underlying element of fatalism increases doubt since "Allah leads astray those whom He pleases and guides whom He pleases" (surah 14:4).[31] Ultimately, the more work that is required of someone to obtain heaven, the more hopeless heaven becomes.[32]

Hence, it is imperative that a Christian explain clearly the finished work of Christ on the cross and stand firmly on the exclusivity of the gospel of Christ (John 14:6; Acts 4:12). For someone who is wrapped up in the futility of a works-based salvation, the words of Christ on the cross, "It is finished!" (John 19:30), can be an oasis of hope and a balm of healing.

But Muslims have legitimate questions which must be answered including, How can another man die for me? And isn't salvation too easy in Christianity? These questions are intimately related to the atonement of Jesus Christ. On the one hand, Christians must point out the necessity of the atonement of Christ for forgiveness of sin (Heb 9:22). The cross of Christ reminds us of a God who is both loving and just. Both of these attributes are seen in that God sent His Son to pay the penalty of sin on our behalf (John 3:16). In Islam, Allah's justice is at best questionable since he allows those into heaven whose sins remain unpunished. Islamic justice is akin to a judge who

---

[31] In Bukhari's Hadith, we find that even Muhammad doubted his final destiny. He stated, "By Allah, though I am the Apostle of Allah, yet I do not know what Allah will do with me" (5.266).

[32] Consider this one fact: The pilgrimage to Mecca is required of all Muslims who can afford it (surah 3:97), yet less than 10 percent of all Muslims ever make the pilgrimage.

allows a murderer to go free by allowing other works to rectify the crime. Though perhaps a murderer, punishment does not seem necessary since he may have been a good father, a good husband, or just a good person. Additionally, although guilty of multiple heinous acts, the criminal is not merely given a pass but is rewarded with the greatest benefits the judge can bestow upon him. So is the case in Islam when the Muslim is given Paradise even though his life is weighed down with sin and guilt. Only in Christianity are all sins paid for—either by each individual at the judgment (Rev 20:11–15) or by Christ on the cross (Matt 26:46).

The latter question raised by Muslims is answered by recognizing the cruel death of Christ and the daily death of the believer to self. Salvation, so rich and free, is nonetheless costly to our Savior, who has transformed the Christian in order that we may be conformed to His image (Rom 12:1–2; Phil 2:5). Unfortunately, the idea of surrender to Christ is foreign to the vocabulary of many professing Christians and, thus, absent from their witness in front of an unbelieving world.

Due to a works-based salvation, two concepts elude the Muslim mind: unconditional love and eternal security. The Muslim believes that Allah loves him only if he is obedient (surah 2:190). Once again our answer lies within the atonement: "But God demonstrates His own love toward us, in that while we were still sinners, Christ died for us" (Rom 5:8). This unconditional love is based on the fatherhood of God, the relational portrait of a caring father who wishes only the best for His children. Like the wayward son in the Gospel of Luke (15:11–32), our Father promises that "all that I have is yours" (Luke 15:31) because of our relationship with Him, not because of our actions against Him. Indeed, He, our Father, promises, "I will never leave you nor forsake you" (Heb 13:5). Both God the Father and God the Son promise that no one can separate believers from their God (John 10:28–29). Believers in Jesus Christ, the Son of God, will never be orphans but, by the grace of God, will be glorified by God in due time (Rom 8:28–30).

Epistemology: Basing Our Beliefs on the Revelation of God

> Then He said to them, "O foolish ones, and slow of heart
> to believe in all that the prophets have spoken! Ought not
> the Christ to have suffered these things and to enter into His
> glory?" And beginning at Moses and all the Prophets, He ex-
> pounded to them in all the Scriptures the things concerning
> Himself.
>
> Luke 24:25–27 NKJV

Ultimately, the question of epistemology—how do you know what
you know?—comes down to a question of which source you trust. For
those considering Christianity or Islam, there are only three choices:
(1) The Bible is the Word of God; (2) the Qur'an is the Word of God;
or (3) neither is the Word of God.[33] To the Muslim the Qur'an is
the indestructible Word of God. The Qur'an itself states, "We have,
without doubt, sent down the Message; and We will assuredly guard it
(from corruption)" (surah 15:9). Although no miracles are attributed
to Muhammad in the Qur'an (surah 3:183) and the Qur'an itself does
not have predictive prophecy,[34] Muslims quickly assert that the Qur'an
itself is a miracle due to its beauty and unique style.[35] To the Muslim
the Qur'an is the dictated words of Allah given to Muhammad through
the angel Gabriel. On the other hand, orthodox Christians hold to the
plenary (full) verbal inspiration of the Bible; that is, the very words,
letters, and syllables are inspired (Matt 5:17–18), and it is entirely
without error in its contents (2 Tim 3:15–17). The Bible is not private
opinion or mere suggestion, "but holy men of God spoke as they were
moved by the Holy Spirit" (2 Pet 1:21 NKJV).

---

[33] For a popular account of a former Muslim who is a secularist, see Ibn Warraq, *Why I Am
Not a Muslim* (New York: Prometheus, 1995).

[34] Some Muslims take exception to the statement that there are no prophecies in the Qur'an,
specifically pointing to surah 30:2–4, the Roman victory over the Persians. Yet this passage
does not have anything essentially supernatural about it and is hardly a long-term prophecy of
any sort. See Norman L. Geisler and Abdul Saleeb, *The Crescent in Light of the Cross*, 2nd ed.
(Grand Rapids: Baker, 2002), 200–1.

[35] Many Muslim scholars, eager to attribute miracles and prophecies to the Qur'an, speak of
categories such as numeric miracles. For example, it is alleged that the word *day* is mentioned
365 times in the Qur'an and that the words *life* and *death* are each mentioned 145 times (see
the popular site www.islamicity.com for such attribution).

The two sacred texts are antithetical to each other on the essential points of each faith. One must come to the conclusion that either Jesus died on the cross (Matt 26; Mark 14) or He did not (surah 4:157–58). Either Jesus is God (John 1:1–18) and rewards those who deemed Him the Son of God (Matt 16:18), or He was created from dust (surah 3:47) and denounced any such attempt at deifying Him (surah 5:116). Either Jesus declared that He completed the work of salvation (John 19:30), or we must work for our salvation (surah 23:1–11). From creation to the fall, from the flood to the sacrifice of Abraham's son, from the prophets to the apostles, the Bible and the Qur'an significantly differ in their contents. Even one's belief of how to view the Bible is determined by which source is deemed reliable. Muhammad argued that the Qur'an superseded the Bible, asserting, "O people of the Book! There has come to you our Messenger, revealing to you much that you used to hide in the Book, and passing over much (that is now unnecessary): there has come to you from Allah a (new) light and a perspicuous Book" (surah 5:15).

According to Islam the Qur'an abrogates the Scripture and nullifies any of the contents and/or interpretations of the Bible which disagree with the Qur'an. Ironically, this area of revelation poses the greatest difficulty to Islam. Both Islam and Christianity purport not only the inspiration of their holy books but their preservation as well (surah 85:22; Matt 5:17–18). However, Islam denies the present inspiration of the Bible, believing the Bible has been distorted (by the Jews and Christians). Muslim scholars argue that the Torah (*Taurat*) and the Psalms of David (*Zabur*) were inspired by God and now are altered. Moreover, they believe that the gospel (*Injil*) was inspired by God and now is corrupted. Several questions must be broached: Was God not powerful enough to preserve His written Word? Was man powerful enough to corrupt that which God wrote? Perhaps, since God is all-powerful, did He cause His Word to be corrupted? Finally, why should believers trust that the Qur'an will be "guarded from corruption" when the Torah, Psalms of David, and gospel fell prey to man's distortion?

Christians must remember that our faith rises or falls on the foundation of our faith: the Lord Jesus Christ as revealed in the Scripture. Any other foundation will eventually crumble whether rationalism, experientialism, or otherwise. Whenever we base our faith on that which is subjective or contingent, we will utterly fail and, worse, elevate ourselves to deity. We must base our faith not in the limited knowledge within ourselves or the subjective faith outside ourselves but instead on the eternal promises of Him who is above us and gave us His Holy Word.

Part 5

POSTMODERNISM AND RELATIVISM

Chapter 14

THE CHALLENGES OF POSTMODERNISM

J. P. Moreland

An important and, sadly, often neglected component of Christian apologetics is the task of showing how Christian ideas enhance and do explanatory work across the academic disciplines and how rival worldviews harm and fail to do commensurate work in those same fields. And given that the various aspects of the image of God are recalcitrant facts for rival worldviews such as naturalism and post-modernism, one would expect that in those fields that examine that image, Christianity would enhance and its rivals would harm work and practice in these fields in particular. Nowhere is this more obvi-ous than in the field of psychology. In what follows I want to delimit some significant features of postmodernism relevant to the practice of therapy and counseling and show how these postmodern features wreak havoc in that practice.

For at least two reasons, the effective Christian counselor must keep in touch with the intellectual currents of the day. For one thing ideological trends have an impact on academic disciplines, and psy-chology and theology are no exceptions to this rule. For example, dur-ing the arid days of positivism in the first half of the twentieth century, philosophical behaviorism was all the rage. Apprised of those trends, one can be more discerning while reading in one's field. Further, ideo-logical trends contain ideas that shape the emotions, thoughts, and behaviors of patients; so counselors should be able to address those ideas as part of their therapeutic package. Currently, postmodernism is an intellectual trend that Christian counselors would do well to understand. With this in mind, I shall offer a summary of postmodern thought, followed by an analysis of four aspects of postmodernism especially relevant to the Christian counselor.

What Is Postmodernism?

Postmodernism is a loose coalition of diverse thinkers from several different academic disciplines, so it is difficult to characterize postmodernism in a way that would be fair to this diversity. Still it is possible to provide a fairly accurate characterization of postmodernism in general since its friends and foes understand it well enough to debate its strengths and weaknesses.[1]

Postmodernism is both a historical, chronological notion and a philosophical ideology. Understood historically, postmodernism refers to a period of thought that follows and is a reaction to the period called modernity. Modernity is the period of European thought that developed out of the Renaissance (1300–1550) and flourished in the Enlightenment (c. 1650–1800) in the ideas of people like Descartes, Locke, Berkeley, Hume, Leibniz, and Kant. In the chronological sense, postmodernism is sometimes called "post modernism." So understood, it is fair to say that postmodernism is often guilty of a simplistic characterization of modernity because the thinkers in that period were far from monolithic. Indeed, Descartes, Hume, and Kant have elements in their thought that are more at home in postmodernism than they are in the so-called modern era. Nevertheless, setting historical accuracy aside, the chronological notion of postmodernism depicts it as an era that began in and, in some sense, replaces modernity.

As a philosophical standpoint, postmodernism is primarily a reinterpretation of what knowledge is and what counts as knowledge. More broadly, it represents a form of cultural relativism about such things as reality, truth, reason, value, linguistic meaning, the self, and other

[1] For a helpful introduction to postmodernism, see Joseph Natoli, *A Primer to Postmodernity* (Oxford: Blackwell, 1997).

notions. On a postmodernist view there is no such thing as objective reality, truth, value, reason, and so forth. All these are social constructions, creations of linguistic practices and, as such, are relative not to individuals but to social groups that share a narrative. Roughly, a narrative is a perspective such as Marxism, atheism, or Christianity that is embedded in the group's social and linguistic practices. Important postmodern thinkers are Friedrich Nietzsche, Ludwig Wittgenstein, Jacques Derrida, Thomas Kuhn, Michel Foucault, Martin Heidegger, and Jean-François Lyotard.

My purpose in this essay is to tease out implications of postmodernism relevant to Christian counselors; it is not to provide a philosophical critique of it. Still, I cannot resist offering one criticism. Put simply, postmodernism is self-refuting. Postmodernists appear to claim that their own assertions about the modern era, about how language and consciousness work, and so forth are true and rational; and they write literary texts and protest when people misinterpret the authorial intent in their own writings. In these and other ways postmodernism seems to be self-refuting.

Sometimes postmodernists respond by denying that they take their own assertions and writing to be true, rational, constituted by their own authorial intent, and so forth. If these claims are correct, then they would, indeed, save postmodernism from self-refutation. But this response must be rejected. When one actually reads carefully postmodernist writings, it is hard to avoid the impression that they do, indeed, present themselves as true, rational, and so on. In this sense, though on the defensive, postmodernists may deny that their writings exhibit these features; nevertheless an examination of those writings seems to undermine those denials.

How Does Postmodernism Impact Counseling?

At least four implications of postmodernism strike at the core of Christian counseling. The first two follow from the fact that, according to postmodernism, the self is a social construction, a creation of language, an objectification of the first-person pronoun I; and, as such, the self is a culturally relative, historically conditioned construct. As Philip Cushman asserts, "There is no universal, transhistorical self, only local selves; no universal theory about the self, only local theories."[2]

Two things follow from this. First, there is no unity to the self and no enduring ego.[3] Rather the self is a bundle of social roles and relations that are expressions of the arbitrary flux of the group. This has disastrous implications for helping people separate and individuate in any objective sense. If postmodernism is true, all that can happen is for a patient to disown one arbitrary, socially constructed self while standing in another one. One wonders if such a trip is worth the effort. Further, on this view there is no point in taking personal responsibility for one's pathologies since it is always open to a patient simply to distance from an arbitrary, fleeting constructed self in which the pathology is embedded.

Second, as postmodern critic Terry Eagleton points out, since the self is a passive social construction, "there are no subjects sufficiently coherent to undertake . . . actions."[4] Active agency and free action disappear under the postmodern cloud of constructivism. Thus, postmodern thought is on a collision course with important developments in psychological theory during the last ten years which have emphasized the self as an active, free agent. Moreover, as Immanuel Kant wisely noted, the goal of the moral life and, presumably, of therapy, is the production of a good will, of a person who freely and rationally chooses to live a virtuous life that honors the moral law. If this goal is removed from therapy, as it must be for postmodernists, it becomes opaque as to just exactly what therapists, especially Christian therapists, are trying to accomplish.

Third, postmodernism leads to the institutionalization of anger. Postmodernists are preoccupied with power struggles that surround

---

[2] Philip Cushman, "Why the Self Is Empty: Toward a Historically Situated Psychology," *American Psychologist* 45 (1990): 599.
[3] For more on the self and the soul, see J. P. Moreland and Scott Rae, *Body and Soul* (Downers Grove, Ill.: InterVarsity, 2000); J. P. Moreland, "Restoring the Substance to the Soul of Psychology," *Journal of Psychology and Theology* 26 (1998): 29–43.
[4] Terry Eagleton, *The Illusions of Postmodernism* (Oxford: Blackwell, 1996), 27–28.

language use and social practice, and they see themselves as part of a missionary movement to liberate powerless, oppressed victims from dominance. They often practice a "hermeneutics of suspicion" in which they interpret body language, speech, and written communication not in terms of the communicators' own intentions but in terms of their attempt to victimize and dominate "the other" as understood according to the postmodernists' interpretive agenda (e.g., feminism, gay rights, and so forth). To be sure, power issues are a legitimate aspect of language, though one hardly needs postmodernism to see this. But by making power struggles and victimization a central focus of the postmodern crusade, the movement dignifies anger by institutionalizing it and placing it on ideological high ground, and it creates anger by fostering relational suspicion according to which there is a victimizer under every linguistic tree. America is a country of angry people, and postmodernism is to be blamed for its share in creating this situation.

Finally, with its relativization of truth, postmodernism has contributed to the absolutization of desire satisfaction. With truth dethroned as a guide for life, something had to take its place. And the heir to the throne is the absolute importance of satisfying one's desire. Postmodernism helps to prop up this value in the culture by its denial of truth and reason, along with its promulgation of a naive and destructive notion of tolerance. Christian therapists know that some beliefs and behaviors—for example, child molestation—should not be tolerated, and they also know that a healthy person is one who can cultivate good desires and control bad ones. Ironically, due to the implications of postmodern ideology, a movement that seeks to liberate victims actually creates the conditions under which that liberation is impossible. And that should be a matter of concern for us all.

The Christian worldview, with its emphasis on the existence of truth and goodness and on the reality of personal identity and responsibility, helps us address problems discussed in psychology. The Christian faith furnishes us with a wide range of answers and resources that are lacking within a postmodern framework. And this fact is an indication of Christianity's convincingness, integrity, and intellectual plausibility over against its competitors, including postmodernism.

Chapter 15

IS MORALITY RELATIVE?*

Francis J. Beckwith

I have participated in a number of public discussions on the question of abortion. Inevitably, either my opponent or a member of the audience will make the assertion, "Don't like abortion? Don't have one," followed by rousing applause by like-minded audience members. This assertion, though common, reveals not only a deep misunderstanding about the nature of the abortion debate but also a confusion about what it means to say that something is morally wrong.

The culprit, I believe, is moral relativism—the view that when it comes to questions of morality, there is no absolute or objective right and wrong; moral rules are merely personal preferences and/or the result of one's cultural, sexual, or ethnic orientation. So choosing an abortion—like choosing an automobile, a vacation spot, or dessert—is merely a matter of preference. Some people like Häagen Daz; others like abortion—to each his own. Just as it is wrong for one to judge another's taste in ice cream, it is wrong for one to judge another's reproductive choices and to ask for the law to reflect that judgment.

* This chapter is adapted from "Why I Am Not a Relativist," which appeared in *Why I Am a Christian*, ed. Norman L. Geisler and Paul Hoffman (Grand Rapids, Mich.: Baker, 2001). Chapter 2 of my book, *Defending Life: A Moral and Legal Case against Abortion Choice* (New York: Cambridge University Press, 2007) is also adapted from the 2001 piece but differs little from this present chapter, which I tinkered with in small ways to fit in with the editors' purpose.

Many people, however, see relativism as necessary for promoting tolerance, nonjudgmentalism, and inclusiveness; for they think if one believes one's moral position is correct and others' incorrect one is closed minded and intolerant. I will argue in this chapter that not only do the arguments for relativism fail but also that relativism itself cannot live up to its own reputation; for it is promoted by its proponents as the only correct view on morality and thus entails intolerance (rightly understood), judgmentalism, and exclusiveness.

Christianity teaches that objective moral norms apply to all persons in all places in all times. Relativism says that there are no such norms. If relativism is incorrect, Christianity cannot be dismissed on the grounds that it affirms objective moral norms. Thus, a critique of relativism plays an important role in supporting the Christian faith.

Moral Relativism and Moral Discourse[1]

Moral relativism has stunted the ability of many to grasp the nature of moral claims. Some people in our culture often confuse *preference claims* with *moral claims* or reduce the latter to the former. To understand what I mean by this, consider two statements:[2]

1. I like vanilla ice cream.
2. Killing people without justification is wrong.

The first statement is a preference claim since it is a description of a person's subjective taste. It is not a *normative* claim. It is not a claim about what one ought or ought not to do. It is not saying, "Since I like vanilla ice cream, the government ought to coerce you to eat it as well," or, "Everyone in the world ought to like vanilla ice cream, too." A claim of subjective preference tells us nothing about what one *ought to* think or do. For example, if someone were to say, "I like to torture

---

[1] The ideas and argument of this section have been significantly shaped by Hadley Arkes, *First Things: An Inquiry into the First Principles of Morals and Justice* (Princeton, N.J.: Princeton University Press, 1986), 20–22.

[2] Arkes's work (ibid.) was instrumental in helping me to understand better the differences between the two statements.

children for fun," this would tell us nothing about whether it is wrong or right to torture children for fun.

The second claim, however, is different. It has little if anything to do with what one likes or dislikes. In fact, one may *prefer* to kill another person without justification and still know that it is morally wrong to do so. This statement is a *moral claim*. It is not a descriptive claim, for it does not tell us what, why, or how things are, or how a majority of people in fact behave and/or think. Nor is it a preference claim, for it does not tell us what anyone's subjective preference may be or how one prefers to behave and/or think. Rather, it is a claim about what persons *ought to do*, which may be contrary to how persons in fact behave and/or how they prefer to behave.

Unfortunately, the espousal of moral relativism has made it difficult for many people in our culture to distinguish between preference claims and moral claims. Rather than pondering and struggling with arguments for and against a particular moral perspective, people sometimes reduce the disagreement to a question of "personal preference" or "subjective opinion." For example, some who defend the abortion-choice position sometimes tell pro-lifers: "Don't like abortion? Then don't have one." This instruction reduces the abortion debate to a preference claim. That is, the objective moral rightness or wrongness of abortion (i.e., whether it involves the unjustified killing of a being who is fully human) is declared without argument not to be relevant. But this is clearly a mistake, for those who oppose abortion do so because they believe that the unborn during most if not all of a woman's pregnancy is a full-fledged member of the human community and that it is *prima facie* wrong, both objectively and universally, to kill such a being. For this reason, when the pro-lifer hears the abortion-choice advocate tell her that if she doesn't like abortion, she doesn't have to have one, it sounds to her as if the abortion-choicer advocate is saying, "Don't like murder? Then don't kill any innocent persons."

Understandably, the pro-lifer, committed to objective moral norms, finds such rhetoric perplexing as well as unpersuasive. Of course, many sophisticated abortion-choice advocates are opponents of moral relativism as well.[3] But it just seems that in the popular debate abortion-choice advocates tend to reduce the issue of abortion to a matter of preference and thus seem to have been more affected by moral relativism than have their opponents. (But they are *not completely* affected, for they do appeal to "fundamental rights" which are typically grounded in some objective morality.)[4] The pro-lifer's arguments may be flawed, but the abortion-choice advocate does not critique those flawed arguments when he mistakenly turns a serious moral disagreement into a debate over preferences.

Arguments for Moral Relativism

Two arguments are often used to defend moral relativism. The first is the argument from cultural and individual differences, and the second is the argument from tolerance.

1. *Argument from Cultural and Individual Differences.* In this argument the relativist concludes that there are no objective moral norms because cultures and individuals disagree on moral issues. In order to defend this premise, the relativist typically cites a number of examples such as cross-cultural and intracultural differences over the morality of sexual practices, abortion, war, and capital punishment. In the words of Hadley Arkes, an opponent of moral relativism, "In one society, a widow is burned on the funeral pyre of her husband; in another, she is burned on the beach in Miami. In one society, people complain to the chef about the roast beef; in another, they send back the roast beef and eat the chef."[5] There are at least five problems with this argument.

First, relativism does not follow from disagreement. The fact that people disagree about something does not mean that there is no truth of the matter. For example, if you and I were to disagree on the question of whether the earth is round, our disagreement would certainly not

---

[3] See, for example, David Boonin, *In Defense of Abortion* (New York: Cambridge University Press, 2003), 13–14.

[4] For an assessment of the apparent incoherence of this position, see Hadley Arkes, *Natural Rights and the Right to Choose* (New York: Cambridge University Press, 2002).

[5] Arkes, *First Things*, 149.

be proof that the earth has *no* shape. The fact that a skinhead (a type of young neo-Nazi) and I may disagree on the question of whether we should treat people equally and with fairness is certainly not sufficient reason to conclude that equality and fairness are not objective moral truths. Even if individuals and cultures hold no values in common, it does not follow from this that nobody is right or wrong about what is moral truth. That is, there could be a mistaken individual or culture, such as Adolf Hitler and Nazi Germany.

If the mere fact of disagreement were sufficient to conclude that objective norms do not exist, then we would have to believe that there is no objectively correct position on such issues as slavery, genocide, and child molestation; for the slave owner, genocidal maniac, and pedophile have an opinion that differs from the one held by those of us who condemn their actions. In the end, moral disagreement proves nothing.

Second, disagreement counts against relativism. Suppose, however, that the relativist, despite the logical failure of his case, sticks to his guns and maintains that disagreement over objective norms proves the correctness of relativism. But this will not work. For the relativist has set down a principle—disagreement means there is no truth—that unravels his own case. After all, some of us believe that relativism is a mistaken view. We, in other words, *disagree* with the relativist over the nature of morality. We believe that objective moral norms exist whereas the relativist does not. But, according to the relativist's own principle—disagreement means there is no truth—he ought to abandon his opinion that relativism is the correct position. And to make matters worse for the relativist, his principle is a proposition for which there is no universal agreement and thus on its own grounds must be rejected. As Arkes points out, "My disagreement establishes that the proposition [i.e., disagreement means there is no truth] does not enjoy a universal assent, and by the very terms of the proposition, that should be quite sufficient to determine *its own invalidity*."[6]

Third, disagreement is overrated. Although people and cultures disagree on moral issues, it does not follow from this that they do not

[6] Ibid., 132.

share the same principles or that there are not moral norms binding on all nations in all times and in all places. Take for example the Salem witch trials. In 1692, in the colony of Massachusetts, nearly three dozen citizens (mostly women) were put to death as punishment for allegedly practicing witchcraft.[7] We do not execute witches today but not because our moral principles have changed. Rather, the reason we don't execute witches is because we do not believe, as some of the seventeenth-century residents of Salem did, that the practice of witchcraft has a fatal effect on the community. Even if one believes, as I do, that the trials and executions of these alleged witches were travesties of justice, based on flimsy evidence and trumped-up charges fueled by hysteria,[8] the principle to which the trials' apologists appealed seems *prima facie* correct: communities and their leaders should support and enforce policies that advance the public good. After all, suppose we had good evidence that the practice of witchcraft did affect people in the same way second-hand cigarette smoke affects the nonsmoker. We would alter practices to take this into consideration. We might set up nonwitch sections in restaurants and ban the casting of spells on interstate airplane flights. The upshot of all this is that advancing the public good is a principle of just government that we share with the seventeenth-century residents of Salem but we have good reason to believe they were factually wrong about the effect of witchcraft on the achievement of that good and/or that religious liberty better advances the public good than does religious coercion (even if one may have good reason to believe that the practice of witchcraft is in fact not good).[9]

---

[7] See Tim Sutter, "Salem Witchcraft: The Events and Causes of the Salem Witch Trials" (2003), *The Salem Witch Trials* (Web site) at http://www.salemwitchtrials.com/salemwitchcraft.html (12 July 2006).

[8] Ibid.

[9] I say the latter because it seems to me that if certain religious traditions may have rational warrant, it would not be irrational for believers in those traditions legitimately to judge certain practices (e.g., witchcraft) as evil without criminalizing the practice. For some interesting arguments on the rationality of certain religious traditions, see Alvin Plantinga, *Warranted Christian Belief* (New York: Oxford University Press, 2003); and Francis J. Beckwith, William Lane Craig, and J. P. Moreland, eds., *To Everyone an Answer: A Case for the Christian Worldview* (Downers Grove, Ill.: InterVarsity, 2004).

Consider again the issue of abortion. The conventional wisdom is that the moral and legal debate over abortion is a dispute between two factions that hold incommensurable value systems. But the conventional wisdom is mistaken, for these factions hold many moral principles in common.

a. Each side believes that all human persons possess certain rights regardless of whether their governments protect these rights. That is why both sides appeal to what each believes is a fundamental right. The pro-life advocate appeals to "life" whereas the abortion-choice advocate appeals to "liberty" (or "choice"). Both believe that a constitutional regime, in order to be just, must uphold fundamental rights.

b. Each side believes that its position best exemplifies its opponent's fundamental value. The abortion-choice advocate does not deny that "life" is a value but argues that his position's appeal to human liberty is a necessary ingredient by which an individual can pursue the fullest and most complete life possible.

On the other hand, the pro-life advocate does not eschew "liberty." She believes that all human liberty is at least limited by another human person's right to life. For example, one has a right to pursue freely any goal one believes is consistent with one's happiness, such as attending a Los Angeles Lakers basketball game. One has, however, no right to pursue freely this goal at the expense of another's life or liberty, such as running over pedestrians with one's car so that one can get to the game on time. And, of course, the pro-life advocate argues that the unborn are persons with a full right to life. And because the act of abortion typically results in the death of the unborn, abortion, with few exceptions, is not morally justified and for that reason ought to be made illegal.

Abortion-choice advocates do not deny that human persons have a right to life. They just believe that this right to life is not extended to the unborn because they are not full members of the human community and/or they are not entitled to use the mother's body against her will. Pro-lifers, on the other hand, do not deny that people have the liberty to make choices they believe are in their best interests. They just believe that this liberty does not entail the right to choose abortion; for such a choice conflicts with the life, liberty, and interests of another human being (the fetus), who is defenseless, weak, and vulnerable and has a natural claim upon his parents' care, both pre- and postnatally. Thus, when all is said and done, the debate over abortion is not really about conflicting moral systems. After all, imagine that a pro-life politician were to say the following in a campaign speech: "My party's platform affirms a woman's right to terminate her pregnancy if and only if it does not result in the death of her unborn child." Disagreement over such a plank would not be over the morality of killing human persons; it would be over the metaphysical question of whether the unborn human is included in that category.

Fourth, absurd consequences follow from moral relativism.

a. If there are no objective moral norms that apply to all persons in all times and in all places, then certain moral judgments, such as the following, cannot be universally true: Mother Teresa was morally better than Adolf Hitler; rape is always wrong; and it is wrong to torture babies for fun. But to deny that these judgments are not universally true seems absurd. For there seem to be some moral judgments that are absolutely correct regardless of what cultures or individuals may think.

b. If the relativist claims that morality is relative to the individual, what happens when individual moralities conflict? For example, suppose Jeffrey Dahmer's morality permits him to cannibalize his neighbor, but his neighbor disagrees. What would the relativist suggest be done in this case, since, according to this form of relativism, nobody's morality is in principle superior to any other? In addition, if the moral life is no more than a reflection of people's individual tastes, preferences, and orientations, then we cannot tell young people that it is morally wrong to lie, steal, cheat, smoke, abuse drugs, kill their newborns, and drop out of school even though these behaviors may be consistent with the students' own personal tastes, preferences, and/or orientations.

c. Even if the relativist were to make the more modest claim that morality is not relative to the individual but to the individual's culture, that one is only obligated to follow the dictates of one's society, other problems follow.

In the first place the cultural relativist's position is self-refuting. A claim is self-refuting when it is inconsistent with itself. For example, if I were to say, "I cannot communicate," that would be self-refuting since I would in fact be communicating to you the claim that I cannot communicate.

How is cultural relativism self-refuting? The supporter of cultural relativism maintains that there are no objective and universal moral norms and for that reason all individuals ought to follow the moral norms of their own culture. But the cultural relativist is making an absolute and universal moral claim—namely, that individuals are morally obligated to follow the moral norms of their own culture. So, if this moral norm is absolute and universal, then cultural relativism is false. But if this moral norm is neither absolute nor universal, then cultural relativism is still false; for in that case I would not have a moral obligation to follow the moral norms of my culture.

In the second place, because each of us belongs to a number of different "societies" or "cultures," which one of them should be followed when they conflict? For example, suppose a woman named Carla is a resident of a liberal upscale neighborhood in Hollywood, California, attends a Christian church, and is a partner in a prestigious law firm. In her neighborhood, having an adulterous affair is considered "enlightened," and those who do not pursue such unions are considered repressed prudes. At her church, however, adultery is condemned as sinful while at her law firm adultery is neither encouraged nor discouraged. Suppose further that Carla chooses to commit adultery in the firm's back office with a fellow churchgoer, Winston, who resides in a conservative neighborhood in which adultery is condemned. The office, it turns out, is adjacent to the church as well as precisely halfway between Carla's neighborhood and Winston's neighborhood. It is not clear which society is morally relevant.[10]

---

[10] J. P. Moreland offers a similar illustration in J. P. Moreland, *Scaling the Secular City* (Grand Rapids: Baker, 1987), 92.

In the third place, there can be no moral progress or moral reformers. If morality is reducible to culture, then there can be no real
moral progress. The only way one can say that a culture is *getting better*, or progressing, is if there are objective moral norms that are not
dependent on culture to which a society may draw closer. But if what
is morally good is merely what one's culture says is morally good,
then we can only say that cultural norms change, not that the society
is progressing or getting better. Yet, it seems, for example, that the
abolition of slavery and the establishment of civil rights of African-
Americans in the United States were instances of moral progress. In
addition, those that led these movements, the moral reformers such as
William Wilberforce, Harriet Beecher Stowe, and Martin Luther King
Jr., could not have been morally correct if cultural relativism is true.
As J. P. Moreland notes:

> Moral reformers, by definition, *change* a society's code by
> arguing that it is somehow morally inadequate. But if [cul-
> tural] relativism is true, an act is right if and only if it is in
> society's code; so the reformer is by definition immoral (since
> he adopts a set of values outside the society's code and at-
> tempts to change that code in keeping with these values). . . .
> Any moral view which implies that is surely false.[11]

Thus, in order to remain consistent, the cultural relativist must deny
that there can be any real moral progress or any real moral reformers.
For such judgments presuppose the existence of real, objective, moral
norms.

    2. *The Argument from Tolerance.* Many people see relativism as nec-
essary for promoting tolerance, nonjudgmentalism, and inclusiveness;
for they think if you believe your moral position is correct and others'
incorrect, you are closed minded and intolerant. They usually base
this premise on the well-known differences of opinion on morality
between cultures and individuals. So the moral relativist embraces the
view that one should not judge other cultures and individuals, for to
do so would be intolerant. There are at least three problems with this

---

[11] Ibid., 243.

argument, all of which maintain that tolerance (rightly understood) and relativism are actually *incompatible* with each other.

First, tolerance supports objective morality, not relativism. If everyone ought to be tolerant, then tolerance is an objective moral norm. And therefore, moral relativism is false. So, ironically, the call to tolerance by relativists presupposes the existence of at least one nonrelative, universal, and objective norm: tolerance. Also, tolerance presupposes that there is something good about being tolerant, such as being able to learn from others with whom one disagrees or to impart knowledge and wisdom to that person. But that presupposes objective moral values—namely, that knowledge and wisdom are good things. Moreover, tolerance presupposes that someone may be correct about his or her moral perspective. That is to say, it seems that part of the motivation for advocating tolerance is to encourage people to be open to the possibility that one may be able to gain truth and insight (including moral truth and insight) from another who may possess it. If that is the case, then there are objective moral truths that one can learn.

In addition, tolerance presupposes a moral judgment of another's viewpoint. That is to say, I can only be tolerant of those ideas that I think are mistaken. I am not tolerant of that with which I agree; I embrace it. And I am not tolerant of that for which I have no interest (e.g., European professional soccer); I merely have benign neglect for it. (That is, I don't care one way or another.) Consider the following example. Suppose I tell a friend that I believe that homosexuality is immoral. And suppose my friend requests that I be tolerant toward homosexuals in my community. If I accept this advice and choose to be civil, respectful, and gracious to gay men and women with whom I have contact, while at the same time judging their sexual practices as immoral, it seems that I would be truly tolerant. But suppose someone says that my judging of homosexuality as immoral still makes me "intolerant." At that point, given my understanding of "tolerance," I have no idea what I am supposed to do. For if I change my view of homosexuality and say either that it is not immoral or that I have no opinion (i.e., I have benign neglect), then I cannot be tolerant; for I can only be tolerant of that which I believe is wrong or mistaken. On the other hand, if judging another's position as wrong or mistaken makes one intolerant, then the person who judges my negative assessment of homosexuality is, by that person's own definition, intolerant. But that is absurd. For if *tolerance* means that one ought not to judge a view as morally wrong, then it seems to be consistent with either embracing the view or having benign neglect for it. If that is the case, then tolerance has lost its meaning and is simply a cover for trying to shame and coerce others not to disagree publicly (and/or perhaps privately) with one's controversial and disputed position on human sexuality. This, ironically, is an example of intolerance (as traditionally understood). So it seems to me that the appeal to tolerance, once we have a clear understanding of its meaning, is *inconsistent* with relativism.

Second, relativism is itself a closed-minded and intolerant position. After all, the relativist dogmatically asserts that there is no moral truth. To illustrate this, consider a dialogue (based loosely on a real-life exchange) between a high-school teacher and her student Elizabeth.[12] The teacher instructs her class, "Welcome, students. This is the first day of class, and so I want to lay down some ground rules. First, since no one has the truth about morality, you should be open minded to the opinions of your fellow students."

The teacher recognizes the raised hand of Elizabeth, who asks, "If nobody has the truth, isn't that a good reason for me not to listen to my fellow students? After all, if nobody has the truth, why should I waste my time listening to other people and their opinions? What's the point? Only if somebody has the truth does it make sense to be open-minded. Don't you agree?"

"No, I don't. Are you claiming to know the truth? Isn't that a bit arrogant and dogmatic?"

"Not at all. Rather I think it's dogmatic, as well as arrogant, to assert that no single person on Earth knows the truth. After all, have you met every person in the world and quizzed them exhaustively? If not, how can you make such a claim? Also, I believe it is actually the opposite of arrogance to say that I will alter my opinions to fit the truth

---

[12] This dialogue is presented in slightly different form in Francis J. Beckwith and Gregory P. Koukl, *Relativism: Feet Firmly Planted in Mid-Air* (Grand Rapids: Baker, 1998), 74.

whenever and wherever I find it. And if I happen to think that I have good reason to believe I do know the truth and would like to share it with you, why wouldn't you listen to me? Why would you automatically discredit my opinion before it is even uttered? I thought we were supposed to listen to everyone's opinion."

"This should prove to be an interesting semester."

Another student blurts out, "Ain't that the truth," provoking the class to laughter.

Third, relativism is judgmental, exclusivist, and partisan. This may seem like an odd thing to say since the relativist would like you to think his viewpoint is nonjudgmental, inclusivist, and neutral when it comes to moral beliefs. But consider the following: (a) The relativist says that if you believe in objective moral truth, you are *wrong*. Hence, relativism is judgmental. (b) It follows from this that relativism is *excluding* your beliefs from the realm of legitimate options. Thus, relativism is exclusivist. And (c) because relativism is exclusivist, all nonrelativists are automatically not members of the "correct thinking" party. So relativism is partisan.

Tolerance only makes sense within the framework of a moral order, for it is within such a framework that one can morally justify tolerating some things while not tolerating others. For tolerance without a moral framework, or absolute tolerance, leads to a dogmatic relativism and thus to an intolerance of any viewpoint that does not embrace relativism. It is no wonder that in such a climate of "tolerance" any person who maintains that there is an objective moral order to which society ought to subscribe is greeted with contempt.

Reasoning about Moral Matters

Morality is clearly more than mere reasoning just as architecture is more than mere mathematics. One can immediately grasp as well as appreciate the moral virtue of Mother Teresa or the monumental elegance of the Eiffel Tower without having studied Thomas Reid's moral philosophy or mastered geometry and calculus. Nevertheless, just as one cannot build the Eiffel Tower without mastering certain mathematical disciplines, one cannot attribute the label *just* or *right* to one's point of view without offering justification for its rightness.

The logic of moral reasoning has been part and parcel of our discourse for as long as human beings have occupied the earth. It has stirred souls, shamed sinners, moved nations, energized social movements, and provided for us a potent grammar in numerous areas of private and public life. Consider just one example, though numerous others could be conscripted for our purposes.

In his failed 1858 bid for a U.S. Senate seat from Illinois, Abraham Lincoln engaged in a series of public debates with his Democratic opponent, Stephen A. Douglas. Among the many topics on which they disputed was the question of whether U.S. territories should be allowed by the federal government to permit slavery if they so chose. Douglas maintained that although he believed slavery was wrong (i.e., he personally opposed it), he was not willing to require that the federal government eliminate slavery; for to do so would be to violate the principle of popular sovereignty (i.e., that local majorities should be permitted to vote on such issues free of any and all federal constraints).[13] But, as Lincoln aptly pointed out:

> When Judge Douglas says he "don't care whether slavery is voted up or down," . . . he cannot thus argue logically if he sees anything wrong in it. . . . He cannot say that he would as soon see a wrong voted up as voted down. When Judge Douglas says that whoever, or whatever community, wants slaves, they have a right to have them, he is perfectly logical if there is nothing wrong in the institution; but if you admit that it is wrong, he cannot logically say that anybody has a right to do a wrong.[14]

Lincoln, a practical man with uncommon wisdom, grasped an important conceptual truth not often apprehended by those, such as Douglas, who inadvertently stumble into the arena of moral reasoning and think they are somewhere else: to claim that something is a wrong

---

[13] Arkes, *First Things*, 24.
[14] *The Collected Works of Abraham Lincoln*, ed. Roy P. Basler (New Brunswick, N.J.: Rutgers University Press, 1953), 3: 256–57, as quoted in Arkes, *First Things*, 24.

is to claim that it is impermissible, but it would inexorably follow from that truth that one cannot claim one has a *right* to perform the wrong, for that would mean the impermissible is permissible.[15] Or, as Arkes puts it: "Once we come to the recognition that any act stands in the class of a wrong . . . the logic of that recognition forbids us from treating that act any longer as a matter merely of personal taste or private choice."[16]

In notes he had prepared for himself, Lincoln provided another example of principled moral reasoning in assessing the sorts of arguments that his contemporaries put forth to defend the enslavement of black people by white people:

> You say A. is white and B. is black. It is *color*, then: the lighter having the right to enslave the darker? Take care. By this rule, you are to be a slave to the first man you meet, with a fairer skin than your own.
>
> You do not mean *color* exactly?—You mean the whites are *intellectually* the superiors of the blacks, and therefore, have the right to enslave them? Take care again. By this rule, you are to be a slave to the first man you meet, with an intellect superior to your own.
>
> But, say you, it is a question of interest; and, if you can make it your *interest*, you have the right to enslave another. Very well. And if he can make it his interest, he has the right to enslave you.[17]

Lincoln was making the point that if one were to apply the arguments for slavery to the prospective and current slave owners, whites, then one has put in place premises that may be employed by the government to undermine the rights of all human beings under its authority.[18] For the premises of the pro-slavery arguments contain propositions that appeal to degreed properties that carry no moral

---

[15] Arkes, *First Things*, 24–25.
[16] Ibid., 25.
[17] *The Collected Works of Abraham Lincoln*, 2:222, as quoted in Arkes, *First Things*, 43–44 (emphasis in original).
[18] Arkes, *First Things*, 43.

weight—color, intellect, and interest—when it comes to the question of human equality. Lincoln's assessment of these arguments is an impressive example of moral reasoning.

Conclusion

Moral relativism is a philosophical failure. The two main arguments for moral relativism—the argument from disagreement and the argument from tolerance—are seriously flawed in numerous ways. Given the failure of moral relativism, it seems reasonable to believe in objective morality. Moreover, there is a logic of moral reasoning that has been employed by numerous people throughout the ages for the purpose of providing for their fellow citizens moral clarity and/or moral justification.

Chapter 16

REFLECTIONS ON MCLAREN AND THE EMERGING CHURCH

R. Scott Smith

A significant topic that is capturing the attention of Christians is the emerging church (hereafter, EC). Many senior pastors, parents, and other laypeople have heard about it, or at least of some of the leading authors in the field, such as Brian McLaren. Often, however, I have found that people in these groups know little about the topic, or what McLaren and others actually are saying. But they are concerned, usually because they have heard that in some way or other, EC ideas draw upon postmodernism. On the other hand, many youth workers have been exposed to and influenced by EC ideas, such as through the influence of Youth Specialties or the writings of McLaren, Tony Jones (the national coordinator for Emergent U.S.), and others, whether in books or on Internet blogs.

I wrote *Truth and the New Kind of Christian: The Emerging Effects of Postmodernism in the Church* (Crossway, 2005) for a lay audience on the EC and Christian postmodernism. As a result, I have had several interesting opportunities and experiences. For instance, when I was speaking at my own church about McLaren's views, a friend came up afterwards to talk. He was about fifty years old, a former elder who also had served on staff with me at a major Christian organization. When he read *A New Kind of Christian*, he felt like McLaren put his finger on the reasons for some of the painful experiences my friend

had encountered in conservative, evangelical churches and that organization.[1] I don't think my friend is alone; I too have had some similar
experiences, and I think many others have also. McLaren resonates
with people at a key level in terms of the problems with the contemporary, American evangelical church, which he thinks are due to the
influences of modernity.

Since the book was released, I have had much more interaction
with Jones, various bloggers (some of whom are academics) who are
both for and against the EC, and even McLaren himself. Those conversations have been worthwhile and insightful as they have allowed
me opportunities to interact with and influence those who are part of
the EC, hear their responses and criticisms of my works, and better
understand their perspectives. Some of these criticisms have prompted
my need to reply in a more public way.

Thus, I will summarize my findings from my *Truth* book to give
an introduction to the subject of the EC in terms of its strengths but
also its weaknesses. Next, I will give an update of the conversations
about that book by sketching McLaren's main replies, to which I will
respond. Last, I will survey and reply to the significant criticism of my
ideas offered by James K. A. Smith (or simply "Jamie"), a philosopher
at Calvin College, which, if correct, would rebut my main concern in
Truth about the EC.

McLaren and the Emerging Church:
A Concise Summary of *Truth*

McLaren was an evangelical pastor, but he encountered various
expectations and situations that made him feel like giving up the
pastorate. He expected that he had to have "bombproof" answers to
peoples' questions, but some issues seem to defy such certainty. He
also believed that the gospel and the Christian life could be reduced to
simple laws, yet he found that few things in life could be that simple.
Moreover, he observed that far too many Christians were arrogant and
inauthentic instead of living as humble servants of Jesus.

---

[1] Brian McLaren, *A New Kind of Christian* (San Francisco: Jossey-Bass, 2001).

McLaren's expectations were formed by a particular conception, or framework. When these challenges arose, they helped precipitate a crisis which seemingly could not be answered adequately by that framework. To be a Christian in that same way would perpetuate this crisis. But he also resonated with some peoples' suggestions about changes at work in the Industrial Age and that our Industrial Age faith would change too. Moreover, he met some people who modeled what a "new kind" of Christian might look like.

In *A New Kind of Christian*, McLaren takes up these and other topics through two fictional characters, Dan Poole, an evangelical pastor in a crisis like McLaren's, and Neo Edward Oliver ("Neo"), the only person with whom Dan can confide. To Dan's surprise, Neo can identify with and even help explain the causes of Dan's experiences. Neo helps identify the source of Dan's crisis with his modern expectations of how the Christian life should be lived, but those expectations and mind-set do not fit in a changing, increasingly postmodern culture. Neo advises Dan to find a "new way" of being a Christian in postmodern times.

What are some of the traits of the modern period, and how has it influenced both the broader culture as well as the church? Instead of providing a philosophical analysis, McLaren tends to focus on more sociological factors that have impacted both. This tends to make his characterization and assessment of modernity highly thought-provoking.

First, McLaren says modernity (roughly mid-1500s to mid-to-late 1900s) has fostered a desire to conquer and control, for instance, through colonization, imperialism, and especially by trying to master our world through science and technology. But this desire has impacted the church, too, when it has tried to exert control by getting a particular political agenda passed into law. Evangelistic "crusades" also imply the idea of a military conquest. Moreover, Christians tend to view evangelism as encounters to convert the person by winning an argument, as though rational acceptance of the truths as presented is all that the person needs to become a follower of Jesus. But in that way we often fail to value a genuine friendship with people. In short, McLaren thinks that methodology is *coercive*.

Second, the modern era is marked by a quest for certainty and absolute knowledge. For instance, philosophers attempted to find indubitable, universal foundations of knowledge. This "Cartesian foundationalism" has impacted Christians to believe they must have utter certainty in their Christian beliefs, without room for doubts, which must result from their lack of faith. Requiring certainty fosters a third trait, that we become critical and must debunk anyone who disagrees with us. Similarly, Christians often feel they have to prove anyone wrong who disagrees with them, which results in a defensive apologetic. In that process their faith tends to be treated as a rigid belief system that must be accepted instead of a unique, joyful way of living, loving, and serving.[2]

Third, McLaren thinks modernity is the age of the machine, with mechanistic views of the universe, human beings, and more. Similarly, Christians have accepted this kind of view by treating the Christian life and their relationship with God as simple steps to perform. This treats the Christian life like a "program" of proper inputs which yield appropriate outputs.

Fourth, modernity has emphasized inordinately the autonomous individual, who can legislate his own morals and also thinks he does not need God or others. Likewise, the church has perpetuated this individualism to the detriment of the body of Christ. This mind-set carries over in a rampant consumerism in culture, in which goods and services are persistently niche marketed to individuals, with the message of acquiring more and more to fulfill ourselves. The church, too, has become a purveyor of religious goods and services to meet individuals' needs, who come to services to get what they want but then leave and do not contribute to the life of the church. In modernity's consumeristic orientation, too often the church has competed for "market share" and "clientele" with other businesses and organizations that vie for our attention and loyalties. Instead, the church needs to be a community that is faithful to the Lord Jesus by being a people who are engaged in a mission, to help reconcile the entire world under Jesus as Lord.

[2] Brian McLaren, *More Ready Than You Realize* (Grand Rapids: Zondervan, 2002), 41–42.

Fifth, modernity has influenced society to value analysis as the highest form of thought, and science provides the tools to master all of reality. Scientists search for a grand theory of everything, in which all of reality could be categorized, explained, and mastered by science. Similarly, Christians have developed systematic theologies to categorize and understand all doctrine. But this tends to reduce God to something we can master.

In contrast, McLaren thinks Christians need to observe several cultural changes in the emerging postmodern culture. Postmoderns are quick to detect inauthenticity in people, and they are looking for genuine friendships, particularly in community. Moreover, postmodern people are not looking for a God shrunken down to modern tastes; they are looking for a God who transcends us, who is worthy of our worship, and yet also is immanent with us.

Philosophical changes are also taking place. Through Neo, McLaren states that postmodernism has successfully "deconstructed," or taken apart, modern thought and exposed it as just another attempt to impose a will to power over people, by telling a story that we can know indubitable truths through reason. But this story, like all others, is told from a particular historical context. Moreover, our viewpoints are always finite, limited, and they have blind spots. We never can be purely objective and lay aside our biases and the influences of our historical, cultural context, especially the pervasive role of language in shaping our perspectives.

Along these lines McLaren makes some provocative comments. Neo tells Dan that history began with our ability to write it,[3] as though events and the language used to describe them are inseparable. Elsewhere Neo tells us that a huge part of who we are flows from language.[4] But does Neo mean our self-understanding, which we express in language, or does he mean something more? Neo also remarks that we are "stuck" in language.[5] Perhaps this means that we work within the limitations of language (understood as verbal and nonverbal

---

[3] McLaren, *New Kind*, 15.
[4] Ibid., 100.
[5] Brian McLaren, *The Story We Find Ourselves In* (San Francisco: Jossey-Bass, 2003), 28.

behaviors) to express our thoughts, feelings, desires, etc., to others. But if it means that we cannot escape the influences of language, to know reality as it truly is in itself, then we have a much stronger claim.

Finally, Neo explains that though we all live on Earth, we still live in different universes, depending on the kind of God we believe in and our understanding of the master story in which we are a part.[6] Sometimes we may speak of living in completely different worlds, in that our experiences and cultures can be so radically different, like the differences I experienced between living in the United States versus in the Congo. But Neo says we live in different *universes, not different understandings* of the same one.

In summary, McLaren advocates that since the culture is going postmodern, Christians need to contextualize the gospel to reach postmoderns. This is a good missiological insight. Yet McLaren also seems to recommend that we need to reconceive the faith in light of postmodern insights, which have successfully deconstructed modern thought.

In reply, I noted several of McLaren's key contributions, including his stressing our need to live authentically. Postmoderns rightly expect Christians to live authentically if they are truly followers of Christ. Moreover, at least in the United States, we have so many failures of political leaders, such that people tend to assume that politicians are basically looking out for themselves. This collapse of confidence has also hit the church because of the many moral failures of its leaders. Many tend to assume that religious leaders are not really serving God but are just trying to impose their own power over others.

More briefly, McLaren rightly highlights the importance of the body of Christ and the need for Christians to live out the "one anothers" of the faith. He also has provided stimulating ways to consider how modernity has affected the culture and the church. And he is helpful in drawing our attention to the need to be missions minded and how we can use stories powerfully to communicate truths to postmoderns.

---

[6] McLaren, *New Kind*, 161.

But I also raised various concerns with McLaren's ideas. I questioned whether we truly need to embrace a postmodern way of being a Christian to solve the problems he has identified. One counterexample I considered is my church, Trinity Evangelical Free Church in Redlands, California. I argued that Trinity has embraced several of the traits McLaren says mark a postmodern way of being a Christian, such as (1) being missions minded, both globally and locally; (2) serving in practical ways the needs of the disadvantaged in our community; (3) stressing and building community in a variety of ways, even by providing "Pathways" support groups for people facing various struggles; and (4) showing compassion to people in need. Our pastoral staff teaches and models that living the Christian life is far more complex than applying just a system of simple formulas. We also realize that there are important insights to be gained from good psychology, good philosophy, and more. We recognize that life sometimes throws challenging circumstances at us, such as when a person cheats on one's spouse or someone receives a diagnosis of cancer. That is a reason we encourage people to be in a small group, since all of us will face significant challenges and trials every few years. We need others who can help share our "overburdens" and thus fulfill the law of Christ (Gal 6:2).

My church also has embraced a more foundationalist view of knowledge, yet we don't require certainty in our beliefs.[7] Trinity is a church of compassionate, missions-minded people who believe in the authority and inerrancy of Scripture but who do not reduce the Christian life to a set of simplistic formulas. We value community and long to glorify God in our worship as well as in the faithful teaching

[7] Unlike Cartesian foundationalism, a "modest" foundationalism is less vulnerable to skeptical charges that if we cannot be certain, we cannot have knowledge. There are precious few beliefs we may have in life that are utterly certain, that we cannot *possibly* (even *conceivably*) be mistaken, so if we maintain the Cartesian standard, we find ourselves vulnerable to the skeptical query, "Isn't it just *possible* that you are mistaken?" In *Truth*, I develop reasons we can have knowledge without certainty. Traditionally, knowledge has been understood as justified true belief. To have knowledge, I need adequate justification (reasons, or evidence, in support of a belief) for my believing it to be true. Justification can vary in degrees among beliefs, and some beliefs may have such large degrees of justification that I have no good reasons to doubt them (e.g., I think the evidence in support of Jesus' resurrection is overwhelmingly in favor of its being true). But that stance does not require that I cannot possibly (however minutely) be mistaken. See *Truth*, 110–21.

and practice of God's Word. We hold it to be the foundation of our faith. Though we could be mistaken about that, we believe the Bible to be our foundation, due to a careful examination of the evidence, including truths found in other disciplines.

I think Trinity Church is not alone in these traits; if so, such churches are counterexamples to McLaren's claim that to overcome the corrosive effects of modernity we need to embrace a new way of being a Christian in postmodern times.

Updates on the Conversation: McLaren's Replies

After *Criswell Theological Review* published an article by McLaren, along with my essay on his views, McLaren e-mailed me some cordial, helpful feedback.[8] He thought that while I described his view accurately in several places, I seriously misdescribed his ideas elsewhere. In particular, while I accurately depicted him as saying that Christians need to learn a new way of being a Christian in the emerging, postmodern culture, nonetheless he felt I misstated this view whenever I portrayed him as saying that we need to embrace a postmodern way of being a Christian.

While subtle, I think McLaren is right to point out this difference and inaccuracy in my two descriptions. McLaren explicitly stated in our "e-dialogue" that he does *not* advocate embracing a postmodern way of being Christians. That would be parallel to being Christians in an American, Republican, Democratic, or communist way. Rather, "I would want them to do the reverse, to engage with their culture in a faithfully Christian way—missionally, strategically, thoughtfully, wisely, incarnationally—so that their Christian faith would give them an alternative, Spirit-empowered way of living—whether they are in a postmodern, modern, American, Republican, Democratic, or communist setting."[9]

This dialogue emphasizes the point that Christians' primary allegiance needs to be to the Lord Jesus, regardless of cultural setting.

---

[8] See my "Some Suggestions for Brian McLaren (and his Critics)," *Criswell Theological Review* (2006): 67–86.

[9] Brian McLaren, in his "cordial response to R. Scott Smith," e-mail dated 6 June 2006.

It also shows the importance of feedback, even when I thought I accurately reflected his views in both ways. I think McLaren is right that there is a difference between my two descriptions, even though when I wrote them, I thought I was just rephrasing the same idea in different words.

Still there are important issues of substance here. McLaren also has said that postmodernism has *successfully* deconstructed modernity's key ideas; so we ought to develop new ways of thinking about the faith. Accordingly, we *should not* see the truth of our faith as an abstract set of disembodied propositions, apart from their narrative context. Thus, we *should* change how we witness from a presentation of "abstract" laws to telling the story of Jesus. Accordingly, it seems that embracing a new way of being a Christian in postmodern times involves accepting at least some postmodern insights. If so, then to what extent is there a real difference between embracing a new way of being a Christian in postmodern times and adopting a postmodern view of being a Christian?

McLaren rephrased that question as follows: to what extent is there "a *real* difference between embracing a new way of being a Christian in postmodern times, and adopting a way of being a Christian that has become aware both of the distortions of modernity (I think I call them 'modern viruses' in one of my books) and the dangers of postmodernity"?[10] To answer, McLaren referred in part to his many writings, including "the tendency in modernity to reduce the gospel from a global redeeming narrative about the coming of the kingdom of God through Christ to information (laws, steps, whatever) about how to go to heaven. Of special concern to me is the way the gospel has been compromised first by its alliance with violence (first via Constantine's empire and, more recently, via modern colonialism)."[11]

This segment, as well as other parts of his reply, illustrates his concern with postmodern conversation as primarily ethical and sociological and not epistemological. McLaren is not formally trained as

---

[10] Brian McLaren in the second part of his "cordial response to R. Scott Smith," e-mail dated 17 July 2006.
[11] Ibid.

a philosopher. Here his concern is with how particular views helped foster and sanction the use of violence in association with the gospel. Whether violence (such as in war) can ever be justified is a subject for more discussion elsewhere. But McLaren has other ethical concerns with the implications of modernity. For instance:

> I am less concerned to argue for or against foundational-ism than I am to ask questions like these: why did so many Christians of the modern era—who I assume were as sincere, intelligent, pious, and honest as any of us, likely more so— find it so easy to participate in colonialism, racism, slavery, environmental irresponsibility, mistreatment of women, mili-tarism, and a careless attitude toward the poor? Why did their theologies make them concerned about scores of rather petty issues while ignoring these larger issues, or even worse, while defending the wrong side of these larger issues?[12]

These are *very* important questions, ones we often do not grapple with enough. They also help clarify McLaren's standpoint. Discussion over these kinds of ethical issues could be fruitful with McLaren and other people inclined toward the EC. Even so, there are important ethical implications of epistemologies, especially if postmoderns have successfully deconstructed modernity and if we therefore should see the faith not as a set of abstract principles but as making sense only in the context of the Christian story. That conclusion has implica-tions for how we should live so as to witness. So I think the way forward is both-and: I encourage McLaren to examine more closely the philosophy associated with many postmoderns' thoughts, and their implications, even ethically. Additionally, I think that dialogue with EC members can help other Christians see possible blind spots they may have to ethical implications of the ways they tend to live out the faith.

I have found McLaren and others in the EC to be sincere about wanting to engage in dialogue about their views. If conversation (*not* a monologue) is undertaken in a spirit of graciousness, to seek under-

---

[12] Ibid.

standing of a person's point of view by first listening to, and reading carefully, what someone has to say, along with attention to the factors that have helped shape that person's outlook, conversation can be fruitful. I have found that people then are open to hear my ideas since I want to respect them as people and listen to their ideas. We can work to clarify our ideas, and actually get down to discussing important issues, in the context of a friendly dialogue that does not ignore truth. And there are important issues, including the truth of core doctrines, which we will take up in the next section.

However, there is another epistemological issue that I discussed with McLaren, namely, the criticisms Jamie Smith raised against my views. McLaren mentioned that he found Jamie's perspectives "very helpful," and so it behooves us to turn to examine Jamie's contentions.[13]

Updates on the Conversation: Jamie Smith's Criticism

In both *Truth* as well as my essays in *Christianity and the Postmodern Turn*, I argued that the views of McLaren, Stan Grenz, John Franke, Brad Kallenberg, and Stanley Hauerwas have important implications, especially for core doctrines.[14] That is, if (1) there is no unbiased, neutral place to stand; (2) we always know truths from particular, historically contingent settings; (3) we cannot transcend the pervasive influences of language upon our views of reality, to know reality as it is; (4) "language does not represent reality, it constitutes reality" (Kallenberg);[15] (5) history itself began with our ability to write it (McLaren); then it seems we *make* our worlds, or our reality, by how we talk in the languages of our communities. And if there is no essence to language but there are only many languages, then there are as many worlds (with their own truths) as there are languages. As Grenz

---

[13] Ibid.

[14] See my two essays, "Christian Postmodernism and the Linguistic Turn," and "Postmodernism and the Priority of the Language-World Relation," in *Christianity and the Postmodern Turn*, ed. Myron B. Penner (Grand Rapids, Mich.: Brazos, 2005).

[15] Brad J. Kallenberg, *Ethics as Grammar: Changing the Postmodern Subject* (Notre Dame: University of Notre Dame Press, 2001), 234.

and Franke write, "We do not inhabit the 'world-in-itself'; instead, we live in a linguistic world of our own making."[16]

Using that interpretation, I went on to apply this view to several core doctrines of orthodox theology, such as the nature of God, the prospects for revelation, the incarnation, and more; and in each case this view will do great violence to them. God Himself and the incarnation will be constructs of our language. We also could never access the meaning God intended when He gave special revelation in Scripture; instead, we always would be working on the "inside" of our language and be unable to know what God intended. We end up constructing the meaning of Scripture. Call this my *first* interpretation.

In response to my first essay in *Christianity and the Postmodern Turn*, Jamie avers that "the very experience of the things themselves is a matter of interpretation."[17] Moreover, "that interpreting the world as creation is, I would argue, the *true* interpretation, does not negate its status as an interpretation or 'conditioned seeing' (contra 'direct acquaintance')."[18] He then associates this belief with his understanding of the "Calvin school": "I think that presuppositional apologetics . . . rejects classical apologetics because it recognizes the truth of the postfoundationalist claim that *everything is interpretation*."[19] So a crucial difference between Jamie's and my views is that we disagree over our ability to be directly acquainted with reality.

In *Truth*, as well as the *Postmodern Turn*, I was trying to address the idea that we cannot have direct access to reality. However, in retrospect, I may have portrayed it in a way that was somewhat inaccurate. I interpreted some writers as claiming that the real world is (in itself) indeterminate and inaccessible, whereas we have constructed the world we live in by the use of our language in a particular community. In turn, Jamie argued that my criticisms are misguided because I have a "restrictive understanding of language" since both language and its

---

[16] Stanley Grenz and John Franke, *Beyond Foundationalism: Shaping Theology in a Postmodern Context* (Louisville: Westminster John Knox, 2001), 53.

[17] James K. A. Smith, "Who's Afraid of Postmodernism? A Response to the 'Biola School,'" in *Christianity and the Postmodern Turn*, ed. Myron B. Penner (Grand Rapids, Mich.: Brazos, 2005), 218.

[18] Ibid. (emphasis in original).

[19] Ibid. (emphasis mine).

users are part of the world.[20] Moreover, the world we inhabit is "always already *interpreted* within a framework of signs or a semiotic system."[21] But these points do not entail the "kind of stilted Kantianism that Scott paints."[22]

Therefore, let me offer a *second*, revised interpretation of what Jamie, McLaren, and several others are claiming: there is a real world, but there is no knowledge by direct acquaintance. All experience and all knowledge are interpreted. On this view we do not "construct" our worlds, but we do interpret them, and that necessarily involves our particular historical location, including (crucially) our language. Like my first interpretation, we never can achieve epistemically an "objective" (i.e., neutral, unbiased) vantage point from which we can gaze directly at and know "objective" reality (i.e., metaphysically, the world as it really is, apart from interpretations). On neither my first nor my second interpretation would McLaren, Jamie, or others deny that there is a real world that exists apart from our experiences or interpretations. But rather than constructing our world, on this second interpretation we always bring with us our interpretive "glasses" to any experience or any act of knowing such that *everything* (even the gospel) is an interpretation.[23]

Jamie is right to call attention to the focus on interpretation, and not so much epistemology, in the postmodern "turn." And he has made clearer the nature of some of the claims I have been at pains to interpret. I think Jamie is right, for all of the authors I have been examining affirm that there is a real world, which fits better with Jamie's view that everything is interpretation.

Still, on this view I do not think we will be able to know reality. In one place Jamie considers part of Disney's *The Little Mermaid* movie.[24] Ariel, the mermaid who wants to experience life in the human world, has seen and collected various artifacts from it. Scuttle the sea gull

---

[20] Ibid., 222.
[21] Ibid. (emphasis in original).
[22] Ibid.
[23] James K. A. Smith, *Who's Afraid of Postmodernism? Taking Derrida, Lyotard, and Foucault to Church* (Grand Rapids: Baker Academic, 2006), 42–51.
[24] Ibid., 40–42.

helps her by adding to her collection what we know as a fork, but he calls it a "dinglehopper," which he explains is to be used to comb hair. When Ariel gets her chance to experience life in the human world, she even eats with the prince. Imagine his surprise when she starts combing her hair with her fork at the dinner table!

Jamie then explains his point:

> This thing—this strangely shaped piece of metal—even when we find it sitting on the table right in front of us, is subject to interpretation. Given our horizons of expectation, our past history, what we've been told, and thus a whole host of presuppositions that we bring to the experience, we immediately see the object as a fork (and find it difficult to see it as anything *but* a fork). But for Ariel—with her different history, different experience, and thus different presuppositions—the item is interpreted as a dinglehopper. While it might seem as though we don't interpret the object, we actually go through the interpretive process so quickly, without even thinking about it, that it seems as if we're not engaged in interpretation. But the speed with which the object is construed as a fork does not negate the fact of interpretation or the interpretive process involved. So we never get past texts and interpretations to things "simply as they are" in any kind of unmediated fashion.[25]

On Jamie's view, when Ariel saw a particular metal object, she did not see the object itself, but she saw it as a dinglehopper, whereas the prince and we see it as a fork. Still, she, as well as the rest of us, sees something. But what is that "something"? Perhaps it is the metal. But on Jamie's claims, when we each experience the metal in the object, we are not experiencing it directly; instead we (each) are experiencing something else *as* being metal. Or perhaps we are seeing the shape. But, again, we are not experiencing it directly; instead we (each) experience something else *as* being a shape. The same result obtains with any quality of this object (or even that "it" is an *object*), such that

---

[25] Ibid., 41–42 (emphasis in original).

none of us can experience or know the object or any of its qualities. Essentially, though we may rightly affirm that the real world exists, with real things and real people, it seems that in Jamie's view, we never can get to know them at all if there is no experience, or knowledge, by direct acquaintance. Anything we try to know (epistemically, or even in the sense of knowing a person in a relationship) always seems to elude our grasp.[26]

But that result leaves us in a poor position to know anything about the world, or even that there is a real world, or any reality in it, including ourselves. That result has serious implications for Christians and Christianity. We do not seem able to know, for example, that God has spoken to us, or that Jesus died for our sins and arose from the dead on the third day. But that situation is utterly foreign to the New Testament writers. As but one example, the apostle John wrote about several things we can know to be true, including that the Word of Life has come in the flesh (1 John 1:1–3), that Christians can have eternal life (5:3), and much more. The view that everything is interpretation cannot explain how we can (and do) know many things, and it will serve to undermine the confidence that the apostles intended for Christians to have in the truths of the faith.

Conclusion

We need to consider carefully the various problems McLaren has identified with the contemporary evangelical church. There can be forms of bondage from the influence of modernity upon Christians. But our primary need for emergence is not from modernity's influences; it is from a deeper, more pervasive kind of bondage, one that transcends times, cultures, and even languages—namely, sin. To emerge from that will require that we know the truth, so we should not embrace a view that will serve to undermine that. And knowing truth will require our holding fast to the truth in the Word of God, which is able to cut through our sin in all its many forms (Heb 4:12–13).

[26] I do not have space to develop this argument here. But I intend to argue more fully in a future manuscript, *In Search of Moral Knowledge: Rethinking Ethics and the Fact-Value Dichotomy* (presently unpublished).

Part 6

PRACTICAL
APPLICATION

Chapter 17

DEALING WITH EMOTIONAL DOUBT

Gary R. Habermas

F ew issues plague believers more frequently than doubts concerning Christianity in general or their own faith in particular. After all, if my faith is centrally important to me and I have what I think are serious questions about it, it could be disturbing, especially if I do not seek out someone with whom I may discuss it.

The situation is further exacerbated by the many incorrect ideas concerning doubt. Few topics are accompanied by more false views or faulty information. For example, the following are all arguably false to a large degree: doubt is relatively rare; biblical heroes never or seldom questioned God; doubt is unbelief and is always the opposite of faith; it is the unpardonable sin or at least always a sinful practice; it cannot or seldom produces positive results; it is always solved by a study of Christian evidences; it never bothers unbelievers; doubt grows worse as we get older.[1]

I will define religious doubt as uncertainty regarding God or our relationship to Him. Although non-Christians reportedly also experience religious uncertainty,[2] I am treating specifically Christian doubt.

---

[1] For a discussion of these and other incorrect comments on the subject of religious doubt, see Gary Habermas, *Dealing with Doubt* (Chicago: Moody, 1990), 12–19 and Gary Habermas, *The Thomas Factor: Using Your Doubts to Grow Closer to God* (Nashville: Broadman & Holman, 1999), chapter 2.

[2] See C. S. Lewis's comments about his doubts while he was an atheist in *Mere Christianity* (New York: Macmillan, 1952), 123.

Within this definition I have identified three primary families of doubt: factual, emotional, and volitional uncertainty.[3] Questions can arise in several forms, such as challenges to the truth of Christianity, the assurance of one's own faith, or concerns regarding pain, suffering, or the perception of unanswered prayer.

In this essay I will address what is perhaps the most common as well as the most painful variety of religious doubt—that which is emotional in nature.[4] My goal is to present a pastoral perspective that could possibly help to alleviate some of the most painful side effects of this uncertainty.[5]

Identifying Emotional Doubt

Emotional doubt is identified not so much by the sorts of questions that are asked but by the underlying reasons for those questions. While it frequently masquerades as factual doubt, asking what may sound like evidential sorts of issues, the chief basis out of which these questions come is not solved by answering the questions, as is factual doubt. This is why emotional doubters often think that they are just one more apologetics book away from solving their pain, but their momentary hope is usually followed once again by another emotional challenge.

So the pertinent issue here is the proper identification of emotional doubt. This is a crucial point because if the family of doubt is misidentified, the chances of achieving substantial benefits are reduced.

Emotional doubt can arise from a large variety of factors but most often emerges in the aftermath of one's emotional hurts. For example, medical background and issues (including heredity or sickness),

---

[3] Since human nature combines factual, emotional, and volitional elements, among others, doubt is frequently a case of mixing and matching different issues and causes. So more than one area of turmoil may well be present. Still it is necessary for the pastor or friend to pick out the most prominent source(s), and work on that.

[4] For many details that cannot be discussed here, see my two books on this subject, *Dealing with Doubt* and *The Thomas Factor*. Both texts are available without charge on my Web site: www.garyhabermas.com.

[5] Please note that I am not a psychologist, a counselor, or a psychiatrist. Thus, this treatment is not psychological or psychiatric but pastoral and biblical.

psychological factors (including anxiety or depression), as well as childhood or more recent hurts (death, divorce, or other breakups) can all be highly relevant factors. But even the lack of sleep, a good diet, or regular exercise can contribute much, as can peer pressure.

Throughout, perhaps the chief characteristic of emotional doubt is judging issues by one's feelings—how the questioner *feels* when these subjects arise or how the issues *affect* the individual. Unfortunately, the person usually does not realize that he is reacting less to the questions themselves and more to the *results*.

We have said that the questions often concern not the factual data itself but one's response to these questions. Perhaps the single most telling indication of the emotional component is the well-placed, "What if?" comeback, whether spoken or implied. Here, doubters are not questioning the data but the observation that, although the evidence appears to be solid and they are inclined to accept it, they *could* be mistaken. Often the follow-up challenge to produce some noteworthy issues is answered by the rejoinder, "Well, I don't see any obvious factual problems. But *what if* we are still mistaken somehow?"

Interestingly, emotional doubters who are most interested in their own salvation may report that they only want to be sure that they're a Christian, that they are really in love with Jesus. But then they may go on to allow that, while they seem to have those feelings and desires, they could possibly be misleading themselves. The latter may even be buttressed with Scripture, such as Matt 7:22–23! Strangely enough, it seldom seems to occur to such persons that we generally only worry about things that are close to the top of our personal list of concerns, betraying the fact that we probably are in love with Jesus, after all!

Another common thought occurring to emotional doubters seems to be that, although they do not know why, perhaps they are going to hell. If informal surveys help, many Christians even visualize this possibility, often at night, with Jesus extending His left arm to them at judgment, directing them to eternal punishment. Another text might even be cited for this (Matt 25:41–46).

It should not be surprising, then, if emotional doubters indicate to their pastor or best friend that the entire situation has left them feeling worn out and defeated. Their descriptions are sometimes wrought with emotional language. To those who know them best, they have frequently grown distraught by the constant questioning of their most cherished beliefs. Probing may indicate that they are focusing on remote possibilities that are not governed by the rules of evidence. Sometimes their questions are even immune to the facts. After all, any case produced by a pastor can be confronted with the well-placed challenge, "But what if . . . ?"

Therefore, the key to identifying emotional uncertainty often involves picking out any painful or distressed feelings *behind* the questions or issues. It means developing an ear for cases where producing a list of strong evidences may seem to work for a few days, perhaps even producing a momentary emotional "high," followed by the diminishing assurance that may result again in feelings of turmoil.

Understanding Emotional Pain

Some Christians mistrust the theories and techniques of psychologists and professional counselors, often because they are unable to distinguish biblical from unbiblical ideas. I am neither a psychologist nor a professional counselor; I am presenting here a biblical or pastoral treatment of doubt. But many strong Christian counseling writings are available for application to a biblical or pastoral setting.[6]

One crucial observation, which specialists often explain is based on a solid experimental foundation, seems to be counter to what most people think. What and how we think greatly influences both our feel-

---

[6] Some of these works include the following: William Backus and Marie Chapian, *Telling Yourself the Truth* (Minneapolis: Bethany, 2000); William Backus and Marie Chapian, *Why Do I Do What I Don't Want to Do?* (Minneapolis: Bethany, 1984); William Backus, *Telling the Truth to Troubled People* (Minneapolis: Bethany, 1985); William Backus, *The Good News about Worry* (Minneapolis: Bethany, 1991); Tim Clinton and Gary Sibcy, *Attachments: Why You Love, Feel and Act the Way You Do* (Brentwood, N.J.: Integrity, 2002); Gary Collins, *The Biblical Basis of Christian Counseling for People Helpers: Relating the Basic Teachings of Scripture to People's Problems* (Colorado Springs: NavPress, 1993); David Stoop, *You Are What You Think* (Grand Rapids: Revell, 1996); Chris Thurman, *The Lies We Believe* (Nashville: Thomas Nelson, 1989).

ings and our behavior. The result is that the most prominent influence on our emotional and volitional struggles is *not* the painful things that happen to us in life, but what we *say* or *think* to ourselves *concerning* these things in our lives. In other words, while our circumstances can contribute, how we *download* our experiences, and most of all, what we tell ourselves *about* them is the most significant factor in our emotional lives. If we say or think hurtful or incorrect things about what happens to us, we are candidates for emotional pain.[7]

Along this line, consider the following thoughts by Christian psychologists:

> Most of our unhappiness and emotional struggles are caused by the lies we tell ourselves.[8]

> The bottom line is that we mold our emotional lives by the way we choose to think about what happens to us. To think otherwise is to be emotionally irresponsible. . . . How we respond is, after all, our choice alone.[9]

> We have been taught to believe that our feelings and emotions are determined by the events in our lives. . . . The truth is that our emotions and behavior are *not* dependent on what is going on around us in our environment.[10]

> [Two crucial principles:] 1. Our Thoughts Create Our Emotions, [and] 2. Our Thoughts Affect Our Behavior.[11]

> *What you think and believe determines how you feel and what you do.*[12]

> Misbeliefs are the direct cause of emotional turmoil, maladaptive behavior and most so-called "mental illness."[13]

[7] For example, Backus and Chapian, *Telling Yourself the Truth*, chapters 1–3 (esp. pp. 9, 27); Stoop, *You Are What You Think,* esp. chapters 2–3; Thurman, *The Lies We Believe,* esp. chapters 1–2.

[8] Thurman, *The Lies We Believe,* 22. In Thurman, for emphasis, this sentence was printed throughout in uppercase letters.

[9] Ibid., 54.

[10] Stoop, *You Are What You Think*, 28.

[11] Ibid., 35.

[12] Backus and Chapian, *Telling Yourself the Truth*, 22 (their emphasis).

[13] Ibid., 17.

If the direction of these comments is accurate, then how we think *about* the things in our lives is more crucial to our health that the actual circumstances themselves, including what happens to us. This means that we could well be the cause of most of our own emotional pain! And if emotional pain is, as some claim, often the worst pain we will ever experience, then we may cause much if not most of the worst pain in our lives! That we can control this pain level is simply incredible.

Following this further, the real and sometimes difficult suffering of emotional doubters is perhaps (if not probably) the primary result of their own poor thinking strategies. In fact, changing their thinking will at least present a strong possibility of lessening that pain. Imagine that we may hold the key to our own suffering as expressed in our emotional doubt! The world around us may not change, but our assurance can remain in spite of our situations!

This is why a study of Christian evidences may be helpful but will usually not solve the issues or take away the pain of emotional doubt. It might be likened to taking the wrong medicine for what ails us: we often continue to hurt. Thus, knowing that Christianity is true can serve as a strong foundation to which we return; but to treat the emotional issues we must direct ourselves to what we tell ourselves. As we will see, not only are there several helpful action plans that will often promote substantial healing, but this entire process is thoroughly in line with the repeated emphasis of Scripture.

Developing Some Strategies for Treating Emotional Doubt

There is more than one way to deal with emotional doubt. As we have noted, we react to our thoughts; and if we think things that are untrue or hurtful, we ought not be surprised if these ideas cause us confusion and suffering.

One popular method is to identify the lies or misbeliefs that we tell ourselves, followed by our aggressively disputing them.[14] Emotional

---

[14] Scripture often affirms that pain and other negative circumstances result from improper statements or beliefs. Conversely, blessings result from speaking the truth, both to ourselves and to others. See Ps 39:2; Prov 10:21; 12:18,25; 18:21; 26:20,22; Rom 1:25; 1 Cor 10:12; Jas 1:13–17; 4:1–8; cf. Eph 5:19.

doubters often repeat thoughts like these: "What if Christianity is false?" or, "What if I didn't say the right words when I decided to follow Christ?" or, "You know, I could arrive at the final judgment and hear Jesus tell me to depart from His presence." When challenged about such beliefs, these doubters might retort, "I'm not being irrational. This is possible, isn't it? People can be mistaken. The Bible even says so." But if the theory we have discussed above is true, these are *precisely* the sorts of comments that can cause us much pain. Persisting in these and other thoughts, then, adds more pain to our pain, literally increasing our level of discomfort.

Let's look at our examples. Often when I ask if doubters think that the facts of the Christian gospel are false, they respond, "No, not at all. I think that they are true. But *what if* they are untrue, anyway? *What if* we got it all wrong? It's *possible*, you know." But even if this "what if" scenario is possible, is it *probably true*? The strongest evidences for Christianity are those that precisely confirm the gospel data, the center of our faith. By acknowledging their beliefs while still "what if-ing" *about* them, these doubters are admitting that they are preferring *possibilities* to *probabilities*. But who bases life-and-death decisions on mere possibilities? If we did that, we'd never drive on the roads, never go out of our homes, or never even eat food! To favor this "what if" reasoning elsewhere, then, might actually mean favoring *improbabilities* as the guide to life!

To confront the lies in this first example, we can make a list of the historical facts that confirm the gospel. Then we can examine the differences between possibilities and probabilities and how we make potentially life-and-death decisions every day based on the facts. By so doing, we are arguing against the false assumptions of these doubts.

Or in the next two examples, is it likely that those who understand the gospel message and decide to trust the Lord, casting themselves on His mercy, do not find salvation? Does the New Testament support this sort of unhelpful reasoning? Just like today, we find repeatedly that when people heard the gospel message and responded in faith, they became believers and were counted among the elect.[15] Sure, from time to time, we do hear that some of those who professed belief never meant it, but by far the most common scenario was the simple observation that those who believed had truly become Christians. We are not told that they did anything extraordinary or thought about the many possible meanings of their words. They simply believed and became Christians. This is significant.

Thus, one of the chief issues here is that the "supposals" of emotional doubters are *irrational*. Why? Of course the ideas behind these destructive thoughts may be *possible*. But preferring (barely?) *possible* scenarios to *probable* ones is neither rational, nor healthy, nor truthful, nor biblical. As we have said, you cannot make everyday life-and-death decisions by this method. Therefore, emotional doubters need to argue with themselves, engaging these unlikely scenarios in dialogue. They must contend with themselves forcefully that these thoughts are *unlikely*, even *highly unlikely*. No wonder these thoughts cause pain; they are simply untrue. Wonderfully, our emotions can serve here as truth detectors! Our God-given emotions sound off in pain when we attempt to base our lives on falsehoods.

One way to argue with ourselves is to dispute repeatedly: God is interested in our heart condition. Those who respond simply and sincerely, as children do, are saved. So when we understand the gospel message and do our best to trust the Lord in light of it, salvation is the normal result. This is the way it happened in the New Testament, and it is still the case today. Then truth needs to be *practiced* until it sticks. Thoughts to the contrary need to be cut off immediately and forcefully: "Stop it. All you are doing is being irrational and contributing to your own pain. Can you live like this in everyday life?"

This entire process begins only as we grow intimately attuned to our own thoughts. Whenever we tell ourselves things that are probably untrue, we need to catch them right away. This should be followed by a vigorous series of arguments against this idea. "That's

---

[15] 1 Cor 1:6; 12:27; 15:1–2; Gal 3:26; Eph 1:13–14; Col 1:6; 1 Thess 1:4; 5:5; 2 Thess 1:10; 2:13–17; 1 Pet 5:4,10; 2 Pet 1:5–11; 1 John 5:13.

not true because . . ." is the proper comeback, followed by several truthful rebuttals.[16]

In this way it is possible to weed out the thoughts at the root of our pain and discomfort. As Backus and Chapian assert, "You *can* change your emotions, you *can* be an adjusted and happy human being, no matter what you have experienced in your life and no matter what your circumstances are."[17]

Besides disputing our false thoughts, we should apply other disciplines (both mental and physical) in their place, in order to correct our emotional musings. The apostle Paul provides an excellent example in Phil 4:6–9. To counteract our anxious thoughts, he suggests *prayer, thanksgiving, and praise*, along with *exchanging* our anxious thoughts for godly truths, and *practicing* these things.

In this text Paul does not tell us more specifically how to pray (v. 6). However, Peter explains that we ought to cast our anxious thoughts on God (1 Pet 5:7). Other biblical passages also tell us to pray through emotional times.[18] Of course, the key is to leave these issues with the Lord!

Helpfully, Paul then says that we should offer thanksgiving (v. 6) and praise (v. 8) during these troubled occasions. In Scripture this is a common prescription.[19] When lecturing on this topic, I usually pause at this point and ask the audience what they have observed whenever they give thanks or praise during a time of emotional upheaval. Voices proclaim variously that these practices help them to refocus their attention on the Lord, to realize their blessings, to place the area of upheaval into the broader context of their lives, or to step momentarily away from the issues. They report that the pain usually subsides, sometimes rather quickly. The answers are so unanimous in their liberating experience with praise and thanksgiving that I have definitely gained

---

[16] For other specific suggestions on how to confront various lies, see Habermas, *The Thomas Factor*, chapter 6.

[17] Backus and Chapian, *Telling Yourself the Truth*, 24 (their emphasis).

[18] For examples, see Pss 34:4–8; 55:4–8,16–17,22; 57:2–3; 94:18–19; 119:145–147; Eph 6:18; cf. Matt 7:7–11; 1 Thess 5:17.

[19] Some instances include Pss 30:4–5; 42:5,11; 43:5; 56:4,10–11; Eph 5:20; 1 Thess 5:16,18.

a new appreciation for these practices. I also wonder why we do not practice them more frequently and systematically.

Then Paul encourages the believer to replace his anxious thoughts with a variety of truthful substitutes (v. 8). As we have already noted, this is the same process that is encouraged by many contemporary counselors. It removes the poison from our minds. And it, too, is frequently commanded in Scripture.[20] It seems that believers have simply not understood the power of biblically correct thinking and speaking. We cause pain in ourselves and others, sometimes without meaning to do so, due to our disobedience.

From the many biblical injunctions regarding treating our times of emotional distress, it seems clear that there is no specific, particular path that must be pursued, least of all in a particular order. The implication, then, is that believers are free to "mix and match" practices that both teach God's truths and at the same time relieve the emotional suffering that comes from this species of religious doubt.

Although we cannot discuss here some of the other disciplines that are helpful during times of emotional doubt, many other options exist. These include such avenues as corporate worship, meditation, memorizing appropriate Scripture texts especially for use during difficult times, keeping a journal, or talking with a friend.[21] Like a many-faceted diamond, each path contains its own remedies for application to specific and personal situations. The key is to practice these truths.

Applying Truth to Stubborn Conditions

A few comments on the application of these procedures may be helpful. Especially since the topic of emotional religious doubt is so tricky, it is not likely that simply stating the above points will make them obvious. I would not want someone to stop pursuing the remedy because something did not seem to work the first or second time. Here are a few common "sticking points."

---

[20] See Pss 39:2; 56:3–4; 73:26; 119:148; 143:3–6; Prov 14:30; 15:13,15b; 17:22; Lam 3:19–24; Rom 12:1–2; Col 3:1–2.
[21] For more than a dozen suggestions of mental and physical disciplines that can be applied to emotional doubt, see Habermas, *The Thomas Factor*, chapters 7–8.

1. Believers often report that they fail at precisely the initial point of locating their misbeliefs since they are so often unaware of these ideas. Role-playing with these doubters frequently confirms their observations. After all, we are not used to disputing our own thinking because we accept it so readily!

One helpful suggestion is to begin not by looking for the lies themselves but to become attuned to sudden changes in our mental outlook throughout the day. As the old saying goes, "Where there's smoke, there's fire." So after the "pain alarm" sounds and we notice our emotional mind-set, we should immediately pause and ask ourselves: "What did I just say to myself?" or, "What was I just thinking?" It will probably take some time to get used to it, but after practice it should grow easier and easier to get back to our original thought. When we do, that is precisely the time to pounce on the lies, as pointed out above.

2. How do we handle *truthful* thoughts that seem to cause us pain—such as might come after we *really do* flunk an exam, lose our job, or get sick? In these cases the external situation might be true, but what we tell ourselves *about* the situation is still false. And the latter causes most of the pain. So it is here that we must protest.

For example, it is still untrue that these actual events *caused* most of our emotions. So to blame our resulting emotional states on the actual events is still a case of mistaken identity! We must dispute the mistaken portion of the situation, which most likely caused the majority of the pain. When we flunked the exam, we may have added to our thinking that *we must be stupid*. Or, if we got fired, *we probably won't achieve our life goals*. Or if we are sick, *we'll probably die, and that's the worst thing that can ever happen to me*.

We must detect the lies in our thinking. Really being sick is not the lie. But telling ourselves that we will probably die and that is the worst thing that can happen *are* lies. First, only one sickness ever ends in our death! But we seldom take the time to reflect on this afterwards. We repeat the worst; and then when we get better, we acknowledge, *that wasn't so bad after all*. But in the meantime, our misbeliefs may have caused ourselves (and perhaps others) a lot of pain.

Second, even dying is *by no means* the worst thing that can happen to us. To spend eternity apart from the Lord is far, far worse. As Paul does in 2 Cor 4:16–18, then, we must reinforce the truth of eternity by meditating on God's truth, for it is far better than earthly life (see also Phil 1:21–23). So while life can still hurt, eternal life needs to be celebrated. This truth must sink deeply into our minds (Col 3:2).

In these examples it is not the truth that hurts. It's the untruth that lurks in the shadows and gets inserted so quickly afterwards that we seldom even notice the shift. We do not even have to say the actual words to ourselves. Simply thinking a few things in "code" will often suffice to cause the pain when we know what those simple words mean. Thus, "Oh, no . . ." or, "Here we go again . . ." can certainly set off the painful reaction. Mental images can do it, too. We can think far faster than we speak, and we usually know what we mean by these loaded phrases and images.[22]

3. What if, once the misbelief is discovered, we are not good at arguing with ourselves? In this case it might be helpful to take a sheet of paper and divide the page into two sections. Whenever we detect a lie, we can number it and record it in the left column. On the right side, corresponding to that lie, we can number as many points of refutation as we can detect for that particular untruth. Ideally, every lie on the left will be refuted by several points down the right side. We are looking for strong reasons that specific misbelief is false. Adding other lies and their corresponding refutations to this list can provide a helpful reference that will presumably be helpful during these and other times of doubt.[23]

4. Earlier we mentioned a common, often agonizing, question that frequently nags at emotional doubters. "How do I know that I *really* do believe in the Lord?" We must ask an amazingly simply question at this point. Do we normally worry most of all about things that are unimportant to us? For example, does the health of people we do not

[22] Stoop, *You Are What You Think*, 30–31.
[23] Thurman, *The Lies We Believe*, should be helpful in providing such lists because he arranges chapters 2–6 and especially appendixes A and B by providing many truths that counter particular lies.

even know matter more to us than the health of our *own* children? Here emotional doubters have revealed too much of their own heart's desire. That their faith may be the most crucial item in their lives betrays the fact that they are most likely deeply in love with the Lord. Thus, their repeated worries provide one of the best reasons to think that they are actually believers!

5. An additional hint is that the more *forceful* we are with ourselves in disputing our misbeliefs, the more likely it is that we will react properly to our own directions. In other words, soft words and halting convictions while arguing with ourselves will often produce diminished effects.[24] We might even convince ourselves in reverse, thereby deepening our pain! As in everyday life, more forceful statements and unwavering convictions will be heeded far more frequently! Preaching to ourselves can be helpful here.

One suggestion is that, when we dispute our lies, we could imagine taking both hands, grabbing our collar, and pulling ourselves close, so that we can speak directly in our own face! Then we may be more willing to listen. Our questions might include, "Do you hear me? Yes, I'm talking to *you*!" or, "What, exactly, is the basis for that baloney? Where did you ever get *that* crazy idea?" Though it may sound comical, we need to get our own attention!

6. When do we most need to practice this truth-telling? It makes sense to apply the techniques most rigorously when we are in the most pain. But this is also the time when it will probably be the most difficult to apply these truths, due to the amount of distraction during those emotional moments. So we need to learn the techniques before we really need them. Therefore, the next best time to practice truth-telling is when we do not need it as much since if we know ourselves, we will realize the likelihood that, given our personality, doubt will most likely rear its head from time to time.

Therefore, the process should be learned and practiced as part of the normal course of spiritual and healthy living. Additional lessons can be applicable to a wide range of situations.

---

[24] Windy Dryden and Raymond DiGiuseppe, *A Primer on Rational-Emotive Therapy* (Champaign, Ill.: Research Press, 1990), 49, 57, 86–87, 91.

Conclusion

We have said that emotional doubt is probably the most common and the most painful species of religious uncertainty. Sometimes it simply demands our attention. The many unexpected twists and turns related to this topic further complicate the healing process. But it can often or even usually be treated in a manner that can at least reduce, if not substantially heal, its most painful aspects. The key is the regular practice of any number of disciplines that not only divert our attention but which also get at the roots of the doubt by replacing the misbeliefs with truth. The lies need to be uprooted forcefully and removed one by one, while the firm application of truth promotes healing.

The key is to *practice the truth*. It may take some time. But the result of regularly and forcefully practicing God's truth as the antidote to our erroneous thinking can bring the peace that the Bible promises so readily (Isa 26:3; 32:17; Phil 4:7,9).

Chapter 18

APOLOGETICS FOR AN EMERGING GENERATION

Sean McDowell

The lunch bell rang, and Mike sheepishly slipped into my class-room, slouched into a desk, and buried his face in his folded arms. As a typical high school sophomore, he didn't want to appear "uncool" in front of friends, so he came to talk to me when no other students would be around. As I approached, he sat up, looked me in the eyes, and said abruptly, "Mr. McDowell, we need to talk. I think I am losing my faith."

Like many young people, Mike was caught up in his day-to-day routine without much thoughtful reflection about his Christian be-liefs. The night before we talked, he came across an atheist Web site that raised difficult questions about his beliefs. Lacking the intellectual tools and the confidence to answer the challenges, he started to won-der: *Can I trust the Bible? Is evolution true? Isn't it intolerant to believe that Jesus is the only way? How could a loving God who is all-powerful and who could prevent evil allow it to happen?* Doubts such as these came crashing down like bricks to assail and overpower his confidence in God.

Fortunately, Mike trusted me enough to enlist my guidance dur-ing this challenging part of his faith journey, and over the next few months we spent many lunch hours exploring crucial apologetics questions. We examined the Bible's authenticity as well as extrabiblical evidence for Christianity's truth claims in history, philosophy, and science. Mike appreciated having a knowledgeable adult to help him through the hard questions and later shared with me that had I not been there, he likely would have jettisoned his faith.

Not only is apologetics training critical for discipleship, as Mike demonstrates, but it is also important in evangelism. Dave Geisler, founder of Meekness and Truth Ministries, recently wanted to find out what non-Christian students consider the greatest obstacles to evangelism. What barriers are preventing young people from becoming followers of Jesus today? He interviewed students at the University of Texas–Austin and recorded the three most popular responses. In an open-ended survey, the top three concerns students expressed were, "Can everyone be right?" "Is the Bible reliable?" and "Who is Jesus Christ?"[1] Many students today have intellectual questions about the truth of Christianity that are preventing them from becoming followers of Jesus.

The Apologetics Difference

The message is clear: apologetics training is (or should be!) a critical component in the discipleship and evangelism of today's youth. All young people inevitably will wrestle with deep questions about truth, whether while they are in high school, during college, or when they get out in the "real world." We must train young people to love God not only with their hearts and souls but with their *minds* (Matt 22:37) as well and to be able to offer a defense of their faith to all those who ask (1 Pet 3:15).

For the past decade or longer, the Christian marketplace has been flooded with books about how to do ministry in a postmodern world. Their authors rightly have pointed out many cultural changes due to postmodernism but often have failed to realize how much has actually remained the same. I am perplexed when I read contemporary writers, particularly some in the emerging church movement, who question

---

[1] Dave Geisler, "Evangelism Training for the New Millennium: Conversational Evangelism," www.meeknessandtruth.org.

the need for apologetics in ministry to postmodern youth. My experience has been that young people today, even in our postmodern culture, are deeply interested in apologetic questions.

Sociologist Christian Smith, who has conducted one of the most extensive research studies of culture and contemporary youth, points out that youth today are not in need of a "radically new 'postmodern' type of program or ministry."[2] Smith believes, instead, that one of the key things young people need is to be challenged to consider *why they believe what they believe* and to learn *how to articulate* their faith. Living the Christian life with consistency and conviction can be an attractive witness to teens, but this must not deter us from following the biblical command to give an apologetic for the truthfulness of Christianity.

My experience has been that, especially when given the privacy of a note card to respond, both Christian and non-Christian students often ask the tough questions and are interested in reasons for belief in Christianity and its claims. In speaking engagements throughout the United States, I have collected thousands of these questions from curious students. "How can I know God is real?" "How can there be only one right religion?" These types of questions demand an apologetic response by an adult mentor or leader who is well versed in apologetics issues. We need to give our youth reasons Christianity is objectively true, why the Bible is God's inspired and infallible Word, and how we know Jesus' resurrection from the dead is more than mere mythology or an elaborate hoax. If we cannot rise to the task, we run the risk of losing our children and generations to follow. One might argue that such a disturbing and tragic loss already has begun.

The Loss of Faith

In the past years between 55 and 66 percent of churched young people have said that the church will play a part in their lives when they leave home. Now only 33 percent of churched youth say that.[3]

[2] Christian Smith, *Soul Searching: The Religious and Spiritual Lives of American Teenagers* (New York: Oxford University Press, 2005), 266.
[3] George Barna, *Real Teens* (Ventura, Calif.: Regal, 2001), 136.

That is consistent with what various youth leaders have confessed to me. Many youth leaders estimate that between 58 and 90 percent of young people are leaving the traditional church after high school, and few are returning. Why is this so?

Thousands of teenagers who claimed no religious system of belief said, when interviewed for the 2005 National Study of Youth and Religion, that they had been raised to be religious but over time had become "nonreligious."[4] The teenagers were asked, in an open-ended question with no set answers from which to choose, why they left the faith in which they were raised. The most common answer (32 percent) was *intellectual skepticism*. Their answers included, "Some stuff was too far-fetched for me to believe in," "I think scientifically there is no proof," and, "There were too many questions that can't be answered."[5] Many young people are leaving faith behind because the Christian community is failing to engage their minds as well as their hearts.

Radio talk show host Dennis Prager once did a program on couples who had experienced the sudden death of a child. He found that a high percentage of their marriages ended after the incident. He wanted to know *why* so many couples divorced after facing such tragedy. After interviewing hundreds of couples, he found one common element among those who were able to weather the storm: they had developed a philosophy of life (a worldview) into which they could fit their tragedy when it occurred.[6] Those who give thoughtful reflection to the reality of suffering *ahead of time* have far greater odds of holding fast to their faith when tragedy strikes. The same is true for the faith of young people. We must equip youth with a biblical worldview *beforehand* to withstand the moral and intellectual pressures of life in the real world.

David Wheaton was one of the top professional tennis players in the world, winning the Grand Slam Cup and attaining a world ranking of twelve. Although he grew up in a traditional Christian home

[4] Smith, *Soul Searching*, 89. The Web site for the National Study of Youth and Religion is www.youthandreligion.org.
[5] Ibid.
[6] Dennis Prager, *Happiness Is a Serious Problem* (New York: Harper Collins, 1999), 117.

with thoughtful and loving parents, he was simply unprepared for secular college life. His faith was crushed when one of his first class discussions involved mocking the Bible as stupid. The moral and intellectual challenges of college were simply too great for him to bear. This is why he concludes, "The majority of Christian teens are spiritually unprepared for the most challenging transition they will ever make in life."[7] As a result, he says, we must equip young people with the ability to defend their faith *before* they are challenged in the real world.

David Kinnaman, the strategic leader of the Barna Group, explained, "Much of the ministry to teenagers in America needs an overhaul—not because churches fail to attract significant numbers of young people, but because so much of those efforts are not creating a sustainable faith beyond high school. . . . Youth ministry fails too often at discipleship and faith formation."[8] According to Kinnaman, an important step for youth workers to engender young people with a sustainable faith "is to develop teenagers' ability to think and process the complexities of life from a biblical viewpoint."[9] As parents, educators, and youth ministers, we can give young people a priceless gift by helping them think biblically and defend their faith *before* they leave our sphere of influence.

The Crisis of Belief

Most adults are concerned about the behavior of young people. Few, however, go deeper to the source of their behavior: their beliefs. Glenn Schultz demonstrates how beliefs influence behavior in his book *Kingdom Education*: "At the foundation of a person's life we find his beliefs. These beliefs shape his values, and his values drive his actions."[10] If we want to shape the behavior of young people, we

[7] David Wheaton, *University of Destruction* (Minneapolis, Minn.: Bethany House, 2005), 15.
[8] "Most Twentysomethings Put Christianity on the Shelf Following Spiritually Active Teen Years," *The Barna Update*, 11 September 2006, www.barna.org/FlexPage.aspx?Page=BarnaUpdate&BarnaUpdateID=245.
[9] Ibid.
[10] Glenn Schultz, *Kingdom Education* (Nashville: LifeWay, 1998), 39.

must guide them to truthful beliefs about the world and help them to strengthen and build on their existing true beliefs and convictions.

People act on what they believe—not on what they *say* they believe, or *want* to believe, but what they *truly* believe. Young people who have a biblical worldview are not only less likely to leave the faith; they are more likely to practice it in their own lives, and those who believe that God truly has spoken through the Bible are far more likely to follow it than are those who are not so convinced. Teens who trust in God's plan for purity, for example, are much more likely to abstain from impure acts.

This is why it is so critical to help our youth come to terms with their *actual* beliefs and to help address their doubts, questions, uncertainties, and fears honestly. This doesn't mean that we should pretend to have all the answers (teens are far too savvy today to believe that anyone has it all figured out) but that we should guide them lovingly to a greater understanding of the truth.

Given the importance of truthful beliefs, we should be deeply concerned about our youth today. In his top religious trends of 2005, George Barna concluded:

> American Christians are biblically illiterate. Although most of them contend that the Bible contains truth and is worth knowing, and most of them argue that they know all of the relevant truths and principles, our research shows otherwise. . . . The younger a person is, the less they understand about the Christian faith. . . . With fewer and fewer parents teaching their kids much of anything related to matters of faith, young people's belief systems are the product of the mass media.[11]

Consider some of the beliefs of conservative Protestant youth:[12]

- Eighteen percent believe that God is either a personal being who created the world but is not involved in it today (as in

---

[11] George Barna, "Barna Reviews Top Religious Trends of 2005," *Barna Update*, 20 December 2005.
[12] Smith, *Soul Searching*, 41–45, 74.

deism) or an impersonal entity, something like a cosmic force (as in pantheism).

- Twenty-three percent are not assured of the existence of miracles.
- Thirty-three percent either "definitely" or "maybe" believe in reincarnation.
- Forty-two percent are not assured of the existence of evil spirits.
- Forty-eight percent believe many religions may be true.

Take a moment to consider the implication of these statistics. How can our young people have vibrant prayer lives when nearly one in five (18 percent) does not believe God is personally involved in the world today? How can they avoid falling into "the snare of the devil" (1 Tim 3:7) when more than two in five (42 percent) are not even assured of the existence of evil spirits? How, finally, can they confidently believe that Jesus is "the way, and the truth, and the life" (John 14:6), when nearly one in two believes that many religions may be true?

This is why Paul attaches such prime importance for spiritual transformation on the training of the mind: "And do not be conformed to this world, but be transformed by the renewing of your mind" (Rom 12:2). Helping our youth, then, to transform their reasoning and understanding and to become like Jesus begins with helping them think like Jesus and put those thoughts into action. This involves asking not just, "What would Jesus do?" but more importantly, "*Why* would Jesus do what He would?"

In *The Scandal of the Evangelical Conscience*, author Ron Sider concludes that people who have a biblical worldview demonstrate genuinely different behavior. They are nine times more likely to avoid adults-only material on the Internet, three times as likely not to use tobacco products, and twice as likely to volunteer to help the poor.[13] People's beliefs about God, the world, and truth itself *do* make a difference in their practice of the Christian faith.

---

[13] Ron Sider, *The Scandal of the Evangelical Conscience* (Grand Rapids: Baker, 2005), 128.

The Confusion about Truth

This past summer I was the guest speaker at a youth Bible camp in Northern California. The theme throughout the week was Matt 22:37—loving God with all our heart, soul, and mind. I taught from passages such as 1 Sam 16:7, which show that God judges the heart rather than appearance, and encouraged the students to consider Jesus' teaching in Matt 10:28: "Do not fear those who kill the body but are unable to kill the soul; but rather fear Him who is able to destroy both soul and body in hell." I challenged them to use their minds to consider the claims of Jesus as the sole means of salvation (Acts 4:12).

I asked the campers for feedback at the end of the week, and their responses shocked me. One camper summed it up in these words: "We like his stories, but that's just *his* truth. I don't want to judge him, but I have a different truth." Her response probably should not have surprised me as it did, especially since recent studies reveal that the majority of our youth (81 percent) have adopted the view that "all truth is relative to the individual and his/her circumstances."[14] The common attitude toward religion and morality is, "Something may be true for you, but not true for me." Many young people claim to be Christians, but I can't help but wonder how many truly understand that Christianity is *the* truth, the *only* hope for salvation, and the *sole* opportunity for a relationship with the living God who created the universe.

Christian Smith demonstrates that for youth today the "very idea of religious truth is attenuated, shifted from older realist and universalist notions of objective Truth to more personalized and relative versions of 'truth for me' and 'truth for you.'"[15] Smith says we often hear youth proclaim, "Who am I to judge?" "If that's what they choose, whatever," and, "If it works for them, fine." Many youth see truth pragmatically as that which "works" in their lives, rather than upholding the classical view of truth as "that which corresponds to reality." If Hugh Hefner's hedonistic motto, "If it feels good, do it," characterized

---

[14] George Barna, *Real Teens* (Ventura, Calif.: Regal, 2001), 92.
[15] Smith, *Soul Searching*, 144.

the 1960s, today's youth seem to buy the rallying cry of relativism, "If it works for you, it's right."

The Division of Truth

Why do youth think they can pick and choose religious beliefs as if they were merely choosing movies to watch or iTunes to download? In *Total Truth*, Nancy Pearcey explains that contemporary culture holds widely divergent opinions about the concept of truth itself. According to Pearcey, culture has drawn a dividing line between the sacred and the secular, and ascribed religion, morality, and "private" understanding to the sacred, subjective realm, and science and "public" knowledge to the secular, objective realm.[16] "In short," she writes, "the private sphere is awash in moral relativism. . . . Religion is not considered an objective truth to which we *submit*, but only a matter of personal taste which we choose."[17] As Pearcey has realized, religious and moral claims are considered matters of personal preference rather than knowledge claims about the real world.

As a result of this cultural divide, teenagers have been trained to compartmentalize their belief in God away from their daily lives—to keep their beliefs about God in the private, subjective realm and not to consider them objective knowledge. This compartmentalization is revealed most clearly in the way youth prioritize spirituality.

A study by the Harvard University Institute of Politics revealed that 70 percent of students consider religion "somewhat" or "very" important in their lives.[18] This at first may seem like a sign of spiritual vigor, but when researchers asked students what they got excited about, what pressing issues they were dealing with, and what experiences or routines seemed most important in their lives, their answers were radically different. Rather than talking about their religious identities, beliefs, or practices, most teens talked about their friends, their My Space accounts, music, romantic interests, or other personal issues.

---

[16] Nancy Pearcey, *Total Truth* (Wheaton, Ill.: Crossway, 2004), 20.
[17] Ibid., 20.
[18] As cited in "Youth Culture Update," *YouthWorker Journal*, July/August 2006, 9.

Christian Smith observed, "What a number of teens apparently mean in reporting that religion is very important in their lives is that religion is very important in the strictly religious sector of their lives. Religion influences them religiously—that is, when it comes to church attendance, basic beliefs, prayer, and so on—but not necessarily in other ways."[19] He then concluded, "What our interviews almost never uncovered among teens was a view that religion summons people to embrace an obedience to truth regardless of the personal consequences or rewards."[20]

This division into realms of truth poses no problem for some religions, but biblical scrutiny exposes it as incompatible with orthodox Christianity. We must help young people grasp that what makes Christianity unique is that it is identified with the life, work, character, and person of Jesus Christ—who walked on the Earth two thousand years ago and claimed to be both the Son of God and God in the flesh.

Many religions of the world are based on timeless principles, but Christianity is based primarily on the historical resurrection of Jesus. Paul makes this clear in 1 Cor 15:17: "If Christ has not been raised, your faith is worthless; you are still in your sins." Christianity is "total truth," in that it encompasses all of reality, sacred as well as secular, public as well as private.

One of the greatest obstacles we face in ministry to youth today is their distorted view of truth. This is why I spend nearly three weeks teaching my high school seniors about the nature of truth. Paul warns us in his second letter to the church in Thessalonica that people perish for not loving truth (2 Thess 2:8–10). Unless we rebuild the foundations of truth among our youth, they will be "tossed here and there by waves and carried about by every wind of doctrine, by the trickery of men" (Eph 4:14).

Do Youth Really Care about Truth?

Philosopher Francis Beckwith once had a skeptical student who questioned him every day in his ethics class. One day she asked, with

---

[19] Smith, *Soul Searching*, 138.
[20] Ibid., 149.

an air of superiority, as though her question would undo her professor's philosophical foundations, "Dr. Beckwith, why is truth *so* important?" After thinking for a moment he replied, "Well, would you like the *true* answer or the *false* one?" In other words, her very question assumed the existence, knowability, and importance of truth. It is impossible to survive without being concerned for truth.

Deeply rooted in the hearts of young people is the awareness that truth is a necessary bedrock for life. We often dismiss the fact that youth believe in truth, that they want truth, and that they organize their lives around what they believe is ultimately true. They just need help to clear away the misconceptions about truth that they unwittingly have adopted from our culture.

Dan Kimball, pastor at Vintage Faith Church, reinforces this truth in his book *The Emerging Church*: "I am finding that emerging generations really aren't opposed to truth and biblical morals. When people sense that you aren't just dogmatically opinionated due to blind faith and that you aren't just attacking other people's beliefs out of fear, they are remarkably open to intelligent and loving discussion about choice and truth."[21] I have found that although they clearly are turned off by people who arrogantly think they have all the answers, *young people respond positively to someone who can lovingly lead them to truth.*

The purpose of apologetics is *not* merely to win an argument but to draw people into a loving relationship with their Creator. It often is our attitude that speaks more powerfully than our words; thus, if we have the greatest arguments in the world but have not love, it profits us nothing (1 Cor 13:1–3). The old axiom, "People don't care how much you know unless they know how much you care" still applies.

More than ever we need to follow the advice of Peter and give our youth reasons for believing in the truth that concurs with reality yet do it with gentleness and respect. Living the truth is just as important as defending it, especially for a generation that judges truth by how well it "works." This crucial concept is worth repeating: *living the truth before a teenager is just as important as defending it.*

---

[21] Dan Kimball, *The Emerging Church* (Grand Rapids: Zondervan, 2003), 86.

Clearing Up the Confusion

How then do we help young people see that Jesus' claims are about objective reality and simply cannot be true for one person and false for another? I once performed the following experiment with my students. I placed a jar of marbles in front of them and asked, "How many marbles are in the jar?" They responded with different guesses: 221, 168, and so on. Then, after giving them the correct number of 188, I asked, "Which of you is closest to being right?" They all agreed that 168 was the closest guess, and they all agreed that the number of marbles was a matter of fact, not personal preference.

Then I passed out *Starburst* candies to each one of my students and asked, "Which flavor is right?" As you might expect, they all felt this was an unfair question because each person had a preference that was right for him or herself. "That is correct," I concluded. "The right flavor has to do with a person's preferences. It is a matter of subjective opinion or personal preference, not objective fact."

Then I asked, "Are religious claims like the number of marbles in a jar, or are they a matter of personal opinion, like preference for flavors of candy?" Most of my students concluded that religious claims belonged to the category of candy preference. I then opened the door for us to discuss the objective claims of Christianity. I pointed out to my students that Christianity is based on an objective fact in history—the resurrection of Jesus. I reminded them that while many people may reject the historical resurrection of Jesus, it is not the type of claim that can be "true for you but not true for me." The tomb either was empty, or it was occupied on the third day; there is no middle ground. I also pointed out that Christianity has an objective view of creation, the nature of the triune God, the nature of man, and the authenticity of the Bible.

A Strategy for Change

Once we have cleared up the confusion about truth, we have laid the groundwork for beginning to help teenagers understand creation, the historical Jesus, the problem of evil, and other important apologetic issues. In my own work with teens, I have found four helpful strategies.

First, help teens develop the skills of critical thinking. In our fast-paced, image-oriented culture, youth are more persuaded by images and stories than reasoned proofs. Few have cultivated the ability to think critically, yet critical thinking is the skill they need to recognize truth from error. All young people should be able to identify self-refuting statements such as, "There is no truth," *ad hominem* fallacies such as, "Christianity is false because there are so many hypocrites," and appeals to emotion such as, "We must legalize abortion because so many unwanted babies get abused in the world." Basic logic skills are indispensable for training students in apologetics. I regularly bring in to my students examples of logical fallacies from magazines or the newspaper to help them identify poor thinking.

Second, use examples from media to teach biblical truths. Studies indicate that students spend more time interacting with the media outside the classroom (e.g., the Internet, television, video games) than they do interacting with subject material in the classroom, which makes media examples powerful tools. I try to incorporate a media example nearly every time I teach youth. Film clips and song lyrics are great springboards for discussion and thoughtful reflection on issues pertaining to God and society. One of the best lessons I had in high school about thinking biblically and critically was watching *Schindler's List* with my family and interacting with my dad over dinner about truth, morality, and God. I remember that valuable lesson to this day.

Third, ask pointed questions. The best way to help teenagers learn how to defend their faith often is through probing questions and interaction rather than "preaching" or lectures. This is how Jesus Himself taught. When Jesus was challenged or asked a question, He often responded with a question. I often begin a lesson with a thought-provoking question (which also helps me to find out what my students *truly* believe about a subject). For example, I recently asked, "Does it benefit a couple to live together before they get married?" About half of my students thought that it does, and this gave me the chance to challenge their thinking and to help them come to terms with a biblical perspective on marriage.

Fourth, help teenagers put their knowledge into practice. Without application, apologetics is often simply a head game that makes little difference in their lives so we must provide supervised opportunities for them to apply what they have learned in real-world situations. I know of one group, for example, that has taken Christian students on a trip to the University of California at Berkeley[22] to expose them to secular thought *before* they go to college. The youth were not thrown into this situation suddenly but trained for months before the trip on defending the Christian faith. Students got connected with Christian groups on campus but also heard presentations against theism from students involved in Berkeley atheist clubs. The youth were able to interact personally with the atheist students, to ask good questions, and to put their faith on the line. As a result, many of the students walked away with a renewed zeal for learning apologetics.

A Bold Stand for Truth

As I reflect back on my conversations with my student Mike, I realize that his progress developed in a particular fashion. Once Mike realized there were answers to his deepest questions, he started to wonder about how he could share these truths with his non-Christian friends. A key principle that I learned in our discussions is that *when young people find answers to their questions about the Christian faith, they often become bolder in their witness for Christ.* Apologetics training creates confidence and courage. If we want our young people to be bold witnesses for Christ, we must equip them with the intellectual tools to defend their beliefs.

[22] See Brett Kunkle, "You're Taking Students Where?!" Student Impact, Stand to Reason, http://www.str.org/site/DocServer/brettkunklenews0602.pdf_1.pdf?docID=903, and "The Berkeley Mission Report," Student Impact, Stand to Reason, http://www.str.org/site/DocServer/brettkunklenews0603.pdf?docID=882.

CONTRIBUTORS

Francis J. Beckwith
Associate Professor of Philosophy
Baylor University

L. Russ Bush III
Distinguished Professor of Philosophy of Religion/ Director, Center
for Faith and Culture
Southeastern Baptist Theological Seminary

Emir Fethi Caner
Dean of the College at Southwestern
Professor of History
Southwestern Baptist Theological Seminary

Paul Copan
Pledger Family Chair of Philosophy and Ethics
Palm Beach Atlantic University

William Lane Craig
Research Professor of Philosophy
Talbot School of Theology

Craig A. Evans
Payzant Distinguished Professor of New Testament Studies
Acadia Divinity College

R. Douglas Geivett
Professor of Philosophy of Religion and Ethics
Talbot School of Theology

Gary R. Habermas
Distinguished Professor and Chair of Philosophy and Theology
Liberty University

Craig J. Hazen
Professor of Comparative Religion and Apologetics
Biola University

Sean McDowell
Theology/Bible Department Chair
Capistrano Valley Christian Schools

J. P. Moreland
Distinguished Professor of Philosophy
Talbot School of Theology

Michael J. Murray
Arthur and Katherine Shadek Professor in Humanities
Franklin & Marshall College

Harold Netland
Professor of Philosophy of Religion and Intercultural Studies
Trinity Evangelical Divinity School

Charles L. Quarles
Chair of Christian Studies
Louisiana College

Jay Wesley Richards
Research Fellow
Acton Institute

R. Scott Smith
Associate Professor of Ethics and Christian Apologetics
Biola University

N. T. Wright
Bishop of Durham
Durham, England

AUTHOR INDEX

SCRIPTURE INDEX